Michael Lawrence's

Opening Leads

C&T
BRIDGE SUPPLIES
(800) 525-4718

ISBN 1-885691-06-8

Published in the
United States of America
by
C&T Bridge Supplies
3838 Catalina St
Los Alamitos, CA 90720
(310) 598-7010

Opening Leads

Table of Contents

Table of Contents

Introduction

Unless you are an egregious over bidder or hand hog, it is inevitable that you will be on opening lead on about one-fourth of the bridge hands you play. Considering that the opening lead is usually the most important single play of a hand it is pretty important that you get as many opening leads correct as possible.

Unfortunately, the dice are stacked against the opening leader. He only gets to look at thirteen cards, while for all other plays a player can see at least twenty-six. Many players just flip out a card on opening lead, blindly following some rule such as "lead fourth best", "when in doubt, lead trumps", "avoid leading from a king", etc. These players lose many points on their opening leads when there were clues available which should have guided them to the winning lead.

In this book, Mike shows how to change the odds. He not only discusses the various types of leads, but shows how the bidding can produce the vital clues to the winning opening lead. He shows how, by listening to the bidding and examining your hand, you can predict how the play is likely to go, and how you can find the opening lead which will most benefit the defense and thwart declarer's plans before he has begun to carry them out. In addition he introduces a handful of tricks known only in the expert community — a few of which were quite new to me. I can't wait to try them against Mike when I next play him.

There are no assurances that following the ideas in this book will always produce the winning lead. It is still true that opening leads involve more guesswork than any other play, since there is less available information. What you can be assured of is that, if you follow these ideas on opening leads, your opening leads will be more successful on average than they have been. Also, you will enjoy the thrill of putting together the clues from the bidding and picturing what the enemy hands look like and finding the killing opening lead when your picture is correct. Making opening leads can be much more than drudgery or guesswork. They can actually be fun

— Kit Woolsey

FORWARD –
WHAT THIS BOOK IS ABOUT

The First Part

When you are on lead, there are lots of things to think about beginning with the auction and ending with the cards in your hand. Sometimes you have a blind lead, meaning that your opponents have given you little or no information to go on.

Because leads are hard enough when you have bidding to help you and harder still when you haven't a clue, it is a fact that you are going to make a lot of poor leads. I do not know a single expert who will claim to be perfect. In fact, I don't know a single player of any competence that will make this claim. Opening leads are so uncertain an art that if anyone does claim to be a great opening leader, they automatically lose a lot of respect points.

This book is intended to help you improve your leads, but it is also intended to help you cut down on bad leads. It might surprise you to know the number of bad leads which are routinely made. Likewise, you might be surprised to know that there are some good leads that many players refuse to consider, let alone make. This is not a winning combination. It should be changed.

The Second Part

The second section is a quiz which will give you a chance to see the first half of the book in action. As you will see, this quiz is a little different from other quizzes you may have faced in the past.

In General

Much of the time, you will have an easy opening lead. Many hands are blessed with a clear choice which allows you to start the defense on a conscience-free note. I imagine that more than half of the time, you would lead the same thing I would lead and which most other good players would lead. This book is not about these nice times. This book is about the other times when you have no clear lead or when you have conflicting data to think about. In the next two hundred pages or so, I will offer you ideas which will help you through those difficult moments.

There is one thing which I most definitely do not wish to do. I do not want to turn you into someone who looks for a miracle on every hand. Bridge is not played that way. Be content to look for normal good leads. One thing I would like to instill in you is a reflective mood.

This is how you should approach your opening lead. After selecting your choice, mentally hold the card in readiness, and then ask yourself this question.

"I think I have spotted the right lead. Was there anything in that book which suggests I am making the wrong choice?" If you make an honest effort to look at all sides of the question and you resolutely like your choice, then toss it out there and get on with the hand. If you can find a reason that your first choice is not ideal, reconsider the other choices. Keep in mind that not all hands have obvious leads. There will be days where you have to choose between a poor lead, a bad lead, a disgusting lead, and a hideous lead. My best wishes go out to you on those days. When they happen, my advice is to select the 'poor' choice as a least of evils. On other days, the opponents will be in three notrump doubled and your choice of leads will be to lead from the AKQJ of clubs or the AKQ10 of diamonds. You can work this one out without my help. Enjoy yourself.

One thing you must not do after reading this book is to look at every hand and say to yourself that Michael covered this hand exactly and told me what the best lead is. What Michael did do was give you many things to think about, and show you how on one occasion a certain lead might be good, and how on another occasion, a certain lead might be bad.

CHAPTER ONE

THINKING ABOUT YOUR OPENING LEAD

So You Are On Lead.............Again

What do you think about when you are faced with an opening lead problem? Do you look for a nice sequence to lead? Do you look for a singleton? Are you happy when you have a decent five card suit to lead against notrump?

All three of these things will be factors in choosing your opening lead. There are, however, other factors, including one which is the most important of all.

The Auction

The cards you have are important in considering your opening lead. Definitely. But, before looking to your cards for the right choice, you must remember the auction that got your opponents to their final contract.

Here is what I am referring to.

South is in four spades and you are on lead with the West hand. What do you lead?

WEST	The queen of hearts looks tempting and so does the three of diamonds. It
♠ 1083	is easy to make a case for a trump lead too. The one suit I would not lead
♡ QJ1072	is clubs. Leading suits headed by the ace is not good in general against
◊ 3	suit contracts. This is a sufficiently important topic that it has a chapter
♣ AQ76	of its own. In fact, there is a separate chapter on leading singletons, one
	on trump leads, and another on sequence leads. There is a lot to think
	about on opening lead.

So which is best? More importantly, how can you tell?

At this point, you should be complaining that something is lacking here. In fact, something very important is missing. You don't have an auction yet.

Would you believe that the auction is the most important factor in choosing your opening lead? You have to look at your cards, of course, but the bidding is going to be the major key in your choice.

WEST

♠ 1083
♡ QJ1072
◊ 3
♣ AQ76

Here is your hand. What do you lead against four spades after each of the following auctions?

W	N	E	S
	1H	P	1S
P	2S	P	4S
P	P	P	

Lead your singleton diamond. On this sequence, you ignore the heart suit and choose the three of diamonds. This is a clear choice. Once North has bid hearts, you know you won't be able to set up tricks there, so you look elsewhere. With your clubs headed by the ace, you should not lead them without an exceptional reason to do so.

W	N	E	S
			1S
P	2D	P	3D
P	3S	P	4S
P	P	P	

Lead the queen of hearts. Here, leading your singleton diamond is horrible. The opponents have both shown diamond strength. Most likely, leading a diamond will ruin a potential diamond trick your partner might have. If he has the queen of diamonds or possibly four to the jack, he will not appreciate seeing your diamond lead. The queen of hearts, given the auction, is an automatic choice. As before, clubs are not considered.

W	N	E	S
			1S
P	1NT*	P	2H
P	3D	P	3H
P	3S	P	4S
P	P	P	

*Forcing

Lead a trump. Dummy rates to have two spades and one heart. Leading a trump lets you stop one and maybe two heart ruffs in dummy. It sounds like dummy is not happy with this auction. This is more or less what I expect to see in dummy. ♠ 94 ♡ 8 ◊ KQ108652 ♣ J104. Only in the unlucky event that declarer can draw trump and run the diamonds will this lead be wrong. Even the best reasoned leads will be wrong some of the time.

W	N	E	S
			1S
P	2D*	P	3H
P	3S	P	4D
P	4H	P	4S
P	P	P	

*Game forcing

This is not an easy hand to lead from. If you shut your eyes and just listened to the bidding, you would conclude that a club lead was right. The unbid suit is often the right lead and is always worth a thought. On this hand, you have the AQ76 of clubs, which is normally an awful holding to lead from against a suit contract. I think I would make an exception on this hand and lead the ace of clubs. It goes against the grain for me to do this, but the auction does dictate a club lead. If any other lead looked good, I would consider it. On this sequence, the opponents have shown extra strength and fitting cards in both of their side suits. It is likely that the only tricks we have on this hand are clubs, and if we don't get after them, we may not get them.

The four auctions above lead one to this interesting conclusion. When you are on lead, you should, for a moment, review the bidding and determine WITHOUT LOOKING AT YOUR CARDS what the auction suggests you lead. Using the answer as a suggestion, you can then look at your cards and proceed.

REMEMBER to make your opening leads with your ears as much as your fingers.

A Useful And Sobering Fact Of Life

On 20 to 30% of the times you are on lead, you will not be sure of what to lead. Even when you 'know' you are making the right lead, you will find that sometimes it isn't.

W	N	E	S
P	1H	P	2NT
P	3NT	P	P
P			

WEST
♠ QJ1093
♡ J73
◇ 875
♣ Q8

If someone gave this to you as a lead problem, you (and I) would lead the queen of spades with a clear conscience and would consider the problem to be pointless. At the end of the hand, as declarer is scoring up his ten tricks, you notice that your partner had the AKJ102 of clubs. The queen of clubs would have been a killer. Did you do badly? Yes, you did do badly. But you did not do wrongly. You made the normal and correct lead and the cards turned against you in a disgusting way. Rats. Well, I am here to tell you that these things happen. My advice is to do the best you can and be content with a 75 or so percent batting average. Yes, the wild man will make lots of silly leads and will come up roses now and then, but you will come out on top in the long run. Opening leads are a little like the stock market. If you always do the 'right' thing, you will win often, but you won't win always. Do the best you can and suffer the occasional setback.

Other Considerations To Think About

Listening to the auction is a major part of selecting an opening lead. Still, even though paying attention to the auction will give you insights to the best lead, you still have to look at your hand and tie together the cards you see with the auction you heard. The first half of this book will look at many different considerations other than the bidding. Ultimately, you will have all of these things and more to think about when choosing your opening lead.

1.   The bidding.

       How strong was their bidding?
       Do they have a fit?
       Are they stretching?
       Did your partner bid?

2.   Do you have a singleton to lead?

        Is it better to lead a singleton or from an honor sequence such as the KQ98?
        Why?

3.   Could a trump lead be best?
        When and why?
        When and why not?

4.   What honor combinations are best to lead from?

        Are you willing to lead from combinations like Q954 or KJ85 in suits which
        partner has bid? How about when it is an unbid suit?

5.   Do you ever lead a singleton in an unbid suit against notrump?

6.   At notrump, is it better to lead through a suit that dummy bid or into a suit that
        declarer bid?

        Why?

7.   What do you lead when there is no good lead?

        And a hundred more.

On most hands, there is no one single reason for leading one card other than another. The
bidding might tell you to lead a heart. But your diamond holding might be the AKJ and
scream at you that you should lead them instead. How can you tell which urge to follow?

Or worse. What do you do when every card in your hand is stinko? How do you decide
which lead is least horrible?

In the following chapters, I will look at many individual things to think about on opening
lead. Then, in the quiz section, you will find hands that tie them all together.

A Prediction

I expect that some of the material in this book will go against the grain for you and I
promise that not all of the ideas will work immediately for you, nor will they work all the
time for you. I do promise that they will work enough of the time that you should give
them a chance to prove themselves.

CHAPTER TWO

THE TECHNICAL CHOICE OF LEADS – WHICH CARD DO YOU LEAD FROM VARIOUS HOLDINGS?

When Leading Against A Suit Contract

I am not going to present a big list of suit combinations with rules for each of them. You get a little list and some observations. If you are reading this book, you already have a good idea of specific rules. What I will present here is the style of leads that will be used in this book. If your partnership leads differently from what is shown here, nothing is lost. This book, for instance, will lead the ace from an ace-king combination. Your partnership may play that you lead the king from this holding. No matter. The important thing is that you agree on this. NOTE that the material here applies only to the opening lead. In the middle of the hand, you may have reason to lead differently.

1.   <u>Fourth best leads.</u>

     K1074   Lead the four.

     Q8743   Lead the four.

     J96   Lead the six. Sometimes you have to lead from a three card suit.

     A1074   Do not lead this suit. This will be discussed in a later chapter on leading and underleading aces against suit contracts.

     10873   Lead the three.

     7642   See point seven below.

2.   Ace from Ace-King.

AK73   Lead the ace. If you are comfortable leading the king from this holding,
       go ahead and continue doing so. If you are not certain which card is
       right, I suggest, albeit only mildly, that you lead the ace from this
       holding.

3.   Lead the top card from a sequence.

KQ76   Lead the king.

QJ104 Lead the queen.

QJ53   Lead the queen.

J106   Lead the jack.

1093   Lead the ten.

4.   Lead the top card from an interior sequence.

KJ106   Lead the jack.

K1094   Lead the ten.

Q10984 Lead the ten.

A1096   DO NOT LEAD THIS SUIT.

KJ987   Lead the eight. An interior sequence has to be headed by the jack or ten
        to qualify. The 987 interior sequence should be handled as a
        fourth best lead.

K986   Lead the fourth best as in the previous combination.

KQ1092 Lead the king. Interior sequences are led when there is one higher
        card. You can lead the queen from this holding against a notrump
        contract. This is discussed in the chapter on sequence leads.

5.	<u>Lead high from three small if you have raised the suit.</u>

742	If you have *raised* partner, lead the seven.

If you gave a *preference* in this suit, lead the two.

6.	<u>Lead low from three small otherwise.</u>

862	Lead the two. There are many opinions about what to lead from three small cards. It is discussed further in its own chapter later. Hate leading from three small? Me too. See why in the chapter on leading from three small cards.

7.	<u>Judgment when you have four or five small cards.</u>

7652	Leading from four or five little cards against a suit contract isn't very exciting. You can lead the fourth best, which will suggest you have an honor in the suit, or you can lead a high card, which will suggest you have shortness. This is discussed later in its own chapter.

When Leading Against A Notrump Contract

1.	<u>Fourth best leads.</u>

K1074	Lead the four.

Q8743	Lead the four.

J96	Lead the six. Sometimes you have to lead from a three card suit.

A1074	Lead the four. It is OK to underlead an ace against notrump. It is barred to lead an ace or to underlead an ace against a suit contract.

AQ763	Lead the six. You would not lead this suit against a suit contract.

10873	Lead the three.

7642	See point seven below.

2. From suits headed by the AKx(x)

AK73 Lead the king if you have three or four cards. Lead fourth best, in general, if you have five or more. Against notrump, the king lead shows an AKx or a KQx combination.

AKJ105 If you have an exceptionally strong holding, such as the AKJ10x or AKQ105 of a suit, you lead the ace, which asks partner to play an honor if he has one and otherwise to show you how many cards he has in the suit.

	643	
AKJ105		97
	Q82	

West leads the ace. East, if he had an honor, would play it. With two cards, he plays the nine to show that he has two or four cards. West usually can work out the distinction. Had East begun with the 972 of this suit, he would play the two to show an odd number of cards.

3. From suits headed by a sequence.

Lead the top card from a three card sequence such as QJ104. Tend to lead low when your suit is headed by a two card sequence such as KQ75.

KQ76 Lead the six.

QJ53 Lead the three.

QJ104 Lead the queen. When you have a three card sequence, you lead the top card against suits or notrump. (There is a rare exception to this rule. It is discussed in the chapter on leading from sequences.)

KQ6 Lead the king.

J106 Lead the jack.

1093 Lead the ten

986 Lead the nine. This is not a sequence in the normal meaning of the word, but letting partner know you have, or probably have, the nine and eight is important.

4. <u>Lead the top card from an interior sequence.</u>

KJ106   Lead the jack.

K1094   Lead the ten.

Q10984 Lead the ten.

A1096   Lead the ten. You would not lead this suit against a suit contract.

KJ987   Lead the eight. Lead fourth best unless your interior sequence is headed by the ten or higher.

K986   Lead the fourth best as in the previous combination.

5. <u>From three little cards.</u>

752   If partner has bid the suit and you have not raised, lead the little card.

863   In all other cases, lead the top card from three small ones against notrump. Lead the eight, or possibly the six. You do not want partner to waste his energies returning this suit in which you have no personal interest. Leading from three small cards has been debated for years. There are lots of opinions about what is right.

6. <u>Judgment when you have four or five small cards.</u>

7643   Four or five little cards is more appetizing to lead from against notrump than it is against a suit. If you feel this is the best suit for you to be leading, go ahead and make your normal fourth best lead. I will talk about this holding at length later in the book.

7. <u>A special case used only against a notrump contract.</u>

KQ109 Against notrump, you can make a special lead when you have this holding. Lead the queen. If your partner has the jack, he is instructed to play it, regardless of how many cards he has. This lead is made when you have the KQ109 fourth or longer. You should not make this lead from the KQ1053 because it might cost you a trick if partner drops the jack as you are requesting.

```
         7                         If West leads the queen and East drops the jack, South will
KQ1053            J42              have a second stopper in the suit. Save this lead for when
       A986                        you have the required KQ109 or better.
```

Some General Differences Between Leads Versus Notrump Contracts And Leads Versus Suit Contracts

When you are defending against a suit contract, you tend to look for a trick here, a trick there, and perhaps another trick in the wash. Some of the time, your side has enough values that you slaughter the opponents but usually, aside from taking the ace-king and getting a ruff, you don't take more than a couple of tricks in any given suit. Knowing how hard to pursue one suit and when to look elsewhere is one of the arts to defending against a suit contract.

Against notrump, you tend to put many of your eggs in one basket. You try to choose the best suit to attack and for the rest of the hand, continue with this suit. Since you are trying to set up two or three or even four tricks in a given suit, your approach to leading against notrump is different from leading against a suit .

Against a suit contract, you would never lead from the AQ763 of a suit. You would expect that two tricks was all you could get and leading away from the ace would cause you to lose one of them. Against notrump, you would lead this suit because you hope to take four tricks later at the cost of giving one up now. Heck, if your partner has the king, you may take all five tricks.

In general, the choice of cards you lead against notrump is usually the same as against a suit contract. The major difference comes when you have a two card sequence to lead from. With QJ73 of a suit, you would lead the queen against a suit contract. Against notrump, you would lead low. Curiously, if you have a holding such as AK753, you would lead the ace against a suit contract and might consider underleading it against notrump. I will talk more about this in the section on leading from sequences.

CHAPTER THREE

WHAT DOES THE BIDDING SUGGEST LEADING?

Do you study the bidding as it is going on or do you pay just enough attention to it to know when you are on opening lead? Here is a chance to prove it! In this chapter, you will have to determine your lead, not on the cards you hold, but on the bidding sequence. You have to do this because there are no cards in this quiz to lead you astray. When you have cards in your hands, there is a natural tendency to focus on them. Don't fall into this trap. Good opening leads depends very much on how the bidding went and that will be our starting point. Don't despair. You will get some cards soon enough.

Some of the time, your partner will bid something. That is always helpful to you and will help you decide. On some auctions, though, you won't get any help from partner, and will have to rely entirely on other factors.

You are West in the following quiz. No one is vulnerable, ever. Decide, on the basis of the given auction, which suit or suits you should lead, and also which suit or suits you should not be leading. NOTE that there are three sections ranging from uninformative auctions to generally informative auctions to precisely informative auctions.

Uninformative Auctions. The Opponents Were Unable To Describe Their Hands.

# 1	W	N	E	S
		1D	P	1NT
	P	P	P	

What do we know?

South did not bid a major suit. In general, South will not have four of either major and may be short in one or both majors. The same does not hold true for the minors. South would respond one notrump to one diamond with something like this: ♠ J3 ♡ 93 ♢ Q83 ♣ KJ7632. This is not a lovely bid, but it is the correct bid in most systems. This observation suggests leading a major suit against this auction.

Against this, your partner did not choose to bid a major or to make a takeout double. In light of this, you might think that a club lead was a good idea. It would not be impossible for a diamond to be best. If opener has 4-4-3-2 shape and responder has lots of clubs, diamonds may be their weak suit. The sad fact is that in this case, the auction does not give you a strong hint. You will have to look at your cards to see if they can offer any insights. We will do this later. For now, the idea is to see how the bidding gives us something to think about. It may not have helped us on this sequence, but it will help on others.

#2	W	N	E	S	What do we know?
				1C	
	P	1H	P	1NT	South did not rebid one spade. For most players,
	P	P	P		this means they do not have four spades. This suggests a spade lead could be a good idea.

North, on the other hand, may have four spades. He would respond one heart with four hearts and four spades. This makes spades a potentially poor lead. Your partner might have bid spades if he could have done so at the one level. The fact that he didn't mildly suggests against leading a spade.

South did not raise hearts. Perhaps he has two and dummy four. If so, leading a heart could be a good idea. It could be, but if declarer has three hearts or if dummy has five of them, hearts will be a bad choice.

Once again, you have some guideline thoughts, but you still have to look at your hand to see which lead looks best.

#3	W	N	E	S	What do we know?
				1H	
	P	1NT	P	2H	North did not bid spades, so he doesn't have
	P	P	P		four of them. South might have four of them, though.

#4	W	N	E	S	What do we know?
		1D	1S	1NT	
	P	P	P		We know something wonderful this time. East bid. East's overcall gives us every reason to lead a spade. You may find a reason not to, but it is a pretty good hint that a spade is best. It is nice to

16

have a hint from partner. Keep this thought in mind when you are bidding defensively and are wondering whether to overcall. Your partner may be happy to have heard from you if he is on lead. There is another feature about this auction that may help you defend later in the hand. South did not look for hearts. If he had four of them, he might have used the Negative Double. This kind of inference depends in part on the conventions your opponents are playing. It helps to know their tendencies.

#5	W	N	E	S
				1H
	P	2H	P	P
	P			

This is one of the harder auctions to lead against. You know that North has a scattered seven or eight count and those points can be anywhere. Also, since North has a heart fit, he may not have felt like showing a spade suit. North can have any of these hands for his two heart raise.

♠ QJ86	♠ 62	♠ 764	♠ K2	♠ A10764
♡ K82	♡ AJ7	♡ KJ64	♡ J82	♡ Q32
◊ 72	◊ KJ876	◊ QJ6	◊ K	◊ 87
♣ J1063	♣ 765	♣ Q72	♣ J976542	♣ J107

Quite a range. As you can see, North can be loaded in any of the side suits and not have been able to describe that fact in the auction.

#6	W	N	E	S
				1D
	P	P	P	

What do we know?

This is a fairly illustrative auction. You don't know much about the opponents' distribution, but you do know that your partner didn't bid. Partner probably has length in diamonds. It is possible that South has four-four in the majors and just three diamonds. Perhaps a diamond lead is best. Or, failing that, perhaps a club lead is best.

#7	W	N	E	S
	1D	P	1H	1S
	2D	2S	P	P
	P			

What do we know?

Not much. East has four hearts and not much of a hand. I would hope to have an obvious lead since nothing in the bidding suggests a killing lead. Be wary of leading partner's suit when he has responded at the one level and then shuts up. You may choose to lead his suit, but as bids from partner go, this one is not a robust suggestion.

#8	W	N	E	S
	1H	P	2H	2S
	3H	3S	P	P
	P			

What do we know?

East has raised hearts, which shows three hearts and promises around seven points.

West should *think* about leading hearts and will do so in general unless there are reasons not to. I will give you an early insight to an important guideline. RULE. Leading or underleading aces against a suit contract is very bad. If you look at your hearts and find they are headed by the ace and you do not also have the king, you should not lead them. Do not do it. Even though partner raised you, leading a heart is bad. On some hands it will work or perhaps not make a difference, but in the long run, it is an expensive choice. I will talk about this a lot more later.

So far, we haven't seen an auction that gives you a strong indication as to your lead. There is a reason for this. Low level auctions tend to be unrevealing. Hands that are weak can not show all of their features. Following is a hand you have seen many times. Your partner opens one heart. This is your hand.

♠ Q1074 You respond one spade and then, unless forced to do so, tend not to bid
♡ 4 again. For instance, if your partner raised to two spades, you would pass.
◊ 873 Most of the time, your best suit, clubs, is never bid. The same is often true
♣ KQ873 of the opponents' bidding. Their bidding may be unrevealing in the same
way. Take this simple auction by your opponents.

LHO	RHO
1D	1H
1S	1NT

RHO can have any of the six example hands below. It is scary how wide the range of hands is for RHO to have for his auction.

♠ 84	♠ KJ3	♠ 6	♠ Q73	♠ 764	♠ QJ3
♡ AJ763	♡ 10763	♡ AK105	♡ AQ63	♡ J876	♡ 8653
◊ 3	◊ 874	◊ 82	◊ J53	◊ J86	◊ QJ6
♣ QJ874	♣ KQ10	♣ Q106542	♣ 1084	♣ KQ8	♣ Q62

He can have as many as four club stoppers and as few as zero. Likewise, he can have three or four heart stoppers or no heart stoppers. Not an informative sequence for the opening leader.

18

#9	W	N	E	S
				1H
	P	4H	P	P
	P			

You know that dummy is weak, but you know little else. Dummy may have five hearts and five clubs, he may have four hearts and six diamonds, or he might have four hearts and a long spade suit. Declarer hasn't told you much either, other than that he has an opening bid. Opener can have a balanced twelve point minimum up to a twenty count that wisely chose not to bid on after the weak raise to game.

RULE - When the opponents' auction is both weak and unrevealing, you will not have many obvious leads. Sure, you will have some good sequences to lead, but unless your cards dictate a certain lead to you, you may be in the dark. This is a fact. One of the nice things about tournament bridge is that when you don't have many high card points to bid with, the opponents perforce will have them. This may not be fun for you, but you should still be able to find better leads as a result of more information from their auctions. Listen up.

Relatively Informative Auctions: Both Opponents Are Able to Show the General Nature of Their Hands

You will discover that as your opponents' bidding becomes stronger, your opening leads become better and better because you have more information to guide you. It won't always be so since their bidding can be brief. 1NT - 3NT or 2NT - 3NT auctions are irritating to lead against since you know so little other than that they have lots of points. But in general, your opening leads should improve with the increased information you get. Here are some auctions which give you modest information.

#1	W	N	E	S
		1C	P	1D
	P	1S	P	1NT
	P	2NT	P	P
	P			

A heart feels logical. North has denied four hearts and responder probably does not have four hearts. One of the vagaries of opening leads is that you don't know what your opponents' bidding tendencies are. It sounds like South does not have four hearts, but if he belongs to the school that always bids diamonds first, then he may have them. Every partnership, yours, mine, and your neighbor's, has bidding idiosyncrasies that never come out. You can always ask about these things, but it is usually a waste of time. In this book, I will assume standard tendencies unless otherwise noted. If you know your opponents' habits, you may adjust yourself accordingly.

#2	W	N	E	S
				1C
	P	1S	P	2H
	P	2S	P	2NT
	P	P	P	

What do we know?

Opener started with one club and reversed to two hearts. When responder rebid his suit, opener bid two notrump, which ended the auction. This is one of those sequences which is played a number of ways. You might want to know if there are any agreements you should know about. The way to do this is not to ask about each bid. That is too slow. Instead, before making your opening lead, ask if there are any understandings you should know about. For the sake of this hand, you are told that responder was obliged to rebid a five card spade suit if he had one. Opener's two notrump bid was obviously passable so it is fair to assume that responder has five spades and a weak hand.

What should you lead? Should you lead the unbid diamond suit? Should you lead dummy's spade suit? Should you pick on one of opener's suits? If you assume the opponents know what they are doing, you can see that opener tends to have a hand with 1-4-3-5 shape. He has clubs, hearts, and a diamond stopper. It is possible that he has 2-4-2-5 shape, but in the long run, he has closer to the first distribution.

You would be amazed how often it is right to lead spades, the suit that was bid and rebid on your left.

FOOTNOTE TO HAND 2. I commented that if the opponents know what they are doing, you can draw certain inferences. When you are playing a pair that is known to be off the wall, you have harder decisions. Be aware that the worse your opponents, the worse your leads will tend to be. At least your poor leads will often be greeted with poor dummy play. Still, prepare to be frustrated.

#3	W	N	E	S
		1S	P	2H
	P	2S	P	3D
	P	3H	P	4H
	P	P	P	

What do we know?

Opener has some kind of opening bid and responder has hearts and diamonds. On sequences where the opponents show strength and bid around the bush, the unbid suit is a strong candidate for your opening lead. I expect that I will lead a club and will do so unless they are headed by the ace or there is another obvious lead to make.

#4	W	N	E	S
	1C	DBL	2C	2S
	P	P	P	

A competitive sequence where everyone has a say in the bidding. What do you think you should lead?

With your side bidding clubs, a club lead may be right. There is another lead that is worth thinking about. It sounds like North has short clubs for his double. Leading a club isn't automatically a good idea. Maybe a trump is best. If dummy has three spades and two clubs, you may get to take all the trumps out of dummy and stop declarer from getting a single club ruff. Not automatic, but worth thinking about.

#5	W	N	E	S
				1NT
	P	2NT	P	P
	P			

There is a lot of information available to you when the opponents have a notrump auction. You can tell, for instance, within one point how many high cards your partner has. The opponents have twenty-three or twenty-four, so your side has sixteen or seventeen. Deduct your high card points and you know what partner has. Say you have seven points. Your partner has nine or ten. Like magic. This information may help you with your lead, and it will certainly help you with the later defense.

Now, getting back to the opening lead. You know that North did not look for a major suit. This tells you that North has seven or more cards in the minor suits. There is a fair chance that he has four cards in both minors. Opener may have one or both majors, but there is no guarantee. Against this bidding, you should look hard at the major suits. Lead a minor if you must, but think about it carefully.

FOOTNOTE TO HAND 5. Look at the inferences you have on this hand. Compare them with the inferences you would have had the bidding gone 1NT - P - P - P. If this had been the auction, you would not know if dummy had zero points or seven points. Also, since dummy wasn't able to bid, he could have all kinds of distributions. He could be 4-4 in the majors or 4-4 in the minors or 4-4 in any other two suits. Because the bidding didn't tell you much, your opening lead is uninformed and therefore difficult. Sometimes you have an obvious lead, but when you don't you can have a tough time of it. One thing worth noting. When North raised to two notrump, you knew to avoid leading a minor suit. When North passes one notrump, you have no such information. Leading a minor is perfectly OK.

#6	W	N	E	S
				1NT
	P	3NT	P	P
	P			

Curiously, this sequence is not as informative as the previous auction where North raised to two notrump and South passed. Here, where North goes to game, you know that he has at least ten points, generally speaking, but you do not know if he has just ten or up to a fifteen count that didn't want to make a slam try. Also, since North went to three notrump, you didn't get to find out whether South has a minimum or a maximum. On this auction, you know they have twenty-five points up to thirty-two. You do know that responder didn't want to look for a major, but that is about all you know.

Precisely Informative Auctions. The Opponents Bid Back and Forth in Great Detail.

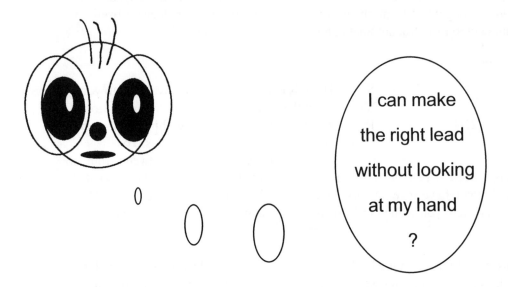

I can make the right lead without looking at my hand ?

Some auctions are very informative. The opponents may have bid circles looking for the right game. They may have taken five rounds to get to slam. Or, they may have taken seven rounds before deciding to avoid a slam. The auction may scream at you what suit to lead. When this happens, you should know the right lead without looking at your hand. This is not unusual.

Leads against long auctions rate to be easier than leads against short ones. This is something worth thinking about when you are bidding and have a choice of making a blunt bid or an insightful one. The less information you give away in the bidding, the less accurate your bidding may be. But in return, you will get more bad leads than the pair which paints an exquisite picture for anyone listening. Even if your opponent finds the best lead against your simpleminded auction, their subsequent defense may suffer from not knowing what you have.

#1	W	N	E	S
		1C	P	1S
	P	2S	P	3C
	P	3D	P	3S
	P	4S	P	P
	P			

They found a spade fit and then made exploratory bids before settling on four spades. South seems to have an invitational hand with four spades. If he had an invitational hand with five spades, he might have made his game try by bidding three spades over two spades. North accepted the game try, but because he bid three diamonds instead of four spades, there is a fair assumption that he has only three trumps. This is not guaranteed, but there is a good hint that they don't have hearts stopped and have chosen a four-three fit as a last resort. I would lead a heart against this bidding about 90% of the time.

#2	W	N	E	S
				1S
	P	2D	P	3D
	P	4S	P	P
	P			

You know they have game strength. Some pairs have special understandings about auctions like this. You can find out by asking if there is anything you should know. You may find out that four spades is a sign-off bid. Or, you may find out that it denies a control in either of the unbid suits. There is another fact you may be able to use. They bid and raised diamonds. If you have four diamonds, you can count on your partner having one or none. Maybe that information will help you with your opening lead.

#3	W	N	E	S
				3NT*
	P	P	P	

*Gambling - Solid suit.
May or may not
have a side honor

South's three notrump bid is alerted as showing a solid minor suit and not more than two or three points on the side. This information can help you with your opening lead. Normally you lead your long suit against notrump. Against this sequence, it has been shown to be effective to lead aces in the hopes of finding declarer's weak spot.

WEST
♠ J8762
♡ AJ4
◇ 2
♣ Q873

Against a 1NT - 3NT auction, you would lead the six of spades and feel secure that you were doing the normal thing. Against South's gambling three notrump bid, you might try the ace of hearts. If spades are going to run right away, you can always switch to them. If hearts are right, at least you are on them right away.

NORTH
♠ AK104
♡ Q86
◇ 85
♣ J1092

WEST
♠ J8762
♡ AJ4
◇ 2
♣ Q873

EAST
♠ 53
♡ K9532
◇ 1043
♣ A64

The ace and jack of hearts gets the defenders the first six tricks. A spade lead gets them the last two tricks. An ace is not always the best lead, but it is worth thinking about.

SOUTH
♠ Q9
♡ 107
◇ AKQJ976
♣ K5

#4	W	N	E	S
		1D	P	1H
	P	3S*	P	4H
	P	P	P	

*Splinter

The auction tells you that North has a game-forcing raise with four hearts and a singleton spade. South didn't want to go further so signed off in four hearts. You know that North has a good hand with shape and you know that your partner didn't double three spades. You have some negative inferences to work with. Perhaps a club is the best attack. Perhaps a trump. You will want to look at your hand, but your choice should ultimately be informed. In the next chapter there are some ideas about what it means if partner doubles three spades.

#5	W	N	E	S
				1H
	P	1S	P	2C
	P	3C	P	3NT
	P	P	P	

You know opener has hearts, clubs, and a diamond stopper. There isn't much room in his hand for many spades. The unbid suit, diamonds, is not a poor choice in general. Before leading one, though, I would give spades a good look first.

CHAPTER FOUR

WHAT CAN YOU EXPECT FROM PARTNER'S HAND?

According to how the bidding went, what do you expect partner to have in various suits? This is important because it will help you decide when to lead from kings and other broken holdings. The following list covers most common situations.

1. Did your partner bid the suit?

2. Did your partner make a takeout double showing the suit?

3. Did your partner bid notrump?

4. Is it an unbid suit?
    A. Did the opponents bid three suits excluding this one?
    B. Did the opponents bid two suits excluding this one?
    C. Did the opponents bid one suit only?
    D. What if no suits were bid?

5. Did your partner make a lead directing double during the auction? Did he pass when he might have doubled?

6. Did your partner make a penalty double at some point in the auction?

7. Did your partner pass your takeout double?

8. Did your partner double the final contract?
    A. Was your side bidding during the auction?
    B. Did your side sit silently until they finished bidding before doubling?

9. How many points does your partner rate to have? What inferences can you draw from his silence?

1. Did Your Partner Bid The Suit?

When partner bids a suit, leading it gets consideration. Keep in mind that partner's suit can range from very weak to very strong. Here are some examples along with inferences.

W	N	E	S
	1S	2C	

If partner overcalled the suit at the two level, it rates to be a very good suit. Barring another obvious lead, leading this suit should work well. If you have an honor to contribute, it is better yet. Leading from holdings such as Q86 or J105 are productive.

W	N	E	S
		2S	

When partner opens with a preempt, his suit is definitely worth leading. The higher the preempt, the better his suit rates to be. Keep in mind that preempts in first and second seat show better suits than preempts in third seat. It will also help you to know your partner's bidding style.

W	N	E	S
	1D	1S	

If partner overcalls at the one level, he usually has a good suit, but there will be exceptions. Unless you have an outstanding alternative, leading this suit is a good idea. Keep in mind that a one level overcall can be made on 109843 if the hand is otherwise good enough. A two level overcall shows a better suit. Frankly, if my partner overcalls one spade and I have the K53 to lead from, I will be happy to do so. Even if it turns out to be a failure, I will be right there to do it again.

W	N	E	S
		1H	

Opening bids in a major imply better suits than opening bids in a minor. Since you will open one heart with 97653 and one club or one diamond with 1073, you can't absolutely count on partner having a good suit, but there is a modest inference that he has some honors. Leading from the king in partner's opened major suit is an OK idea in general. I would be a little slower to lead from the king in partner's opened minor suit.

W	N	E	S
1D	P	1H	

Partner will routinely respond on a crummy four card suit. Still, he shows six or more points, so there is a hope that some of them will be in his suit. In the long run, leading partner's suit in this situation is not my favorite lead.

The main merit in it is that your partner has dropped a mild hint that he has something in the suit. Fortunately, there is usually more bidding to help you choose your lead.

W	N	E	S
			1D
DBL	1H	1S	

If you make a takeout double and partner bids a suit *freely* at the one or two level, he is promising six points or more. Since he will bid a bad four card suit, even freely, he is not promising much in his suit. Don't rush to lead suits bid in this fashion.

W	N	E	S
			1H
DBL	P	1S	

If you make a takeout double and partner answers with a suit after a pass by your LHO, you have no reason to play him for a high card there. All other things being equal, I would prefer to lead a suit partner responded in, but it is a very slight preference. In this case, it is almost as if partner never bid. Obviously, these factors change according to how the bidding goes. If partner responds one spade and later bids again, you will be able to reconsider his spade holding. For now, don't give it much respect. The next auction is an example of this.

W	N	E	S
			1C
DBL	P	1H	2C
2H	3C	3H	4C

Be willing to change your opinion a little. When partner bid one heart, he didn't guarantee a decent suit. He promised four to the five spot or better. In fact, he might not be able to keep that modest promise. He might have been obliged to bid on three little hearts. But, when he bid three hearts, the chances are his suit is decent.

The list above covers some of the common situations where partner can bid a suit. Certainly, the list could have been longer. What is important is that you see how partner came to bid the suit and then whether he continued bidding it.

2. Did Your Partner Make A Takeout Double?

If partner makes a takeout double showing the unbid suits, leading from an honor in one of these suits is a good idea. Partner's takeout double is the moral equivalent to bidding each of the unbid suits. If partner raised you after making a takeout double, it is better yet to lead this suit. Be aware, though, that partner can make a takeout double with as little as three small in one of the unbid suits. This is rare, but possible. All in all, leading a suit that partner has asked for is effective.

3.   Did Your Partner Bid Notrump?

If you have some holding such as the KJxx of a suit and partner has volunteered notrump during the auction, you can consider leading this suit. Hopefully, your partner will have something in the suit to make your lead effective. There are lots of notrump auctions, though, so you mustn't be overly stubborn about this. You are West in the following auctions.

W	N	E	S
1C	1H	1NT	2S
P	P	P	

East clearly has hearts stopped. Leading from the king of hearts can easily be correct. Leading from the king of diamonds, an unbid suit, can also be safe, but be aware that East did not specifically promise good diamonds. He may have them, but does not guarantee them.

W	N	E	S
1C	DBL	1NT	2S
P	3S	P	P
P			

East has shown eight or nine points but does not promise they are anywhere in particular. If you don't have a clear lead, picking on KJxx of any suit is speculative. This auction is interesting in that North's double says he has cards in all of the unbid suits and East's one notrump bid says he has some scattered values.

W	N	E	S
			1H
DBL	1S	1NT	2H
P	P	P	

Partner does not promise spades for his one notrump bid. He is counting on your takeout double for a spade stopper. Leading spades may or may not be effective.

WEST
♠ KJ43
♡ 43
◊ AQ4
♣ Q1094

Lead the ten of clubs. East says he has eight or nine points. Some of them are in hearts. The rest can be anywhere. I think that leading clubs is a better choice than spades since North did specifically say he has some spades. East may or may not have a spade honor. A small aside. Do not lead hearts. Never lead a trump against a contract where one person bid a suit endlessly with no hint of support from his partner.

W	N	E	S
		1NT	2H
P	P	P	

East's one notrump bid on this sequence promises whatever high card range you use for your opening one notrump. If you play fifteen to seventeen or sixteen to eighteen point notrumps, leading from a king or queen in one of the unbid suits is a strong choice. Partner rates to have high card points in all of the suits.

4. Is It An Unbid Suit?

A. Did the opponents bid three suits excluding this one?

B. Did the opponents bid two suits excluding this one?

C. Did the opponents bid one suit only?

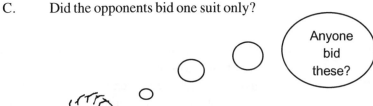

You have probably heard, or been guilty of saying, that a certain suit was unbid and therefore the only possible choice of leads. There is often some truth to this statement. The trick is knowing how much truth is involved. There are three degrees possible.

A.   If the opponents bid three suits there is a decent chance that the fourth suit is a good lead. Even so, the way the opponents bid is pertinent.

W	N	E	S
	1D	P	1S
P	2C	P	2S
P	P	P	

Here, the opponents have bid three suits, which suggests you lead hearts. That is a thoughtful conclusion but does not take everything into account. Responder has a hand in the six to nine point range, which means he may not have shown all of the things he wanted to. It is possible that declarer has four hearts and couldn't bid them. South will bid as shown if he has the following hand.

SOUTH
♠ Q107643
♡ AJ73
♢ —
♣ 732

South can't bid two hearts on the second round since it is forcing and will get the partnership to the three level or higher. We have all had hands like this. We respond one spade only to hear partner rebid two clubs. Two hearts is not feasible since it is forcing and will get us to the three level or higher even if there is a misfit. You have only two choices. You can bid two spades or possibly pass two clubs. Personally, I would want to show the sixth spade and would do so regretting all the while that I couldn't show the hearts.

This auction is just the first example of one of the more frustrating facts of making opening leads. The weaker your opponents' hands, the less information you have to chose your lead. And conversely, the stronger your opponents' hands, the more bids they will make and the better informed you will be as a result. One of the toughest sequences to lead against is an opening one bid that was passed out. Talk about your basic guessing game.

W	N	E	S	
			1C	All you know is that South has three or more clubs and a
P	P	P		minimum of twelve or so points. You will naturally look at your hand and search for inferences, but you have very little to go on other than the fact that your LHO is broke and your partner didn't want to act.

W	N	E	S	
	1S	P	2D	Here, the opponents have enough points that they can afford to show all their features. You can draw some good
P	2S	P	3C	inferences. North shouldn't have a heart suit and South
P	3D	P	3NT	rates to have the minors with some heart strength. Leading
P	P	P		hearts makes sense here.

B. If the opponents have bid two suits, leaving two unbid suits for you to choose from, there is still a suggestion that you look at the unbid suits first when making your opening lead. As before, the stronger the opponents auction, the better chance that they would have shown a suit if they had it.

W	N	E	S	
			1C	This a weak sequence. North can have four spades and not
P	1H	P	2C	enough strength to bid them. As with many weak
P	P	P		sequences, your best chance to work out the opening lead will be by drawing inferences from your own hand about what your partner might have and not have bid.

WEST

♠ Q86
♡ 10974
◊ KJ95
♣ 97

When you have a hand this weak, you can tell that your partner has decent values. His silence suggests he has nothing he could show. Perhaps he has good clubs. Perhaps he has good hearts. Perhaps he has scattered values. He may have four decent spades or four decent diamonds, but he may also have something like the following.

WEST	EAST
♠ Q86	♠ 1053
♡ 10974	♡ AQ83
◇ KJ95	◇ Q6
♣ 97	♣ KQ84

> They bid both of my suits. I couldn't show my hand.

East has a pretty good hand, but there was no point in the bidding for him to show it. The opponents bid both of East's suits, which is a good reason for silence. What West leads is uncertain. One thing West should avoid is a spade. If East had good spades, he might have bid them over one heart. Once you decide to avoid a spade lead, what you should lead will best be known after you see the dummy. On this hand a diamond lead is OK and a heart lead works, as perhaps does a club. But knowing what is right in advance is not possible. My usual reminder is that no matter how hard you try, you will make the wrong lead twenty to thirty percent of the time. Don't let it get you down.

W	N	E	S
	1D	P	1H
P	2H	P	4H
P	P	P	

Both opponents have opening bid strength. One aspect about this sequence is that dummy has a potential source of tricks in diamonds. Avoid leading diamonds unless it is clear to do so. You may be able to draw a conclusion about your partner's failure to bid spades, but it is next to impossible to draw a conclusion about his failure to bid clubs. Spades could be bid at the one level. With ten points and five good spades, East would have bid one spade. East would have to bid two clubs in order to show them. Ten points and five good clubs is not enough to get into the bidding. Keep these negative inferences in mind as well as the positive ones.

C.   If the opponents bid only one suit, you have little to go on other than negative inferences. It is easier to think in terms of what partner might have done than to think in terms of what the opponents might have. This next auction shows a common example of this.

W	N	E	S
			1H
P	2H	P	P
P			

Either opponent can have four spades. North can have five of them! When the opponents bid just one suit and do not show strong hands, as happens here, you often have to look at your own shape and points and try to determine what partner can and can not have.

W	N	E	S
			1H
P	2H	P	P
P			

WEST

♠ J64

♡ K843

◇ Q73

♣ AQ6

You have a lot of high card points so you know East can't have too much. Also, your four cards in hearts tells you that East has one or two hearts. With one or two hearts, East tries to bid on this sequence. The fact that he didn't bid suggests a generally poor hand. If East does have some values, you can't tell where they are.

W	N	E	S
			1H
P	1NT	P	2H
P	P	P	

This is a perplexing auction. You can tell how many points your partner has, but you can't tell much about his distribution. Some sequences are not easy to lead against. This is one such. North's shape can range from a 3-2-4-4 shape to a 1-1-7-4 shape. South can have a 3-6-2-2 hand up to an extreme 4-7-0-2. Admittedly, the wilder patterns are unlikely, but they can exist.

5. Did Your Partner Make A Lead Directing Double? Did He Pass When He Might Have Doubled?

Let me introduce this topic with some questions. Following are sequences where you end up on opening lead. On all of the sequences, North has bid a fourth suit or has made a cue bid. At that point in the auction, East has either passed or doubled, signified by P(X) in the bidding diagram. What do you infer when partner passes and what do you infer when he doubles? This is important material. When you are on lead, you need all the help you can get. A bid from partner of any kind is appreciated. It might be an overcall. It might be a takeout double. It might be a penalty double. And, even though it is not as obvious, your partner's silence might be the key to the killing lead. That is why you must be alert to the things that happened in the bidding and the things that did not happen. On these auctions, there is a specific pregnant moment when partner either does or does not act. You must be aware of these moments and the consequences of what partner chooses to do. You are West. Consider what East's bids show in the following auctions.

	W	N	E	S
#1				1C
	P	1H	P	1S
	P	2D*	P(X)	2NT
	P	3NT	P	P
	P			

*Fourth Suit Forcing

#2	W	N	E	S
				1S
	2C	2D	P	2H
	P	3C	P(X)	3NT
	P	P	P	

#3	W	N	E	S
				1D
	1S	2S	P(X)	3C
	P	3D	P	3NT
	P	P	P	

#4	W	N	E	S
		1H	P	1S
	P	3S	P	4C
	P	4D	P(X)	4NT
	P	5H	P	6S
	P	P	P	

#5	W	N	E	S
				1C
	P	1S	2H	3C
	P	3H	P(X)	3NT
	P	P	P	

#6	W	N	E	S
		1D	2S	3H
	P	3S	P(X)	3NT
	P	P	P	

#7	W	N	E	S
				1H
	P	2C	P	3H
	P	4H	P	4NT
	P	5D	P(X)	6H
	P	P	P	

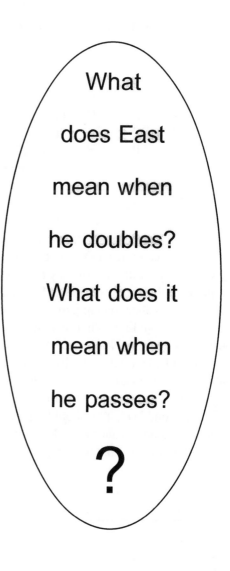

What does East mean when he doubles? What does it mean when he passes?

?

Before continuing decide what it would mean to you if your partner doubled on these seven sequences.

Here are my thoughts on the previous problems.

#1

W	N	E	S	
			1C	Any time the opponents bid the fourth suit, it is likely to
P	1H	P	1S	be suspect. In the same way that you double artificial bids
P	2D*	P(X)	2NT	like Stayman and Jacoby for the lead, you can often
P	3NT	P	P	double a fourth suit for the lead. East might double two
P				diamonds on this sequence with something like the
				following hand.

*Fourth Suit

EAST

♠ 874
♡ K94
♦ KJ985
♣ J8

There is a risk that if you double two diamonds, the opponents will redouble and make it; or they will play the hand especially well in light of your double; or they may even use your double to reach a good contract they otherwise would miss. But against these misfortunes, you have a chance to help partner with his opening lead. The net benefits make it worth doubling. What this means is that when you are on lead against three notrump, you know that East has told you something about his diamonds. If he doubled two diamonds, you will virtually always lead diamonds, and if he passed two diamonds, you will have a negative inference that he doesn't have great diamonds. Be careful not to overreact to this inference. If partner passes two diamonds, you should not infer that he hates a diamond lead. You should infer that he can't demand one. If you have a good diamond holding, go ahead and lead them. If you are thinking of leading a diamond from two small, hoping to find partner's suit, you needn't bother.

#2

W	N	E	S	
			1S	This situation is different. North's three club bid is a cue
2C	2D	P	2H	bid. A common treatment today is to play that this cue bid
P	3C	P(X)	3NT	asks if partner has a club stopper. In this case, South says
P	P	P		he has one and bids three notrump. Let's say you are West
				and you have the KJ7632 of clubs. Should you lead one or
				should you look elsewhere? The answer lies in what East

did over North's cue bid. Did East pass or did he double? In either case, do you know what to make of it? I have two valuable suggestions for you.

Suggestion #1

Here is a treatment which I recommend. If your partner bids a suit and the opponents bid for awhile and later cue bid partner's suit, often looking for three notrump, a double by you tells partner that you have an honor in the suit and are willing to have partner lead the suit. For this purpose, an honor is defined as the ace, king, or queen. You do not promise support. You promise a high card in the suit. You might have two or three clubs to an honor. You might have just a singleton honor.

#3

W	N	E	S
			1D
1S	2S	DBL	

When North cue-bids two spades, East doubles. Does this double have the same meaning as East's double of three clubs in the previous auction? I think there should be a distinction. Here is why. On the prior auction, West overcalled two clubs and the bidding went for one full round before North cue-bid clubs. East had a chance to raise clubs but did not. When North later cue-bid clubs, East, already having denied club support, is able to double to show a club honor. On the auction here, North cue-bids two spades right over the spade overcall. East may wish to raise spades, but not feel like going to the three level.

Suggestion #2

If your partner overcalls and your RHO cue-bids, a double by you should show genuine support for partner. Your support can range from a crummy six point hand up to a huge hand. Here is how you show the difference. This discussion refers to the auction on the top of the page.

EAST
♠ J62
♡ 98653
◊ K8
♣ Q93

Double. You have enough to raise to two spades if it had been possible. Doubling shows this hand. Double does not promise a spade honor. It just says you have a modest hand with spade support. You can have three or four card support.

EAST
♠ K542
♡ 10763
◊ 43
♣ KJ4

Bid three spades. You have four card support to an honor and a decent quality seven high card points along with your shape. You are willing to compete to the three level. The three spade bid shows in the vicinity of eight to ten support points and probably four card support although three is OK if you have good points. Remember that the opponents are bidding strongly so you can tell that your partner has a minimum overcall. No need to raise to the three level with cheese and hand your partner's head to the opponents.

EAST
♠ KJ62
♡ AQ65
◊ 72
♣ J107

In the real world, you won't have many hands as good as this one. If the miracle should ever happen, you can cue-bid three diamonds to tell partner the good news. The expected outcome will be that partner returns to three spades. At least you will feel that you tried.

EAST				
♠ 75	Pass. When your partner overcalls one spade and your RHO cuebids, a
♡ QJ87	double by you should show spade support and six to eight points. This hand
◊ A73	does not have support. You don't want partner to bid more spades and you
♣ 9873	don't want him to lead a spade. Resist the urge to make a silly noise.

#4

W	N	E	S	
	1H	P	1S	This double is just a lead directing order with no other
P	3S	P	4C	hints implied. East has something in diamonds and is
P	4D	P(X)	4NT	suggesting a diamond lead. Nothing special here.
P	5H	P	6S	Typically, East has the KJ8 or better, but even the QJ85
P	P	P		will do in a pinch. As long as you are not doubling them

in a contract they may choose to redouble and play in, you
can whack a cue bid. NOTE that East should not double
four diamonds if he really wants a different lead. Doubling
with J98654 of a suit can get you rich if they play it there, But that won't happen. They
are going to bid something. You may enjoy making a noise with your J98654 of
diamonds, but will you enjoy seeing your partner lead the king of diamonds from the K2
doubleton?

#5

W	N	E	S	
			1C	Here, East overcalls hearts and later doubles a heart cue-
P	1S	2H	3C	bid. This is a meaningful double. It says more than that
P	3H	P(X)	3NT	East thinks he can set three hearts. East is saying he has
P	P	P		good hearts and wants West to lead them. If East does not

have a good suit he can pass, which is a gentle hint to West
to look for another lead. West will probably lead a heart no
matter what he has, but doubling makes sure that West
doesn't find a reason to lead something else.

#6

W	N	E	S	
	1D	2S	3H	This auction differs from the previous auction in that East
P	3S	P(X)	3NT	is making a weak bid. It seems normal to play that East's
P	P	P		double shows good spades. Some scientists use the double

to tell West NOT to lead spades. East presumably wants a
different lead, holding ♠ J87542 ♡ 32 ◊ 5 ♣ KQ94, for
instance. This is actually an OK treatment. East will get a
spade lead most of the time no matter what he does. Using
double to suggest West look elsewhere is not a bad idea.

EXPERT TRICK- This is definitely an optional trick. You can say that when you bid a
suit and later double it, it is a warning that you want a different lead. If you do this, you
must alert your opponents about it.

This next hand shows an example of this science at work. I need not remind you that if you decide to play this, you better be certain that both of you know that this agreement is in effect.

W	N	E	S
	1D	P	1H
1S	3D	P	3S
DBL	3NT	P	P
P			

NOTE. *This hand shows a special trick. Don't try this without a specific discussion with your partner.*

WEST
♠ QJ652
♡ K94
♢ 3
♣ KQJ8

West can use the warning double here. West does not want a spade lead against three notrump, or for that matter, against any other contract that North should declare. West wants a club lead. By doubling three spades, West tells East that there is another lead that West much prefers. Double does not indicate for certain what the other lead is. East does have to work out what is wanted. Usually, East can figure it out. Here, clubs is the unbid suit so it is logical that West wants a club lead.

#7

W	N	E	S
			1H
P	2C	P	3H
P	4H	P	4NT
P	5D	P(X)	6H
P	P	P	

Doubles of responses to Blackwood and Gerber are just lead directing bids. West should lead the suit unless he has a clear other choice.

EAST
♠ 109762
♡ 4
♢ KJ73
♣ K82

Double. West will tend to choose an unbid suit for his opening lead. With spades and diamonds available, he has a choice. You can help him by doubling five diamonds. As noted earlier, you might double five diamonds if your diamonds were a little worse. You could try doubling with the QJ87 of diamonds.

♠ KJ73
♡ 4
♢ 109762
♣ K82

Do you want a diamond lead? Neither would I. Pass five diamonds. Passing does not mean your partner will lead a spade which you very much want, but it will help West decide what to lead. He will, or should, reflect that you did not double five diamonds. This is a common situation. When I am on lead after my RHO has bid Blackwood, one of the automatic things I think about is that partner had a chance to bid over the Blackwood responses. When he does double, you have a strong clue. When he does not double, you have a strong inference.

Some Postmortem Auctions

W	N	E	S
			1H
P	3H	P	4D
?			

This is a reminder auction. Who is going to be on lead when the bidding is over? Assuming they play in hearts, you are on lead. What is the point of doubling if you are the opening leader? Doubling does two things, neither of them good. Your double tells South, who is going to be declarer, that something bad is happening. He will use this information in the bidding and later in the play. The second bad thing is that your double gives them a free round of bidding room. North has two additional bids to make after your double. He can pass, which is informative, and he may redouble, which is frequently used to show a second round control in the suit you just doubled. Doubling a cue bid when you are going to be the opening leader is a free gift to the opponents.

Zia Mahmood, a colorful character (some would use a different term), likes to take advantage of this by making fake doubles. On the auction given, he might double four diamonds with nothing in the suit. This double may confuse their auction and it may confuse declarer in the play. Zia once doubled on the auction above with 9743 of the suit South cue-bid. This had an exemplary effect. North-South were cold for seven in the suit Zia doubled. They did not find their grand slam after this double and they neglected to redouble four diamonds, which would have been almost as good as bidding the grand slam. Try this at your own risk. If it doesn't work, write Zia, care of the ACBL. Don't write me.

Doubling a Splinter Bid

If you play much tournament bridge, this section will be useful for you. One of the conventions you run into in tournaments is the *Splinter Bid*. It works this way. When someone is about to make a strong raise of partner's suit, he can make a jump bid in one of the other suits to indicate that he has a singleton there along with support for partner and enough points for game. In the following auction, North's four diamond bid shows a stiff along with four hearts and thirteen or more points.

SOUTH DEALS
NORTH-SOUTH VULNERABLE

W	N	E	S
			1H
P	4D*	DBL	4H
?			

*Splinter bid

What does East's double mean? Is he showing lots of diamonds and a wish for you to bid five diamonds if you have an appropriate hand? Or is he showing a strong diamond holding that wants you to lead them? He might have something like: ♠ 874 ♡ 93 ◇ KQ109 ♣ 7643. East knows that he can't stand any lead except for diamonds.

Expert Trick - An Artificial Double Of A Splinter Bid

Which meaning for double do you think applies? Or do you think there is another meaning that I haven't shown?

Actually, there is another possible meaning for double. It is interesting. You might play that a double of a splinter bid says nothing about the suit you doubled. (They aren't going to play it here so the double is free in that sense.) Instead, play that the double demands the lead of the lowest unbid suit. In this case, East's double would ask for a club lead.

EAST	With the understanding that you are using the double to ask for the lead of
♠ 97	the lower ranking suit, you should double with this hand. If you pass, your
♡ 106	partner will have a guess as to what to lead and if your partner is as dense
◇ Q8654	about these things as I am, you know he will lead spades too often to suit
♣ AQ65	you. This is an Expert Trick and must be alerted if you use it. You can, if
	you wish, play that the double asks for the highest unbid suit. I think there is

a minuscule advantage in using double to ask for the lowest suit and that is the suggestion I make.

I like using double to ask for the lead of some other suit. You lose the ability to double for the lead of the splintered suit, which is of little consequence. Alternatively, you lose the ability to suggest partner compete in the suit. This is a debatable use since you are making a decision at a high level where the slightest error will be expensive. There is one last benefit of this funny double. If you use this special double, your partner will have an inference when you don't use it. If you use the double of four diamonds to ask for a club lead, then when your partner does not double, you have a hint that he prefers a spade. Life is difficult enough so any little help you can get is useful.

SOUTH DEALS
NORTH-SOUTH VULNERABLE

W	N	E	S
			1H
2C	4C*	DBL	4H
?			

*Splinter bid

This situation is different. West has bid clubs. It is possible that all West needs from East is some club support to go on to five clubs. Here is a useful rule you can adopt. If East doubles four clubs, it shows support and indicates a willingness for West to go on to five clubs. Since East could have bid five clubs instead, West should not play East for a lot. On this auction with favorable vulnerability, East could have this hand for a double: ♠ Q10643 ♡ 83 ◇ 932 ♣ K86. With only three clubs and not much to speak of, doubling is just right. If you play this treatment, you can't double four clubs without real support. If you have K2 of clubs and nothing else, you can't double since it might induce partner to bid again.

SOUTH DEALS
NORTH-SOUTH VULNERABLE

W	N	E	S
			1H
2C	2D	P	2H
P	4C*	DBL	4H
P	P	P	

*Splinter bid

This auction looks similar to the previous one. The big difference is that East did not bid over two diamonds. East can't have real support or he would have bid earlier. When the auction continues and East doubles the delayed splinter, double should just be a lead directing effort. East ought to have the ace or king of clubs.

Sequences where partner doubles an artificial bid are important. Short of bidding a suit, there are few opportunities to get a lead directing noise into the bidding. On the flip side, of course, are the times partner could have doubled and didn't. Don't forget the negative inferences that come with the auction. They are often as strong as the positive inferences. Keep track of the silence as well as the noise.

6. Did Your Partner Make A Penalty Double At Some Point In The Auction?

Be a bit wary of leading a suit that dummy has bid and your partner doubled for penalty. Yor partner will have some values here, but remember that your LHO thought enough of the suit that he was willing to bid it. There is a good chance that declarer will appreciate your giving him some time to set up tricks in the suit. Here are some examples of this.

W	N	E	S
1NT	2H	DBL	2S
DBL	P	P	P

WEST
♠ AQ87
♡ J7
♢ QJ98
♣ AQ8

Should you think about leading a heart? Probably not. South has one or no hearts, so if you lead one, declarer will either get his hands on a quick trick or two or may be able to set up a trick for a later discard. If your hearts were headed by the KQ they would be leadable. In general, leading them isn't rewarding. One specific holding to avoid leading is the doubleton ace. The most likely result will be that you set up dummy's king of hearts.

NORTH
♠ 2
♡ AQ10942
◇ A74
♣ 764

WEST
♠ AQ87
♡ J7
◇ QJ98
♣ AQ8

EAST
♠ 94
♡ K853
◇ K63
♣ J932

SOUTH
♠ KJ10653
♡ 6
◇ 1052
♣ K105

Don't lead the jack of hearts. East's double shows something in hearts, but since West opened one notrump, East does not need really good hearts for a double. West should lead the queen of diamonds. The play can vary, but with a diamond lead the defense will be better placed than with a heart lead. With the jack of hearts lead, dummy takes the ace and leads the queen. Regardless of whether East covers or not, South will get to pitch a loser. The heart lead does not have to work out this way. It could work worse!

There is an aside here worth mentioning. Look at the East hand. Would you double two hearts or just pass it out? If you are a doubler, my congratulations and you don't need to read the rest of this thought. If you are a passer, consider that your side has around twenty-three high card points and at least six hearts. If, in fact, your partner has three hearts, it means you have a large majority of the points and a small majority of the trumps. North is going to find a poor dummy. Whack two hearts with a clear conscience and ruthless expectations. Down one is the least you should expect. NOTE that if South bids something, your points will be useful on defense. North-South are in this one up to their wallets. It will be lucky for them if they escape.

W	N	E	S
1H	2D	P	P
DBL	P	P	3C
P	P	DBL	P
P	P		

This is another sequence where East makes a penalty double of one suit and West ends up on lead against another. West actually did the doubling, but East is the one who has the diamond strength. This sequence is fairly common for pairs that use Negative Doubles. West should not be quick to lead diamonds on this auction just as on the previous hand. East does have something in diamonds, but South has extreme shortness. West may lead a stiff diamond, but should hesitate to lead from two or three of them. On a really bad day, leading a diamond may be the only way declarer can get any diamond tricks. I saw a hand where West led a diamond from three small. Dummy came down with the AKQ107 of diamonds and no quick entry. The worst part of the hand became apparent when declarer showed up with a void. He appreciated the opportunity to discard three losers.

7. Did Your Partner Pass Your Takeout Double?

There are some situations where your lead is mandatory. One instance that everyone knows about is the following. You will find it in every book on bridge. Your RHO opens one of a suit. You double and everyone passes. This was not what you expected when you doubled but it can and does happen. The reason partner passed your takeout double is supposedly that he has a good holding in opener's suit and wishes to defend. Some partners pass your doubles when they shouldn't and when this happens, you are probably going to get a poor result no matter what you lead. Here is a classic case.

SOUTH DEALS
NO ONE VULNERABLE

W	N	E	S
			1S
DBL	P	P	P

NORTH
♠ 52
♡ 109432
◇ 8652
♣ 65

WEST
♠ 7
♡ KJ86
◇ AKJ4
♣ K983

EAST
♠ KJ1098
♡ A5
◇ Q107
♣ Q102

South bids one spade which West doubles. East, with super spades and some high cards too, chooses to pass and play for penalty. How should the defense go? For a second, look at the East-West hands in this light.

SOUTH
♠ AQ643
♡ Q7
◇ 93
♣ AJ74

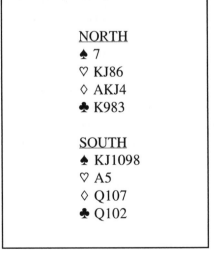

NORTH
♠ 7
♡ KJ86
◇ AKJ4
♣ K983

SOUTH
♠ KJ1098
♡ A5
◇ Q107
♣ Q102

I reversed the cards so that the good spades are now in the South hand. Pretend that you are declaring a four spade contract with the opening lead of the nine of diamonds from West. How do you play the hand? Do you start by taking your high cards in the side suits? No. That is foolish. What you would do is lead trumps. Win the ace of diamonds and lead the seven of trumps to your jack. This happens to lose to the queen. When West leads another diamond, you win and continue trumps. Eventually, you will lose two spades and the ace of clubs. What would you think of a declarer who started the hand by playing three rounds of diamonds, allowing an opponent to ruff in? If the defenders now negotiated a club ruff, thus holding declarer to eight tricks, wouldn't you think that some amount of justice was done?

The same thing applies to the defenders. Go back to the diagram showing all four hands. When East passed the takeout double, he said, in essence, that he wanted to play in a spade contract. East thinks his side can make one or more spades. West must lead a trump in order to stop all the ruffs that declarer will get if the defenders give him time to get them. If West leads the seven of spades and the defenders continue appropriately, one spade doubled will be down four tricks. If the defenders get busy leading hearts and diamonds, declarer will have time to get a diamond ruff in his hand and a club ruff in dummy for down two tricks only. Sloppy defense will lose two tricks.

Don't take this rule to extremes. When you make a takeout double of an opening one bid and partner passes, you should lead a trump.

If you double a weak two bid or a three bid and partner passes, you should not lead a trump. At the one level, you know your partner has great trumps. An opening two or three bid shows a weak hand, but does show a six card suit or better, and usually a pretty good one. Leading a trump will not help you much since you aren't going to be able to draw his trumps as you could after a one bid was doubled and passed out. Instead of leading a trump, you should lead whatever else your instincts suggest. It is true that a trump lead may be best, but there is no indication that this is so.

8. Did Your Partner Double The Final Contract?

A. They Bid a Slam and Your Partner Doubles. The Lightner Double.

When your partner doubles a voluntarily bid slam and you are on lead, he is telling you that he wants you to lead a specific suit. This idea was created by Theodore Lightner in 1929 and has become known appropriately enough as the 'Lightner' double. Ted saw that when his opponents bid slams, they usually made or maybe went down one. Doubling them seldom led to a big penalty. All that happened was that the opponents went down 100 instead of 50 or 200 instead of 100. Against this, the opponents sometimes made their doubled slams and received numbers like 1090 or 1660. You know the numbers I mean. You have to get out a piece of paper to figure them out. In the long run, doubling a slam was not a big gainer for the doubler.

I can see how Ted came up with his double. His opponents bid to a slam and after they made it, Ted saw that if his partner had led a diamond instead of a heart, the slam would have gone down. Since the difference between making a slam and going down is huge, Ted wondered whether there might not be a way to get his partner to lead the right suit. Hence the invention of the 'Lightner' slam double.

It works this way. You are East in the following sequences.

W	N	E	S
			1S
P	2D	P	2S
P	3C	P	3NT
P	6NT	?	

EAST
♠ 8743
♡ J64
♢ AQ76
♣ 83

Sitting East, you can see that North is likely to have the king of diamonds for his two diamond bid. If West should lead a diamond, the slam will go down. But, if West doesn't lead a diamond, the slam may make. Wishing hard for a diamond lead is one approach, but it didn't work for Ted. He observed that if a double asked for dummy's first bid suit, he could, on some hands, ask partner for a certain lead. Using this double, East can double six notrump and West will lead a diamond.

NORTH
♠ K10
♡ Q10
♢ KJ982
♣ AKQJ

WEST
♠ 95
♡ 98752
♢ 104
♣ 9762

EAST
♠ 8743
♡ J64
♢ AQ76
♣ 83

SOUTH
♠ AQJ62
♡ AK3
♢ 53
♣ 1054

Looking at the West hand, would you lead a diamond without the double? Here, the double gains East-West 1090 points which is the difference between making six notrump and going down one, doubled. There is always a chance that South will have the king of diamonds. Is it worth risking a double which will cost you a bundle if it doesn't work? The answer is easy. If doubling gains you more often than failure, you come out ahead. If you agree that North will have the king of diamonds most of the time, they you must agree that doubling will get you many good results in return for one or two bad ones. (You may describe them as unlucky if you prefer.)

You can use the 'Lightner' double against suit slams too. Usually you are indicating a void and want partner to give you a ruff.

NORTH DEALS
NO ONE VULNERABLE

W	N	E	S
	1D	2H	2S
3H	4S	P	4NT
P	5S	P	6S
P	P	?	

EAST
♠ A73
♡ QJ10652
◇ —
♣ 8652

With South declaring six spades, you know a diamond lead will set them. Using the 'Lightner' double, you can double six spades, which will tell partner to lead dummy's first bid suit. This will get you a diamond lead. Down one will be 100 for you so the plus score you get is just a little one. But, you are not getting a minus 980 which would have happened had you passed. The gain to you was 1080 points.

NOTE - Do not double if it will get partner off to a bad lead. This sort of thing has happened. It won't take many hands like the following to make your partner give up the game.

W	N	E	S
	1C	P	1H
P	3H	P	4C
P	4D	P	6H
P	P	P	

EAST
♠ AK5
♡ Q1094
◇ 86532
♣ 4

What lead do you want from your partner? You want a spade lead. If you pass, what will partner lead? He will probably lead a spade. If you double, your partner will say to himself that you must want a special lead. On this bidding, that lead rates to be a club and that is what partner will lead. He will expect you to be ruffing them. You will have the pleasure of watching declarer discard a spade on dummy's ace-king of diamonds and later make the slam, losing one trick to your Q1094 of hearts. Why were the opponents in a slam missing so many important cards? Who knows. What we do know is that if they wish to bid this way, we still have to do the right things to set them. Passing six hearts and beating it a trick or two is a decent enough result. Why double it and persuade partner to get off to an embarrassing lead?

Two Postmortem Thoughts

1.   Partner may be able to draw some inferences from your failure to double the final contract. If partner can eliminate one suit from his consideration, that is a useful step in the right direction. Negative inferences are just as valuable as positive inferences. But they are harder to see and hear. On the previous hand, West would probably have led a spade if East did not double six hearts. Here is another hand from West's point of view. Review the bidding and refer to West's terrible hand. What should West lead?

W	N	E	S
			1H
P	3H	P	3S
P	4C	P	4NT
P	5D	P	6H
P	P	P	

WEST
♠ 10974
♡ 52
◊ 942
♣ 10843

What West should lead is not clear. There are a couple of hints about what to lead and there is an important hint about what not to lead. West, on the merits of his own hand, has little to guide him. West has the fairly strong inference that East doesn't want a diamond lead since he could have doubled the Blackwood response of five diamonds. Doubling Blackwood responses is a good way to help your partner with an opening lead and East's failure to double can be taken as a hint. A lesser hint is that East did not double four clubs. Curiously, a spade lead might be right. South cue-bid them, but he might have only the ace of spades. He could be missing the lesser spade honors. The main point of this problem is that you do consider that partner did not contribute an opinion when he might have done so.

While the majority of doubles of suit contracts are made to get a ruff, there will be some exceptions.

W	N	E	S
	1S	P	2C
P	2H	P	3NT
P	4C	P	4D
P	6C	DBL	P
P	P		

East isn't sure what West will lead. Almost anything is possible. Normally on a sequence like this, your partner will lead an unbid suit. Diamonds are a candidate even though South cue-bid them. Hearts are also possible as are spades. If East wants a heart lead, it is impossible to request one. If East wants a diamond lead, it is also impossible to request one. If East wants a spade lead, he can double, which emphasizes spades, dummy's first bid suit. Should East double with the following hand?

EAST
♠ K10
♡ A9652
♢ 9832
♣ 97

There are fewer certainties when you double a suit slam than when you are doubling a notrump slam. Say South was in six notrump and you were sure North had the ace of spades. If you could double and get a spade lead, you would do so. Unless the opponents have twelve top tricks without needing a heart trick, they will go down. Here, South is in six clubs. A double by you will get a spade lead. But, even if North has the ace of spades, a spade lead won't guarantee setting them. If South has a singleton spade, you will not have a winning spade to cash when you get in with the ace of hearts. Given the dangers, do you think that doubling six clubs is wise?

NORTH
♠ AJ764
♡ KJ104
♢ 4
♣ AJ2

WEST
♠ Q853
♡ 73
♢ J765
♣ 653

EAST
♠ K10
♡ A9652
♢ 9832
♣ 97

SOUTH
♠ 92
♡ Q8
♢ AKQ10
♣ KQ1084

I won't make any promises, but there is a fair clue that suggests you can double. On the second round, South jumped to three notrump. This suggests that South has two spades. If you are willing to take a chance, doubling is reasonable. On this day, a spade lead gets down one. Any other lead gives declarer time to take twelve tricks. East's double is gutsy, but it is also a winner. I suppose it depends on how many tricks South gets to find the appropriate descriptive word for East's double.

2. You can play an addition to the specific rules of a 'Lightner' double. If the opponents bid a slam but do not bid suits along the way, you can use double to tell partner you want a specific lead. Partner may have to think about the situation to come up with the winner, but it should be evident from his hand.

W	N	E	S
			1H
P	4H	P	6H
P	P	DBL	P
P	P		

Say you are West and you hear the opponents bid one heart, four hearts, six hearts, and your partner, who was silent until now, doubles. What do you think is happening?

Does your partner have three or four tricks and is increasing the penalty or does he have some other idea in mind? One thing should be clear. South is not crazy. When he bid six hearts, he expected to make it. If South is a lunatic or if your partner happens to have two or more sure trump tricks, it does not matter what you lead. But if South is a good player, he is not bidding six hearts in the hopes of going down eight hundred. He is bidding six hearts because he hopes to make it. Assuming South has sensible judgment, you do not rate to set six hearts a lot of tricks. The usual goal for the defenders is to set slams by a trick so as to avoid the huge loss that occurs when the slam makes.

The meaning of your partner's double of six hearts is the same as always. He is telling you that if you can find the correct lead, they will go down.

W	N	E	S	
			1H	Here is the bidding again. You will note that on this
P	4H	P	6H	sequence, the opponents did not bid any suits other than
P	P	DBL	P	hearts on the way to slam. East can't use double to specify
P	P			which suit he wants you to lead. The double remains lead

directing, but the message is that East thinks the slam will fail if you can *guess* which suit he wants. Usually the doubler has a void suit and hopes that you can tell from your hand which suit it is.

W	N	E	S	
			1S	This is another uninformative sequence. North jumped to
P	4S	P	4NT	four spades and South tried Blackwood. North didn't have
P	5C	P	6S	any aces, but South still went to slam. East doubles and
P	P	DBL	P	you are on lead with the hand following. What should you
P	P			lead?

WEST

♠ 52
♡ J876542
♢ 6
♣ 874

Without East's double, you would lead the six of diamonds and be pleased you had such a good lead available. If East has the diamond ace or the ace of spades to get in with quickly, you can get a ruff. East's double should stop you for a moment. What do you think East has? If he has the ace-king of any particular suit, he would not double for two reasons. East can't be sure of two tricks. And, to add doubt to the wisdom of doubling with the ace-king of a suit, there is no way for West to know which suit East wants.

Can East have two aces? Not likely. Actually, I have seen people bid this way when missing two aces. Horrible idea. Usually, when someone bids a slam off two aces, they have a void and one of the aces gets ruffed.

Perhaps East has two trump tricks. If so, it doesn't matter what you lead. East will get his tricks.

These things are possible, but they are unlikely. They also reflect bad judgment by one or more of the players at the table. Assume that your partner's double is sane and that he is hinting to you to find a killing lead. On an auction like this one, the reason for the double is almost always a void. On the hand you have, the seven card heart suit is a strong hint that partner wants a heart ruff. Lead a heart and hope you have read it right.

B. They Bid a Game and Your Partner Doubles.

Lead directing doubles can be used against game contracts too. If you and your partner have been in the bidding, you or partner may well double the opponents when they get to game. It is when the opponents have the bidding more or less to themselves that an out-of-the-blue double by your partner can have a special meaning. There are important differences between doubles of three notrump and doubles of suit games.

You Double Three Notrump - Your Side Did Not Bid

W	N	E	S
			1NT
P	3NT	DBL	P
P	P		

The opponents bid to game and your partner, who must have heard the auction, thinks he can set them. What kind of hand will give your partner that idea? One thing the double does not say is that East has lots of points. He won't have that hand since the opponents have shown about twenty-five points or more. The answer is something else entirely. East thinks that the right lead from you will set three notrump. There are many ideas about what this double calls for. Some players think it calls for a club lead. Some think it demands a major suit lead.

Out of all the contrary opinions has come a relatively accepted standard. On the auction above, East's double tells West to make an intelligent guess as to which suit East wants led. Here is the kind of hand that East ought to have.

EAST
♠ KQJ984
♡ A2
♢ 43
♣ 973

Here, East wants a spade lead. With a spade lead, declarer may not have nine winners without some heart tricks. If so, East hopes to run the spades as soon as he gets in with the ace of hearts. East doesn't have a 100% assurance that a spade lead will work, but it is a good shot. Now all that remains is for West to lead the right suit. Usually, this is not hard. East has length in the suit he wants led. It stands to reason that West will not have too many of this suit. Hence the rule. When your partner doubles three notrump and no suits have been bid, you should lead your short suit in expectation of finding partner's suit.

W	N	E	S
			1NT
P	3NT	DBL	P
P	P		

(Repeated for Convenience.)

NORTH
♠ 105
♡ Q7
◇ A10852
♣ K1096

WEST
♠ 32
♡ J9653
◇ QJ6
♣ J84

EAST
♠ KQJ984
♡ A2
◇ 43
♣ 732

SOUTH
♠ A76
♡ K1084
◇ K97
♣ AQ5

If West leads his fourth best heart, the lead he would make without any input from East, South will take at least one spade, two hearts, two diamonds, and four clubs.

If East doubles and if West judges to lead a spade, South won't have time to set up heart tricks or diamond tricks and will go down two tricks. A good result for the convention. Be aware that it is not perfect.

WEST
♠ A10743
♡ J1072
◇ 1082
♣ 9

You are on lead after the bidding goes 1NT - P - 3NT and double by partner. What should West lead? According to the rule, you are supposed to lead your short suit. It looks like partner has clubs and a side entry. Lead the nine of clubs. The result may give you second thoughts about this convention. I know that as East, I wasn't impressed. Here is the complete hand.

NORTH
♠ J
♡ 3
◇ 754
♣ AQ1087543

WEST
♠ A10743
♡ J1072
◇ 1082
♣ 9

EAST
♠ Q952
♡ AKQ954
◇ J6
♣ 2

We can take eleven tricks with a heart lead. We took no tricks with a club lead. Judge for yourself if you agree with this result.

SOUTH
♠ K86
♡ 86
◇ AKQ93
♣ KJ6

On some sequences North and South bid and bid and bid before getting to three notrump. On some sequences, East and West are bidding too. According to how the bidding goes, a final double of three notrump can have different meanings.

W	N	E	S
			1D
P	1H	P	1S
P	2D	P	2NT
P	3NT	DBL	P
P	P		

North-South get to three notrump all by themselves, but they take a long time to do it. South has shown an eighteen point hand and North, who gave a mere preference to two diamonds, admits to having enough to go on to game. East's double is not a double based on the general feeling that they can't make a game. East's double is a demand that West lead a heart. When your side doesn't bid and they get to three notrump, a double by fourth hand asks the opening leader to lead dummy's first suit. On this auction, East is asking for a heart lead. The complete hand:

NORTH
♠ 73
♡ K1074
◇ K763
♣ Q76

WEST
♠ K10852
♡ 852
◇ 9
♣ 10982

EAST
♠ 96
♡ AQJ93
◇ 1054
♣ A54

SOUTH
♠ AQJ4
♡ 6
◇ AQJ82
♣ KJ3

If West is left to his own ears and sight, he will tend to lead the ten of clubs. Without an indication in the bidding from partner, leading from a sequence in the unbid suit is usually a good thing. But not here. A club lead gives South time to get nine tricks. After East's double, though, West has instructions on what to lead and leads hearts. East will win the first trick and will continue hearts, setting up the suit. Sooner or later, East will get in with a club to set three notrump one trick. In fact, if declarer decides to take a spade finesse in hopes of making, he will be down two.

Rules for Doubling Three Notrump When Your Side Did Not Bid

1 If dummy has bid a suit, a double usually requests that you lead dummy's first bid suit.

2 If they bid to three notrump without bidding a suit, a double says East has a good suit that he wants West to lead. West has to use his judgment as to which suit East has. More often than not, the suit East wants will be a major. But it is possible that it is a minor suit. West has to look at his hand to make the decision.

You Double Three Notrump - Your Side Was In The Bidding

Here is another example of a lead directing double of three notrump. Note that in this case, East-West were in the bidding. When your side bids a suit prior to the opponents bidding three notrump, doubles tend to demand the lead of a suit bid by your side.

W	N	E	S
		1C	1NT
P	3NT	P	P
P			

WEST	
♠ J10976	What would you lead against three notrump? Are you impressed enough with
♡ 9864	East's one club bid to lead one or are you going to let South's one notrump
◊ 82	bid worry you that East may have a short club? Admit it. You would either
♣ 42	lead the jack of spades or at least be sorely tempted. After all, East might
	have opened one club with only three clubs. He might be four-four in the
	majors.

Go back to the auction and insert a double for East's final bid. Most doubles, when the opponents bid strongly to game, are lead directing doubles. This one is also. East is asking for the lead of his suit. He wants a club lead. Lead one.

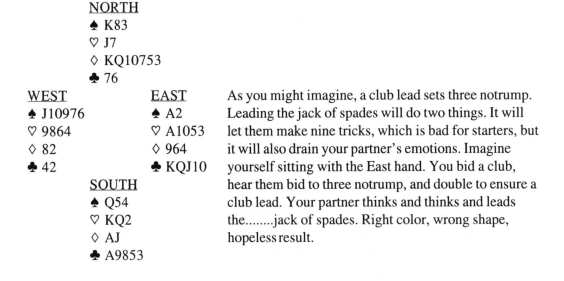

NORTH	
♠ K83	
♡ J7	
◊ KQ10753	
♣ 76	

WEST	EAST	
♠ J10976	♠ A2	As you might imagine, a club lead sets three notrump.
♡ 9864	♡ A1053	Leading the jack of spades will do two things. It will
◊ 82	◊ 964	let them make nine tricks, which is bad for starters, but
♣ 42	♣ KQJ10	it will also drain your partner's emotions. Imagine
		yourself sitting with the East hand. You bid a club,

SOUTH	
♠ Q54	hear them bid to three notrump, and double to ensure a
♡ KQ2	club lead. Your partner thinks and thinks and leads
◊ AJ	the........jack of spades. Right color, wrong shape,
♣ A9853	hopeless result.

Lead directing doubles of three notrump are more frequent than you might think. Once you realize their potential, you will see more and more of them. One caution. Be sure, when you double for a special lead, that the lead is all you need to set them. In my youth, holding KQJ1075 of spades, I doubled three notrump for a spade lead, dummy's first bid suit. Spades was indeed the best lead for our side. The spade lead was less of a triumph than I had wished. It held them to eleven tricks, which was the fewest taken by anyone else in the room. Oh yes, did I mention that they redoubled?

Rules For Doubling Three Notrump When Your Side Bids

These rules assume that the opponents have bid three notrump and your partner has doubled. It is your lead.

1.   If your partner has bid a suit, you should lead it.

2.   If you have bid a suit, you should lead it.

3.   If you and your partner have both bid suits, and partner doubles three notrump, it is uncertain which suit your partner wants. I have seen understandings go both ways with this one. I hesitate to insist on either being right. Since you need a reference, though, I will offer this one. If you and your partner have both bid and the opponents get to three notrump, you can tell whether you or your partner has the stronger hand. I suggest you lead the suit that the stronger hand has bid.

W	N	E	S	
	1S	2C	2D	East's club overcall tends to show more points than West's
2H	2S	P	2NT	two heart bid. Using this guideline, I would lead a club.
P	3NT	DBL	P	This is logical since your partner rates to have some entries
P	P			in addition to his good suit.

A Little Quiz

In the following auctions, what suit is East asking for when he doubles?

W	N	E	S	
	1D	P	1H	Lead a diamond. Your side
P	2C	P	2NT	didn't bid so East's double asks
P	3NT	DBL	P	for dummy's first bid suit.
P	P			

W	N	E	S
			P
P	1H	P	2NT
P	P	DBL	P
P	P		

Lead a heart. The same rules apply in general when you make an unexpected double of two notrump as when you double three notrump. East's double is lead directing for dummy's heart suit. I will touch on this more in a page or two.

W	N	E	S
			1NT
P	2C	P	2S
P	3NT	DBL	P
P	P		

You know that East couldn't double two clubs, so clubs is not the suit. Going back to the earlier guidelines, you will see that East is asking for dummy's first bid suit in the event that your side hasn't bid a suit of its own. On the sequence here, North asked for a major suit and went to three notrump when South bid spades. North has bid hearts, albeit in an indirect fashion. East's double is asking for a heart lead.

W	N	E	S
			1H
2C	2D	P	2NT
P	3NT	DBL	P
P	P		

Your side bid clubs. East's double asks you to lead your club suit.

W	N	E	S
			1S
2C	2D	P	2H
P	3C	P	3NT
P	P	DBL	P
P	P		

Normally, East's double would ask for a club lead. East had a chance to double three clubs to show an honor so you have conflicting input. I think East is actually doubling on a good diamond holding and perhaps some other values. Use your judgment here.

Expert Trick - Getting something out of nothing.

When You Unexpectedly Double A Suit Game

This is a well kept secret. When the opponents bid to a suit game with your side silent, you can double them with lead directing purpose just as you might double a slam. Usually, such a double indicates a void. This brings up an interesting defensive consideration. If your partner doubles for a lead, he will be interested in knowing if you can get in to lead the suit again. Believe it or not, the card you lead should be a suit preference card.

W	N	E	S
			1S
P	2S	P	4S
P	P	DBL	P
P	P		

East thinks a certain lead will set four spades.

WEST
♠ A7
♡ A95
♢ 1086532
♣ 94

Odd. North-South got to game on their own steam and East thinks they can't make it. What does East know that we don't know? It doesn't look like East has a pile of trumps. We have two of them so East has a maximum of three. Can East have aces and kings all over the place? This is also unlikely. If East has enough high cards to set four spades and we have two aces ourselves, it means North-South are bidding with nothing, which is not likely. No. South thought he could make four spades when he bid it, which means he has a good hand.

The likely reason for East to double four spades is that he thinks a certain lead will set it. This is rare, but it happens often enough that you should think about it when the auction goes as indicated. What is most likely happening is that East has a diamond void and wants to start with a diamond ruff. This in itself won't set four spades, but it will give the defenders their best start. You should lead the eight of diamonds. Heck! Lead the ten. This is a suit preference card telling East that you can get in again with a heart return.

```
         NORTH
         ♠ J65
         ♡ K103
         ◇ Q974
         ♣ K87
WEST              EAST
♠ A7              ♠ 942
♡ A95             ♡ J7642
◇ 1086532        ◇ —
♣ 94             ♣ QJ1053
         SOUTH
         ♠ KQ1083
         ♡ Q8
         ◇ AKJ
         ♣ A62
```

North-South bid 1S - 2S - 4S and East doubled. This is the layout that East is hoping for. West leads a diamond which East ruffs. West has an entry and is able to give East another diamond ruff. Down one. East did something good and got rewarded for it. This kind of double does not always work though. It may be that West can't get in soon enough. Or perhaps both North and South have maximum hands and the game is just unbeatable. It happens. Go back for a second and look at the defense from the East hand. West leads a diamond and you ruff. You should know that West will lead a suit preference card in this situation.

This is consistent with the situation where you give partner a ruff in the middle of the hand. You lead a suit preference card for partner to ruff. The situation exists here too. West is expecting East to ruff the opening lead so tries to tell East what to return. The lead was the eight (or ten if West was extravagant) of diamonds. East knows that the right return is a heart and not a club.

One final example. This one is extra special and should wake you out of your doldrums when it happens.

W	N	E	S
		3H	4S
P	P	DBL	P
P	P		

WEST
♠ K4
♡ 7
◇ A62
♣ J1087532

Here we have East, a preemptor, doubling four spades when we expected him to be passing. Barring East losing his mind, always a possibility, you have to assume that he is making an intelligent bid. Looking at your hand, it isn't hard to figure out. East is ruffing clubs.

Proving to him that you are listening and thinking at the same time, you lead the two of clubs. East will ruff and seeing your two will assume that you want, or at least prefer, a diamond return. This will get you two club ruffs, a diamond, your king of spades, and even possibly a heart trick.

Here is partner's hand.

EAST
♠ 95
♡ QJ109832
♢ K1084
♣ —

Your partner preempted in hearts, which meant that he was going to get a heart lead from you against four spades. East, knowing that a heart lead wasn't the best lead for the defense, doubled to alert partner that there was a much better lead available.

Keep the thought in your mind that even when the opponents own the cards and bid slams and games, a lead directing double to tell partner what to lead can save the day. One last example from not so long ago.

W	N	E	S	
			1H	This is also an unexpected effort from East. As a rule,
P	2D	P	3D	when the opponents have a happy auction like this one
P	3H	P	4H	which does not smack of a misfit or lack of values, you
P	P	DBL	P	leave the final contract alone. East might have five good
P	P			hearts and be doubling with sure tricks, but more likely he
				has something devious in mind. Here is your hand.

WEST
♠ QJ1065
♡ 32
♢ 10876
♣ K8

You can tell that East doesn't have a trump stack. What East is doing is asking for an unusual lead. With the opponents bidding diamonds, you can envision East's void. Lead a diamond and start with a ruff. You have some chance of getting in with a club, so I suggest leading the six of diamonds. Good luck. Here is another hand you might have against the same auction. What should you lead this time?

WEST
♠ QJ106
♡ 872
♢ 3
♣ J8652

A very possible situation is that East has the ace of diamonds and can 'see' your singleton. He is telling you to lead diamonds. Normally, leading a singleton in a suit the opponents like is a very poor choice. Without the double, the correct lead would be the queen of spades. With the double, the diamond is best. Following is a possible hand East might have for the double of four hearts.

EAST
♠ 8732
♡ J4
♢ A984
♣ A107

If East trusts the North-South bidding, he might double four hearts with this hand. East can see a diamond, a diamond ruff, a club trick, and another diamond ruff. Without the double, West is unlikely to lead a stiff diamond since it rates to cause more harm than good.

Auctions Where Partner's Double Is Expected

On some sequences the opponents bid something at the end which everyone in the room plus the kibitzers know is going to be doubled. It happens all the time. This auction is typical.

NO ONE VULNERABLE

W	N	E	S
1S	P	2D	2H
2S	3H	3S	4H
4S	5H	DBL	P
P	P		

Here, your side bid to four spades and the opponents sacrificed in five hearts. You will tend to lead a spade or a diamond and you might consider a trump lead. Whatever you do, you will do it according to the cards in your hand. Do not get caught up in looking for a special meaning when partner doubles them unless the double is unexpected. Most doubles are old-fashioned opinions that the opponents are going down.

They Bid a Partscore and Partner Doubles - Two Special Situations

There are two occasions where your partner can double a partscore with the intention of telling you what to lead. Both of them draw on the themes discussed above.

1.   Partner Doubles One or Two Notrump Late in the Auction

When the opponents end in one notrump or two notrump, a double in the passout seat can be used as lead directing.

A.   Partner doubles one notrump late in the auction.

Here are some examples of doubles of one notrump.

W	N	E	S
			1D
P	1H	P	1NT
P	P	DBL	P
P	P	P	

East's double is treated by some players as a reopening double. This is a losing proposition. I am not going into the reasons why it should not be used as a balancing bid. I have already written a book (*The Complete Book on Balancing*) which discusses this. Instead, I intend to remind you that this double is for penalty. Here is an expected hand for East.

EAST
♠ A2
♡ QJ1084
◇ 75
♣ AK73

East can see that with a heart lead, his hand has six potential winners. With North-South stopping in one notrump, it is reasonable that West has a few points. If West leads a heart, the defense is off to a good start and should have the timing to establish and use the heart suit along with whatever other winners are available.

58

```
          NORTH              (The complete hand.)
          ♠ K964
          ♡ K973
          ◊ 32
          ♣ J84
WEST                EAST       The result on this hand is not atypical. North and
♠ J875              ♠ A2       South bid to one notrump in peace and quiet with no
♡ 62                ♡ QJ1084   awareness of their danger. If, at the end of the auction,
◊ QJ84              ◊ 75       East passes, West will lead the five of spades and
♣ Q102             ♣ AK73      declarer will take three spades, two hearts, and two
          SOUTH               diamonds.
          ♠ Q103
          ♡ A5                 If East doubles one notrump, West will lead the six of
          ◊ AK1096            hearts. Now, if South guesses the hand perfectly, he
          ♣ 965               can go down one by playing on spades and working
                              out that West has the jack. If, instead, South takes the
                              heart lead and goes after diamonds, ruin! The
                              defenders will set one notrump three tricks.
```

B.   Partner doubles two notrump late in the auction.

The second situation where you can make a lead directing double of a partscore is when the opponents end up in two notrump. You might not like to remember such hands, but when you think about it, you will probably reflect that you have played in two notrump and gone down three or four tricks on occasion. Usually when this happens, it is because all your finesses were off side. If you agree, then you will agree that when it is the opponents who are going down three tricks, they should be doubled.

The times you whack two notrump are when they bid back and forth and eventually settle in two notrump. If you are in the pass out seat and know from the bidding that they have minimal values AND you know their suits are not breaking, you can double. This is much like the previous double of one notrump shown above.

Here is one example auction where you might double them in two notrump.

W	N	E	S
			1D
P	1S	P	2C
P	2D	P	2NT
P	P	DBL	P
P	P	P	

East rates to have good spades. His hand does not have to be huge because he knows that your partnership has a guaranteed sixteen to eighteen points. The complete hand that led to East's double is on the next page.

W	N	E	S	(This is the auction from the preceding page)
			1D	
P	1S	P	2C	
P	2D	P	2NT	
P	P	DBL	P	
P	P	P		

EAST
♠ AJ1074
♡ 1098
◇ 3
♣ A1063

Why would East double two notrump with this hand? The answer is that East can see three or even four spades if the suit is favorable for East-West. In addition, East knows that West has some points. North-South usually have about twenty-three points when they stop in two notrump. West has about eight points. Perhaps they contain one or two diamond stoppers. East's singleton diamond suggests declarer's main suit is breaking poorly for him. If East is lucky, this will be the complete hand.

NORTH
♠ K863
♡ 654
◇ K87
♣ J52

WEST	**EAST**
♠ Q95	♠ AJ1074
♡ KJ72	♡ 1098
◇ J1095	◇ 3
♣ 74	♣ A1063

If East passes two notrump, West may find a spade lead anyway, but he might talk himself into leading the unbid suit, hearts. When East doubles two notrump, West leads a spade and East shifts to the ten of hearts. South will go down like a brick.

SOUTH
♠ 2
♡ AQ3
◇ AQ642
♣ KQ98

Doubles like this are especially expensive when they fail. If you double one notrump and they make it, they get one hundred and eighty points. This is not good, but it is not quite the heart-thumping misery that an unsuccessful double of two notrump can be. If you double two notrump and they make it, you lose four hundred and sixty or six hundred and sixty points, depending on the vulnerability. You have a lot to gain with a successful double, but the price for a poor decision is hugely expensive. Change the hands slightly, as shown on the next page, and the wisdom of the double is less certain.

                    NORTH
                    ♠ K983
                    ♡ J54
                    ◇ Q1072
                    ♣ 75

WEST   EAST   West leads a spade against this layout and South has
♠ 652   ♠ AJ1074   no trouble coming to eight tricks. Doubling two
♡ K762   ♡ 1098   notrump is especially expensive when it fails. For that
◇ J85   ◇ 3   reason I recommend you try it only at matchpoints. If
♣ QJ2   ♣ A1063   you play IMPs, this kind of action runs too large a
                    SOUTH   risk since you can change a -120 into a - 490.
                    ♠ Q
                    ♡ AQ3
                    ◇ AK964
                    ♣ K984

2.   Partner doubles two of a suit. He is in <u>front</u> of the bidder.

There is a family of sequences where partner double demands a special lead from you.

W	N	E	S
		1H	1S
2H	2S	DBL	P
P	P		

A lesson that takes a few minus 670's or minus 180's to learn is that your side will not get rich doubling the opponents when they have a fit. Worse yet is doubling the opponents when they have a fit and you are in front of the original bidder. On both of the sequences here, East opens the bidding and South overcalls one spade. You make your bid and North raises spades. If East is thinking of doubling, he must remember that he is IN FRONT of the spade bidder. It is amazing how your trump holding can be eaten up by a good declarer. If East has AJ97 of spades, it might look good, but if declarer plays the hand decently, he may be able to avoid more than one spade loser. It would be much better if West had the AJ97 of spades OVER the spade bidder.

W	N	E	S
		1C	1S
2D	2S	DBL	P
P	P		

Here is an excellent rule for you to follow. Do not double them in a low level contract if they have a fit and the bidder is over you *unless you have solid trumps*. You want the QJ109 or the KJ109 or something similar. You want trumps so good that declarer will lose two or three trump tricks no matter what he does.

W	N	E	S
		1H	1S
2H	2S	DBL	P
P	P		

W	N	E	S
		1C	1S
2D	2S	DBL	P
P	P		

This leads to a new rule. If your partner doubles them in two spades on either of the above auctions, you should lead a trump. Among other things, you know partner has only four trumps. They must be good trump to justify a double. You should lead one to make sure they don't get any gratuitous ruffs in.

EAST DEALS
NO ONE VULNERABLE

W	N	E	S
		1H	1S
2H	2S	DBL	P
P	P		

WEST
♠ 72
♡ J75
◊ QJ83
♣ KJ64

Lead the two of spades. You should trust partner to have his double. This is a basic requirement of any bridge decision. Trust your partner. Given that you have faith, you should believe that he has four good spades. You may wonder why you have two spades and your partner four spades when the opponents bid and raised them, but that is not for you to worry about.

Perhaps your RHO overcalled with a four card suit. Perhaps your LHO raised with just two. You don't really care as long as you trust your partner. Incidentally. If you think that partner's double was some kind of special double, you should make sure you are on the same wavelength with him. Even if you have a singleton trump, you should lead it as shown on the next hand.

WEST
♠ 7
♡ J75
◊ QJ832
♣ KJ64

If you choose to pass the double, you should lead the seven of spades. Read and reread the following sentences slowly and carefully and read them again if necessary.

If you double a low level contract where the opponents have a fit and where the original bidder is on your left, you must have great trumps. Your partner should lead one if he chooses to sit for the double.

The same rule applies to your partner's doubles too. Whenever your partner doubles a low level contract where the opponents have a fit and where the original bidder is over your partner, he must have great trumps. You should lead one. Here is the complete hand.

```
              NORTH
              ♠ 862
              ♡ K2
              ◇ K1065
              ♣ Q983
WEST                        EAST
♠ 7                         ♠ KQJ10
♡ J75                       ♡ A10863
◇ QJ832                     ◇ 94
♣ KJ64                      ♣ A7
              SOUTH
              ♠ A9543
              ♡ Q94
              ◇ A7
              ♣ 1052
```

West, trusting his partner, leads the seven of spades. East is able to remove dummy's trumps and by the time the hand is over, East-West have set two spades two tricks, doubled. If West leads a heart, South will get one heart ruff in dummy and that will cost a fortune in matchpoints. The key is that East's trumps are in front of South, who bid them. Change East's spades slightly as in the next hand and you are primed for a disaster.

```
              NORTH
              ♠ J65
              ♡ K2
              ◇ K1065
              ♣ 9873
WEST                        EAST
♠ 7                         ♠ KQ93
♡ J75                       ♡ A10863
◇ QJ832                     ◇ 94
♣ KJ64                      ♣ AQ
              SOUTH
              ♠ A10842
              ♡ Q94
              ◇ A7
              ♣ 1052
```

East's spades are weakened by one point and one spot card and he now has the queen of clubs instead. South will get out for down one now and might even make two spades doubled against poor defense. Do not forget that rule I gave you on the previous page. When your LHO bids a suit and your RHO raises to the two level, do not double without solid trump tricks. Also, be ready for a trump lead from partner. If you have what you promise, this lead will be best. If you don't have what you promise, it won't matter what partner leads.

An aside for West in the above hand. West is not obliged to sit for the double. It is a penalty double in every meaning of the word, but it is not a command. You are allowed and expected to use your judgment. If West had a fourth heart and otherwise the same hand, he should run to three hearts. The hand I gave you here has only one spade, but it also has only three hearts and it does have some high card points. It is correct to pass if partner can be trusted to know what he is doing.

9.   What Inferences Can You Draw If Partner Didn't Bid?

There is an additional important clue to help you with your lead. I have alluded to it already, but it is important enough that it deserves a place in the table of contents. On hands where the opponents have shown weakness, you can draw some conclusions from your partner's silence.

NORTH DEALS
NO ONE VULNERABLE

W	N	E	S
	1D	P	1S
P	2C	P	2S
P	P	P	

WEST
♠ 863
♡ 102
◊ KJ74
♣ QJ92

With hearts being unbid, you would naturally consider them as a possible lead. Looking at this hand, you should have some additional thoughts along these lines: "I have seven high card points and the opponents have stopped in two spades. They have nineteen to twenty-three high card points meaning my partner has ten to fourteen high card points. If my partner has these points, it is likely that he would bid one heart over one diamond if he had five of them. Since my partner did not bid hearts and since I think he is strong enough to bid them if he did have them, I can conclude that hearts is not going to be a great choice."

NORTH
♠ J
♡ K74
◊ AQ962
♣ A1054

WEST	EAST
♠ 863	♠ K104
♡ 102	♡ AJ86
◊ KJ74	◊ 853
♣ QJ92	♣ K87

SOUTH
♠ AQ9752
♡ Q953
◊ 10
♣ 63

East has the expected eleven count, but didn't have the right hand to bid with. If East had a fifth heart, he would have bid over one diamond. As you can see, leading the ten of hearts will be costly if declarer covers with the king at trick one. If West properly concludes hearts do not rate to be a great lead, he may find a club lead, North having bid them notwithstanding. This is, arguably, a hard conclusion to reach.

On the next auction, the opponents have good hands and are able to show most of the features of their hands.

W	N	E	S
			1S
P	2C*	P	2D
P	2S	P	4S
P	P	P	

*Forcing to game

WEST
♠ J63
♡ 102
◇ K1074
♣ QJ92

You have much the same hand as before, but you have different things to think about. Lead the ten of hearts. The opponents have lots of values so your partner has between four and nine points. East can have good hearts and not have been able to bid them at the two level.

NORTH
♠ Q95
♡ K93
◇ 92
♣ AK753

WEST	EAST
♠ J63	♠ 104
♡ 102	♡ AQ864
◇ K1074	◇ 865
♣ QJ92	♣ 1064

SOUTH
♠ AK872
♡ J75
◇ AQJ3
♣ 8

The hand turns out to be just what the doctor ordered. East takes two hearts and gives you a ruff. The king of diamonds is the setting trick. I wish I could tell you that your leads will always work out this way, but I can't give you those assurances. Still, the thinking on these two hands is valid. If either opponent had four hearts, he would have bid them. Also, since your partner has a known weak hand, he couldn't bid hearts even if he had a good suit as happened on this hand. Keep what your partner is doing and isn't doing in mind when you lead.

Most players are good about keeping track of what partner did in the bidding. It is the negative inferences that are often the key to effective decisions at the table. Some of the negative inferences come from your partner. Some of them can come from what your opponents do. You know all about not seeing the forest for the trees. In bridge, you are often called upon to see what is between the trees. The auctions on the next page show you two instances of the spaces between the trees.

#1
NO ONE VULNERABLE
SOUTH DEALS

W	N	E	S
			1NT
P	P	P	

#2
NO ONE VULNERABLE
SOUTH DEALS

W	N	E	S
			1NT
P	3NT	P	P
P			

WEST   What should West lead from this hand after each of the auctions above?
♠ J73
♡ 653
♢ QJ63
♣ Q73

#1   South opened one notrump and played it there. You know East has a pile of
       points. If he had a major suit to bid, he would do so. There are lots of
       conventions which will let you show a hand with a major suit. It is not so easy to
       show a minor. With the world of conventions we have nowadays, it is still hard
       for East to bid clubs or diamonds. East, in my opinion, is more likely to have the
       minor suits. You should consider leading one. My guess would be the three of
       diamonds.

#2   On the second auction, you know East doesn't have much so couldn't think of
       bidding. You have a new inference that you didn't have on auction one. You know
       that North didn't want to look for a major. The odds are that North has seven or
       more minor suit cards. You should lead a major. I would guess to lead the three of
       hearts. Or, if you prefer, lead the six.

A Little Quiz on What to Expect from Partner's Hand

WEST	W	N	E	S
♠ 9764		1D	P	1H
♡ 83	P	3S*	P	4H
◇ 1084	P	P	P	
♣ Q942				

*Singleton spade

This hand is a reflection on your system understandings. If East doubled three spades, do you know what it would mean? You can play that it shows something good in spades and that you can lead them, or you can play that double says East wants the lead of the lowest unbid suit. In this case, double can mean that East *wants* a club lead. This is a point worth discussing.

WEST	W	N	E	S
♠ K108754				1C
♡ 43	2S	3S*	DBL	3NT
◇ 9864	P	P	P	
♣ J				

*Nominally, a game forcing club raise. The usual effect of this cue bid is that South bids three notrump when he has a spade stopper.

Lead a spade if you trust your partner. East's double promises a high card in spades. He should not double without a high honor. Here, East doubled so leading a spade is OK. East will have the ace or queen of spades so the lead will be effective at best and it won't cost a bunch of tricks. If East passes over three spades, you should consider a diamond lead. NOTE that East's double says he has an honor. Had the bidding been 1C - 1S - 2S - DBL, the double would say East has a hand worth raising you to two spades. When you make a weak jump overcall and LHO cue-bids at the three level, it is unimportant to use double to show a raise since you are too high to want to bid again. It is more important to use double to show a high honor in the suit. Remember that opener will bid three notrump much of the time and you will be on lead. Having a leading hint from partner is good news when you get it and inferentially useful when you don't.

WEST	W	N	E	S
♠ 763				1C
♡ J8652	P	1S	P	2C
◇ Q2	P	2D	DBL	2NT
♣ Q73	P	3NT	P	P
	P			

Lead the queen of diamonds. You should be delighted to know that East likes diamonds. Without East's double, you would lead a heart but would not have much enthusiasm for it. What happened here was that North bid what is known as 'Fourth Suit Forcing'. It is common practice nowadays to bid a phony suit in search of information. East rates to have something like the KJ985 of diamonds or some equivalent. If he is not happy to see the queen of diamonds lead, he should not have doubled.

WEST	W	N	E	S
♠ QJ62		1S	2D	2NT
♡ J10753	P	3NT	P	P
◊ 3	P			
♣ J96				

Lead the three of diamonds. Your partner bid two diamonds, vulnerable, and that shows a good suit. If you lead a heart, be prepared for a lecture on overcalling. I like overcalling at the one level with poor suits if the hand is otherwise strong, but at the two level, a good suit is the first requirement. Show partner you were listening to the bidding.

WEST	W	N	E	S
♠ J10875			P	P
♡ 3	P	1D	1H	2NT
◊ J985	P	P	P	
♣ K107				

Go ahead and lead the jack of spades. East overcalled at the one level so his suit doesn't have to be great. Additional reasons for leading a spade are that you have a good suit, you have some entries, and South did not look for a spade contract. There is a decent chance that South is weak in spades.

WEST	W	N	E	S
♠ 10932				1C
♡ J8	P	1D	P	2C
◊ K10763	P	2H	P	3NT
♣ J4	P	P	P	

Lead the two of spades. If you had the seven or eight, leading the ten would be OK. The main point is that you should not lead a heart. It is easy to be suspicious of North's heart bid. East, however, did not double two hearts, so his hearts won't be too good. Remember the bidding. East had a chance to overcall one heart and he didn't. He later had a chance to double two hearts and he didn't.

CHAPTER FIVE

WHAT DO YOU EXPECT EVERYONE TO HAVE?

In some of the prior discussion, I mentioned that you should pay attention to the bidding, even when you have a poor hand. Not only will you learn something about the opponents' hands, you will learn something about partner's hand.

If partner bids during the auction, you will learn something specific.

If partner does not bid, the facts you learn from the opponents along with what you know about your own hand will give you some guidelines. Admittedly, most of this information will become important later during the defense, but some of it can help you on opening lead. One example. You are West.

W	N	E	S
			1C
P	1S	P	1NT
P	P	P	

WEST

♠ Q963
♡ 2
◇ KJ763
♣ J84

You are going to lead a diamond. That part of this hand is easy. Before you do this, just for the record, can you tell who has what in hearts? Does anyone have five of them? Who has four? Who has three?

You know from the fact that they stopped on one notrump that East has some points. On the average, he will have twelve points. He can have a point or two more or less than this.

Do you think that East has six hearts?

No. If he had six of them and twelve points, he would have overcalled two hearts on the first round or bid two hearts when one notrump came around to him. East has four or five hearts with the odds being highly in favor of his having five.

W	N	E	S	
			1C	(Hand and auction repeated)
P	1S	P	1NT	
P	P	P		

WEST   Do you think that North has four hearts?

♠ Q963

♡ 2   Probably not. When opener rebids one notrump, responder tends to show a

◊ KJ763   four card heart suit when he has one. It is likely that North has three hearts.

♣ J84   The reason you expect North to have three hearts is this. South has a

maximum of four hearts. You have one. Your partner, who is known to have a good hand, would bid hearts if he had six of them. He rates to have five of them. This leaves North-South with seven hearts. If you accept that North won't have four of them, it follows that South has four and North three.

ASIDE. On the hand above, you know how many points your partner has before your opening lead. They have from eighteen to twenty-two. You have seven. There is room for partner to have eleven to fifteen points. Since he didn't bid, he rates to have about twelve. On some hands, you won't know how many points your partner has until you see the dummy. On some hands, you won't know what your partner has until the end of the hand. Those are the hardest hands of all. But, on hands where you know his point count immediately or at least on seeing the dummy, you should automatically note that your partner has a certain number of points. You will know how many points partner has at the beginning of the defense and as you see him show up with various high cards, you know how many points he has left at any given stage of the defense.

W	N	E	S
			P
P	1S	P	2D
P	2H	P	2NT
P	3NT	P	P
P			

NORTH

♠ Q10973

♡ AKQJ

◊ Q4

♣ 94

WEST

♠ A8

♡ 9752

◊ K2

♣ K8653

You lead the five of clubs. East plays the ten and declarer the queen. Declarer leads to the ace of hearts and leads a spade to his king, which you take. One very good chance for you is that East has the jack of clubs, in which case you can continue the suit and set it up. Is this a good idea? Yes, it is, but as good an idea as it is, there is a better plan available. When the dummy came down, you should have said to yourself that declarer, who is a passed hand, has eleven or twelve high card points. At trick one, South showed up with the ace and queen of clubs and next showed up with the king of spades. There is room in his hand for another jack or two, but that is all. East must have the ace of diamonds. There is no need for you to lead another club and run into declarer's possible AQJ. Lead the two of diamonds to partner. Getting a club return from his side will be safe for you. This is the entire hand.

```
                 NORTH
                 ♠ Q10973
                 ♡ AKQJ
                 ◊ Q4
                 ♣ 94
WEST                        EAST
♠ A8                        ♠ J654
♡ 9752                      ♡ 103
◊ K2                        ◊ A765
♣ K8653                     ♣ 1072
                 SOUTH
                 ♠ K2
                 ♡ 864
                 ◊ J10983
                 ♣ AQJ
```

On this hand, you were able to use the proven point count to let you find the winning defense. Sometimes the benefits come much later. Sometimes, as late as tricks eleven or twelve, you need to know who has what. Noting and keeping track of the points as they show up is a necessary habit for good defenders.

Many years ago, I was playing in a home game when this uneventful hand appeared. The auction was brief. LHO opened one notrump and RHO raised to three, leaving my partner on lead. This is possibly the only hand you will find in this book where you are not the opening leader. You are in the East seat. Your partner, West, leads the four of diamonds which is fourth best in your methods. Here is what you see. What do you know after seeing the opening lead and the dummy?

NORTH
♠ A73
♡ A8
◊ J862
♣ Q765

EAST
♠ J862
♡ Q73
◊ Q53
♣ J84

Start with the diamonds. How are they located around the table?

West has four diamonds. You know this since he led the four, which is fourth best. Dummy has the two and you have the three. West can not have a five card suit. This means that South has two diamonds.

NORTH   (Repeated for convenience. West leads the
♠ A73   four of diamonds against three notrump)
♡ A8
◊ J862
♣ Q765
            EAST
            ♠ J862
            ♡ Q73
            ◊ Q53
            ♣ J84

How are the hearts and spades distributed?

Against this auction, you tend to lead a major suit. If West had four hearts or four spades,
they would take precedence over a four card diamond suit. This means (I think) that West
has three cards maximum in hearts and in spades. This suggests that South has three or
more spades and five or more hearts. West, remember, is expected to have only three
hearts and this leaves declarer with five of them. Many players open one notrump with
five card majors so this is a possible scenario.

If you know your opponents and know, for instance, that they do not open one notrump
with a good five card major, you might draw the further conclusion that South has five
hearts to the jack or worse. Here is the complete layout of the hand. See if you agree with
the inferences above.

                    NORTH
                    ♠ A73
                    ♡ A8
                    ◊ J862
                    ♣ Q765
WEST   EAST
♠ 1054   ♠ J862
♡ KJ4   ♡ Q73
◊ K1074   ◊ Q53
♣ 932   ♣ J84
            SOUTH
            ♠ KQ9
            ♡ 109652
            ◊ A9
            ♣ AK10

CHAPTER SIX

SHOULD YOU ATTACK OR SHOULD YOU LEAD PASSIVELY?

Beginning with Chapter Seven, you will find numerous specific lead considerations. Among them are leading singletons against suit contracts, leading trump against suit contracts, along with many others. Some leads can be good indeed. But few leads will be good all the time. I can imagine a trump lead being a killer on one hand and an absolute disaster the next. Leading singletons is often the only successful lead. But on some occasions, a singleton lead will be the one and only card that permits their contract to make.

Some leads are too bad to contemplate and are rejected without consideration. With your side silent, leading a singleton against notrump is just about as bad a choice as there is. Leading aces against suit contracts is right up there in the hall of fame for bad leads. Underleading aces against suit contracts is worse yet, if possible.

Before going into the specific leads in Chapter Seven, there is one last element to opening leads that needs attention. It is not technical as are the usual things you think about when you make your opening lead. This element is of a spiritual nature but is just as important as some of the other things you think about when on lead.

Does the Auction Suggest You Go All Out?
Or Does It Suggest Caution?

You have had this happen more than once. The opponents get to a contract, say four hearts, and you make your opening lead. After declarer makes eleven tricks, you look into partner's hand and see that a different lead would have set four hearts. Do you remember this happening to you recently?

W	N	E	S
	1S	P	2H
P	4H	P	P
P			

WEST
♠ 874
♡ 93
◊ K2
♣ J109853

If you lead the safe jack of clubs, declarer will make eleven tricks as long as he doesn't get greedy. Here is the entire hand.

NORTH
♠ AQJ63
♡ AK7
◊ 1084
♣ Q2

WEST
♠ 874
♡ 93
◊ K2
♣ J109853

EAST
♠ 1052
♡ Q84
◊ AJ753
♣ 64

SOUTH
♠ K9
♡ J10652
◊ Q96
♣ AK7

Declarer took the queen of clubs and cashed the ace-king of hearts, refusing the finesse. Switching to spades, South was able to discard two diamonds before East could ruff in. East took the ace of diamonds, but that was the end of the defense. Now that the hand is over, you can see that leading the king of diamonds would have been a great lead. Your partner probably has noticed that too and may even have commented to that effect for you. Should you listen to him? Should you in fact have led the king of diamonds on the go? Here are the things you should consider before deciding on a conservative lead such as the jack of clubs or a dangerous one such as the king of diamonds on the hand here.

#1.   Did the opponents have a strong auction or an uncertain auction? If they bid strongly as they did here, you should realize that they are likely to have their tricks if you give them time to get them. If they staggered into game and did not seem to be happy about doing so, you don't have to be as aggressive because there is a fair chance that they do not have enough tricks unless you hand them a freebie on opening lead. Here, their bidding was strong so you might decide to take a chance on lead. Helping you with this decision is the fact that you have a bad hand. The less you have, the more you can hope for from partner. (See point two below.) All in all, the facts here suggest the king of diamonds is worth trying. Leading doubleton honors is discussed in depth in a later chapter.

Against a suit contract, your decision will usually be less dramatic than on the hand above. More likely will have to choose between a safe lead and leading from a nervous combination such as the K963 of an unbid suit. The aggressive auction above tells you that they have points and a spade suit to use for tricks. It suggests that you lead an unbid suit. If you have the K963, all the better. If their auction was less certain, you might lead passively. For example.

W	N	E	S
			1NT
P	2C	P	2H
P	3H	P	4H
P	P	P	

WEST

♠ A764
♡ 65
◊ K963
♣ Q64

Their bidding was not overwhelming. They have limited points and have no known source of tricks. Leading from the K963 of diamonds into the opening one notrump bidder is dangerous and on this hand should be avoided. You can lead a trump with a clear conscience.

#2.   According to your hand and the bidding, do you expect partner to have any points? If you know that partner is broke, you might choose to be conservative. For instance.

The opponents bid 1NT - 3NT leaving you on lead with a pretty good hand. What is your choice from this collection?

WEST
♠ 865
♡ KJ5
◊ AQ3
♣ KJ53

Your partner has a bad hand. Right? What do you expect him to produce for you if you lead your fourth best club? You may hope for him to have the queen, but he is most likely to have the 864 or worse. If you lead a club, you will probably give declarer one trick and will spend the rest of the defense trying not to give him another. Why, though, do you have to give him one at all? Seeing that East has a Yarborough, you should lead the five of spades. Or, if you wish, lead the six or eight. You don't have to worry about misleading partner because he has virtually nothing to think about. All you wish to do is get out safely and then, on seeing the dummy, to continue as appropriate. Declarer will make this hand if he guesses well or if his dummy has a long suit it can use, but if he has no five card suit to work on and if his guessing is human, like yours and mine, he may find a way to go down. Unless, of course, you give away the setting trick at trick one.

Some General Guidelines

1.   When the opponents bid 1NT - 3NT, you should be aggressive UNLESS you have a hand such as the one above where you know partner is broke.

#1

♠ Q1074   On both of these hands you can hope for values in partner's hand. I
♡ 763   would lead the four of spades on the first hand. As with all speculative
◊ A83   leads, it may not work. The opponents did bid strongly, though, and
♣ J75   attacking is usually a good policy when that happens.

#2

♠ 87   On the second hand, the auction was the same. They bid 1NT - 3NT,
♡ KJ76   which suggests they have enough points to make nine tricks. Attacking
◊ 653   is a good idea. Lead the six of hearts. Remember that your partner rates
♣ QJ63   to have some high card points. You are entitled to hope he can help
             your heart lead. Note that you don't lead a club. This auction suggests
             you lead a major suit. More on this topic later in its own chapter.

2.   When the opponents end up in two notrump, you know they don't have enough points for game. Their limited values may or may not stretch to eight tricks. If their auction does not suggest they have a suit to use for tricks, you may lead passively if no clearly good lead is available.

N	S
	1NT
2NT	P

WEST

♠ 763
♡ J863
◊ Q97
♣ QJ3

Lead a spade. Leading a heart is also acceptable but it is somewhat dangerous. Note that leading a minor suit is a poor choice. North has implied length in the minor suits. Either minor suit might turn out to be dummy's best suit. The important thing here is that their bidding tells you they have twenty-three or so points. If they don't have a long suit, they may have to work hard to make two notrump. In this circumstance, you may consider a quiet defense and start with a neutral spade.

NORTH
- ♠ Q92
- ♡ Q74
- ◇ KJ4
- ♣ 9742

WEST	EAST
♠ 763	♠ A1084
♡ J863	♡ A9
◇ Q97	◇ 8632
♣ QJ3	♣ K65

While making no claims that a spade lead will find this setup, it is easy to see that it is the best lead for the defense. If declarer goes after hearts by leading to the queen, he might get just one trick. If West leads hearts, declarer will get two tricks for sure and West will be left hanging on to his remaining hearts to keep South from getting three heart tricks.

WEST
- ♠ KJ5
- ♡ K1052
- ◇ A105
- ♣ A108

3. The converse is that when the opponents bid to two notrump and show a long suit along the way, you may judge they have their tricks if given time to get at them. Here is a different auction to two notrump. You will note that you have the same hand for your opening lead.

N	S
1D	1H
2D	2NT
P	

This one deserves a little thought. There are major differences between this auction to two notrump and the previous auction.

WEST
- ♠ 763
- ♡ J863
- ◇ Q97
- ♣ QJ3

1. You have been warned, at least tentatively, that your heart suit is not the best lead. In fact, there are times where leading into the bidder is a good idea. It is not so here.

2. You know that dummy has a long diamond suit. This auctions tends to show six diamonds, so there are potential tricks for declarer.

My best guess is to lead the queen of clubs. Both opponents have shown a suit so there is no specific danger that either of them has good clubs. Your partner rates to have eleven points. If he has four clubs or more, this lead will be effective. It deserves a try.

N	S
1D	1H
2D	2NT
P	

(Here is the auction again.)

Below is the hand we would like to find in our dreams.

NORTH
♠ KJ8
♡ 95
◊ A108642
♣ A6

WEST
♠ 763
♡ J863
◊ Q97
♣ QJ3

EAST
♠ A942
♡ AQ
◊ J5
♣ 108752

SOUTH
♠ Q105
♡ K10742
◊ K3
♣ K94

With a passive spade lead, South will end up with two spades, two clubs, five diamonds, and after the war is over will take nine or ten tricks. East doesn't have great spades, remember, because he had a chance to bid over one diamond. If you take an optimistic view and lead clubs, the defense can prevail. You will get the clubs going in time to take three clubs and a trick in each of the other suits. The thoughts on what West should lead against these two auctions are representative of this kind of hand.

4.   This is a hint you have seen already and will use almost daily in your defense. It applies to leads against suits and notrump. While you are thinking about your opening lead, consider whether your partner can have any points. If the auction says he is broke, it will affect your lead. If the auction says he has something, it will also affect your lead.

Now. Having made a preliminary estimate of what partner has, you should, As soon as you see the dummy, make a reassessment. Then, as the play proceeds, keep in mind what partner has left at any given moment in the defense.

If you judge, having seen the dummy, that your partner has eight to twelve points, you must remember this range and adjust your opinion as the play proceeds. If your partner shows up with eleven points, do not start wishing him to have another ace or king. Likewise, if he has shown up with two points by the middle of the hand, you know he still has six or more points waiting to come out.

CHAPTER SEVEN

HOW DO SPOT CARDS AFFECT YOUR LEAD?

(This is the first of four chapters which discuss considerations which pertain to leads versus suits and notrump.)

Spot cards are lovely things. Tens and nines in your long suits are strong cards. Holdings like Q1083 have huge potential. How huge? Let's see.

The opponents get to three notrump and you decide to lead from the Q832 of spades. The entire suit turns out to be as follows.

```
              ♠ K976
  ♠ Q832                ♠ J4
              ♠ A105
```

You lead the two, dummy plays the six, East the jack, and South the ace. If South chooses, he can return the ten of spades. West covers with the queen and dummy's king takes the trick. Later, South can lead the five and if he judges the suit correctly, can finesse the seven and end up with four tricks.

Below is a similar layout which has a couple of key spot cards moved around.

```
              ♠ K763
  ♠ Q1082              ♠ J4
              ♠ A95
```

West leads the two as before and East's jack forces South to play the ace. The defense can continue the suit and will take two tricks in spades. The reason for the improvement is clear. West has spots in the suit. East produces the jack and that is enough for the 10-8 of spades to come on like gangbusters. Amazing.

Giving West the ten of spades in exchange for the trey gains the defenders two tricks.

While suits like K1085 or Q1085 are good choices, given you want to lead that suit, holdings like K974 are useful too. Take this layout. South is in a notrump contract.

♠ 65

♠ K974   ♠ A103

♠ QJ82

West leads the four to East's ace. East returns the ten, covered by declarer's queen. West knows South has the jack so lets South have the trick. (East would return the jack if he had the ten AND the jack.) Later, East returns his last spade and West takes his two tricks. The defenders get three tricks in the suit. West's nine of spades turns out to be worth a trick. Look what happens if West and South trade the eight and nine of spades. That little trade will cost the defenders one full trick.

Spot cards are so important that you should use them to help you with close decisions. Q1083 is better than Q1043 which is better than Q953 which is better than Q843 which is better than Q643. A1085 is better than A1043 which is better than A964, etc. Be aware of your spot cards. Once you see their worth, you will find your opening leads made just a little bit easier.

The opponents have bid 1NT-3NT. You have to lead with this holding.

♠ A4
♡ 93
♢ J6543
♣ QJ109

Even though your diamonds are five cards long, it is right to lead the queen of clubs. Clubs give you two sure tricks. Diamonds might work out better, but the number of times they are successful will not make up for the times where they are a failure. An aside. In Chapter Eighteen, you will see that leading a minor suit against this auction is normally a poor choice since dummy often has length in the minor suit. On this hand, your club spots will be able to cope with dummy having four of them. Your diamond spots might not cope if dummy has four diamonds. I figure that if someone deals me the QJ109 of a suit, it must be for a reason.

CHAPTER EIGHT

LEADING FROM THREE OR FOUR OR FIVE SMALL CARDS

In the introduction, I discussed what you should lead from three little cards. Having an understanding about this is necessary.

Leading From Three Small Cards

You have the 753 of spades and have decided to lead them. Which card should you lead?

There are many schools of thought about this. Believe it or not, you can find support for leading any of the three cards.

You can lead the seven, which is called the "Top of Nothing".

You can lead the five and next play the seven. The idea is that partner will know you don't have a doubleton and won't try to give you a ruff, which might happen if you led the five and followed with the three. This too has a name. It is called "Middle - Up - Down". A shorter name for this is "MUD". Some players feel this is overstating its value as a convention.

Finally, you can lead the three from the 753. Partner will know you don't have a doubleton, but will not know if you have an honor in the suit.

Let me state right now that leading from three small is a tough way to make a living. I do lead from three small now and then, but it is not a constructive lead. Usually when you lead such a suit it is because your partner has bid the suit or because the auction suggests this is the best suit to lead. On occasion, you will lead from three small when all the other choices are worse.

Following are my suggestions.

Leading From Three Small Cards

The first page showed some approaches to leading from three small cards. I am going to take the view that it is right to lead the top card or the bottom card according to a number of factors. Leads from three small cards are not the same against suit contracts and notrump contracts. In addition, it makes a difference whether your side bid the suit.

Versus A Suit Contract

1.   If your partner bid the suit and you raised it, lead the top card.
2.   If your partner bid the suit and you did not raise, lead the little card.
3.   If it is an unbid suit, lead the little card.
4.   If it is a suit bid by the opponents, lead something else if possible.

Versus Notrump

1.   If your partner bid the suit and you did not raise it, lead the little card.
2.   If your partner bid the suit and you did raise, lead the top card.
3.   If it is an unbid suit, lead the top card.
4.   If it is a suit bid by the opponents, lead something else if possible.

Here is a simpler guideline of the above.

Versus A Suit

Lead the little card in all cases except when partner bid the suit and you raised. Be sure to remember that a raise by you is not the same thing as a preference by you.

Versus Notrump

Lead the top card in all cases except when partner bid the suit and you did not raise.

Leading From Three Small When Partner Has Bid The Suit

If you have raised and partner knows you have three of them, it is right to lead the top card. You lead this way regardless of whether the final contract is a suit or notrump. When you lead the top card, partner will realize you don't have an honor but he will remember that you raised so must have three or more cards. He will make an educated play assuming there is one to make.

NO ONE VULNERABLE

W	N	E	S
	1C	1H	1S
2H	2S	3H	3S
P	P	P	

NORTH
♠ AQ92
♡ K106
◊ 975
♣ AJ7

EAST
♠ 4
♡ AJ9843
◊ 108
♣ K654

You are East. West leads the two of hearts. Dummy plays the six. What is your correct play?

What should East play if West leads the seven of hearts?

If you lead as I suggest, East will read the two as being low from three to an honor. East will play the eight knowing that South does not have the queen.

If West leads the seven, East will recognize this as the highest missing spot card and will conclude that South has the queen. East will go up with the ace and avoid losing to South's singleton queen.

Here is an aside to MUDDERS. You are missing the Q752 of hearts. If your partner leads the five, you can't tell whether your partner is leading from the Q75 or the 752. MUD does not help you in this case.

W	N	E	S
	1C	1H	1S
2H	2S	3H	3S
P	P	P	

NORTH
- ♠ AQ92
- ♡ K106
- ◊ 975
- ♣ AJ7

WEST	EAST
♠ 1087	♠ 4
♡ 752	♡ AJ9843
◊ AQJ62	◊ 108
♣ 82	♣ K654

Here is the complete hand. West, who bid two hearts, leads the seven. East goes up with the ace and returns the ten of diamonds. This allows the defenders to take three diamonds and a later club trick. Three spades goes down one. If West starts with the two of hearts, East reasonably might do the wrong thing.

SOUTH
- ♠ KJ653
- ♡ Q
- ◊ K43
- ♣ Q1093

Incidentally, even though this is a book on opening leads, it is useful to look at the East-West bidding. East came in with only eight points when he bid one heart. The good suit and the nice shape allows aggressive bids like this. West raised to two hearts. West's raise is important because it gives East information that allows him to push with three hearts. If East doesn't overcall or if West doesn't raise, North-South get to play in two spades where they will get a plus score. NOTE that the East-West bidding did not get them in trouble. East has six hearts, which is almost as good as having another king. In fact, it turns out that East-West can make three hearts and might make four.

A Coincidence?

Whenever I write a book, the topic of that book seems to crop up at the table more often than at any other time. I started this chapter on a Tuesday and the following afternoon during the first session of a local tournament, this hand occurred. I got to declare the hand in three diamonds against the following defense.

West paid a high price for leading the wrong card here. The price he paid was a trick, but it wasn't the trick that usually gets lost in this situation. Here is the hand and the result that came from West's choice of leads from three small cards.

NO ONE VULNERABLE

W	N	E	S
		1S	P
2S	DBL	P	3D
P	P	P	

NORTH
- ♠ Q10
- ♡ KQ6
- ◊ AQ1085
- ♣ K104

WEST
- ♠ 752
- ♡ J752
- ◊ 9
- ♣ AJ753

EAST
- ♠ AK983
- ♡ A103
- ◊ J43
- ♣ 82

West led the two of spades. East cashed the two top spades and the defenders were out of business. South discarded dummy's six of hearts on the jack of spades and later guessed the clubs to make nine tricks. East commented that he thought West had the jack of spades. Had he known that West did not have it, he would have found the winning defense.

SOUTH
- ♠ J64
- ♡ 984
- ◊ K762
- ♣ Q96

Do you see how East can set three diamonds after winning the first trick?

If East leads back a low heart at trick two, West's jack will force out dummy's queen. When West gets in with the ace of clubs, the defenders will take two heart tricks. This will not happen, of course, if East cashes the top spades.

The clue?

If West leads the seven of spades, East will know that West is leading his top card and will see that South has the jack. The correct defense will be easier to find.

If your partner bid a suit and you didn't raise it, you have a different guideline when leading from three little cards.

If you lead the two from the 752, your partner may hope you have an honor. If you lead the seven, your partner may hope you have a doubleton. Either way, your lead will give your partner some concerns.

I suggest, after a few too many experiences with this kind of lead, that when you have not raised and are leading partner's suit, you should lead the small one. This is true against notrump contracts and suit contracts. The idea is this. You have to tell a lie of sorts. It is better to lead low and show partner how many you have. You hope that partner's suit is so good that he can account for any missing honors. Here is an example of what you hope to achieve.

NO ONE VULNERABLE

W	N	E	S
		1S	1NT
P	2NT	P	3NT
P	P	P	

NORTH
♠ J8
♡ AK8
◊ 853
♣ 109432

WEST	EAST
♠ 752	♠ AK643
♡ J1043	♡ 972
◊ J76	◊ 1092
♣ J75	♣ A8

SOUTH
♠ Q109
♡ Q65
◊ AKQ4
♣ KQ6

West leads a spade against three notrump. East pretty well knows that South has the queen of spades for his notrump bid. What East needs to know is how many spades West has. If West leads the seven, East reasonably can conclude that West has a doubleton. East might win the king of spades and switch to diamonds hoping for West to have the KJx of diamonds. This defense would be necessary if South has four spades since that would give him two spade stoppers. As you can see, the correct defense is for East to continue spades, giving South his trick. Eventually, South will have to play on clubs and East will collect the ace along with his long spades for down one.

The way East works out the correct defense is to have West lead the two of spades showing three or more. East knows that South has the queen of spades but will also know that South has just three of them.

Leading From Three Small Cards When The Opponents Bid The Suit

My suggestion is that you don't find such a lead. If they have bid all four suits and you decide to lead from three little ones because all other leads look worse, I suggest you lead a small card against a suit and a high card against notrump. At the very least, your partner will not try to give you a ruff against a suit contract and your partner will see you are not interested in the suit against a notrump contract. Really, leading from three small is a disgusting alternative. View this discussion in that light and look to your three small cards as a poor choice in general.

Leading From Three Small When It Is An Unbid Suit

Three small remains a crummy lead even if it is an unbid suit. I continue to suggest that leading the top card from three small against notrump will help your partner judge whether or not to continue the suit. It is discouraging when you and your partner lead a suit and continue the suit and then continue it again only to find out that declarer has four winners and your side has none. You would prefer to devote your energies to something constructive. Leading the top card from three small against notrump will help partner know your intentions in that suit, and he will consider that you may want a shift. In the same vein, I suggest leading low against a suit contract.

W	N	E	S
			1C
P	1S	P	2NT
P	3NT	P	P
P			

WEST
♠ 764
♡ 862
◇ AQJ9
♣ 652

You don't want to lead a diamond because it is a near certainty that South has the king. If East has an entry, you would like him to get in and return a diamond. Perhaps you can get four diamond tricks. With this in mind, you might select the eight of hearts. East surely will see that this is not fourth best and may deduce that you want another suit returned.

Really, the science of leading from three small is no science at all. You won't meet an expert who tells you that he *knows* which card to lead from 632. He will give you his rules or his tendencies, but he won't be at all sure what is right. Since it probably won't matter in the long run, I suggest you follow the guidelines above since they will at least keep partner partially in the dark as opposed to permanently in the dark.

MUD, anyone? This is the third possibility for leading from three small cards. From the 752, you lead the five and then follow suit next in whatever fashion you feel will be most helpful to partner. I will state here that I am not a fan of MUD. I used to use it, but it did not do enough good to make up for problems like this one. I already showed you an unflattering example of MUD five pages earlier. Here is another typical problem created by MUD.

W	N	E	S
	1C	P	1S
P	3S	P	4S
P	P	P	

WEST
♠ 1062
♡ A82
♢ 752
♣ J875

This is not a good hand to lead from. No one would fault you for selecting a diamond. Let's say that following the MUD rule, you start with the five of diamonds.

The complete hand.

NORTH
♠ AQJ8
♡ 764
♢ K108
♣ AKQ

WEST
♠ 1062
♡ A82
♢ 752
♣ J875

EAST
♠ 5
♡ J1095
♢ AQ963
♣ 1062

SOUTH
♠ K9743
♡ KQ3
♢ J4
♣ 943

If you are using MUD, and if you choose to lead a diamond, you will lead the five. East wins with the queen. What should East return? East, noticing that the two of diamonds is still missing, might decide West had the 5-2 doubleton. It is possible and if that is what West has led from, a diamond ruff is the best way to start the defense. So East plays the ace of diamonds. West now plays the seven to tell East that he has not led a doubleton. East knows that more diamonds isn't the best defense, so he switches to the jack of hearts. Nice try, but too late. Declarer plays the king of hearts, losing to the ace, and wins the heart return with the queen. After drawing trump, the three of hearts goes on dummy's king of diamonds. A bad hand for MUD. The problem with MUD here is that your partner doesn't know what to do until he sees the second trick, and by that time the information may be worthless.

All in all, I think that it is best to lead low from three small except in the explicit cases where you have raised partner's suit or where you are leading from three small and wish partner to switch rather than continue your lead. In these two cases, leading the top card is OK.

A Summary Of Leading From Three Small

Against a suit contract, your side is often going to lead singletons and doubletons in hope of a ruff. If you lead the top card from three small, your partner will frequently interpret it as being from a doubleton and will continue the suit in search of a ruff. Leading the small one will stop your partner from making that mistake. It is true that he may defend on the hope that you have a high card in the suit, but that is, I think, the lesser danger.

Against a notrump contract, the general goal is to set up a long suit. If you lead a little card from three small, your partner will tend to continue the suit until he runs out of them. This is something you wish to discourage. Leading the top card against notrump will stop partner from wasting time on this suit. He will look elsewhere. In a notrump contract, remember, there is no ruffing. Confusing partner about whether you have two or three cards is not terribly important against a notrump contract.

Leading From Four Or Five Small Cards

Four or five little cards is not much better to lead from than three little cards. In general, I suggest you lead a little card when you have an honor and a high card when you don't. This is OK even against a suit contract. If you lead the eight from the 8753 of a suit, your partner will probably be able to tell from the bidding that you don't have a singleton or doubleton. Against a notrump contract, four cards may end up setting up a trick for you and with five little cards, you may set up two or three tricks. For this reason, against a notrump contract, you will tend to lead a low card from long suits unless you desperately want partner to lead back some other suit.

WEST
♠ A87
♡ 86532
◇ KJ3
♣ A6

If the opponents bid 1NT - 3NT, you should lead the three of hearts. You don't have an honor, but you have five of them and you have some entries to get in with to continue hearts. Leading the three will encourage partner, if he gets in, to continue the suit, which is OK with you in general. Conversely, if the opponents bid 1S - 2S - 4S, you will still lead a heart, but it is probably right to lead the six or even the eight. Here, if your partner gets in, you don't want a heart return. By leading a high heart spot, you will give partner the idea, if he gets in, that hearts is not a good suit for your side. If he is awake, he may stop to think before routinely returning your lead.

A Little Quiz On Leads From Three Small Cards

WEST	W	N	E	S
♠ 763	P	1C	1S	2NT
♡ 83	P	3NT	P	P
◇ Q9542	P			
♣ Q82				

Lead the three of spades. Usually you lead the top card from three small cards against a notrump contract. The one exception is when partner bid the suit and you did not raise.

WEST	W	N	E	S
♠ AJ93				1S
♡ 832	P	2D	P	2NT
◇ Q1043	P	3NT	P	P
♣ Q7	P			

Lead the eight of hearts. South showed five spades and North implied five diamonds. Neither suit is worth leading. Clubs are out of the question. Hearts is really the only suit worth leading. Your partner should recognize the eight as showing no interest in hearts. If he gets in, he will consider switching suits.

WEST	W	N	E	S
♠ Q973		1S	P	2H
♡ Q2	P	3H	P	4H
◇ 764	P	P	P	
♣ AJ83				

Lead the four of diamonds. Against a suit contract, lead low from three little cards. You don't want to lead the seven and have partner try to give you a ruff when, in fact, his time could be better spent attacking elsewhere.

WEST	W	N	E	S
♠ 742			1S	2H
♡ 1073	2S	3H	P	P
◇ K10763	P			
♣ K9				

Lead the seven of spades. You raised spades so leading the seven will not fool partner into thinking you want as ruff. He will realize you are telling him you don't have an honor.

WEST	W	N	E	S
♠ K98			1C	1S
♡ A82	1NT	2S	P	P
◇ Q872	P			
♣ 862				

Lead the two of clubs. You did not raise clubs so leading the eight may influence East into believing you have two of them. It is true that East may think you have a club honor. You have to choose which evil is worse. I suggest that you always lead low from three small cards *except* when you have raised. Your partner will appreciate your consistency.

CHAPTER NINE

LEADING UNSUPPORTED TENS AND NINES

What Should You Lead From 10xx Or 9xx?

There is a follow-up question to the last chapter which needs a look. Leading top from three small is possible on occasion. But tell me. What is a small card? If you decide it is correct to lead the seven from the 743, would it be all right to lead the eight if you had the 843 instead? How about if you have the 943 or the 1043? Would you lead the nine or ten from these combinations?

I know an expert who teaches students that it is right to lead the nine from the 943 and the ten from the 1043.

I have a second opinion about leading from 10xx or 9xx. Leading the top card from these two holdings is a good way to lose the setting trick. Have you ever heard the expression that someone threw away the setting trick? Usually when you hear this, it refers to a defender who discarded the setting trick at trick ten or eleven when they misread the position. A less kind reference is that someone messed up and wantonly threw away the only useful card in their hand. Take your pick of descriptions.

If you insist on leading unsupported tens and nines, you may be guilty of losing the setting trick at trick one, a record that can't be beat and which will be the hit of the midnight postmortems. Here is how you can qualify for this distinction.

W	N	E	S
		1H	1S
2H	2S	3H	4S
P	P	P	

NORTH
♠ K93
♡ Q2
◊ 873
♣ J10652

WEST
♠ A8
♡ 1054
◊ QJ65
♣ 9873

EAST
♠ 52
♡ AJ873
◊ 1092
♣ AKQ

SOUTH
♠ QJ10764
♡ K96
◊ AK4
♣ 4

West, if he leads the ten of hearts, will learn the meaning of hindsight in a hurry. The opening lead is covered by dummy's queen and taken by East's ace. Back comes the ten of diamonds, taken by South's ace. It looks like South has a loser in each suit, but only if you take a shallow look. South has a secret weapon, courtesy of the opening lead. The spade four is led to the king, which happens to win. It would not matter if East turned up with the ace. South would still get to dummy with the nine of spades. The dummy entry is used to lead the two of hearts. Remembering that the lead of the ten marks East with the jack, declarer finesses the nine. This wins, to South's satisfaction and to East's great irritation. Dummy's diamond loser goes on the king of hearts and finally a diamond is ruffed in dummy. If West had led the four of hearts, declarer would only get one heart trick, barring East's doing something silly, and would go down one. See what I mean by leading the setting trick? Here is a little aside for you. Look at the East hand. If West leads the four of hearts, dummy will play the two. East must not play the ace. He has to play the jack at trick one. South will win with the king, but that is the only heart trick for South. If East pounces with the ace, South will be able to discard dummy's diamond.

Following is another example of leading the setting trick. This one is especially irksome since the disaster it causes is known immediately. I will spare you the entire hand. Here is the club suit that caused the problem.

```
         ♣ QJ                          Declarer played in three notrump.  West led the ten of
♣ 1073          ♣ AK864               clubs in response to a lead directing double by East.
         ♣ 952                         East took the first two clubs and continued the suit.
                                       When South won with the nine, East was sad, but that
                                       was nothing to how East felt when West followed suit
                                       to the trick.
```

Although rarer, leading the nine from three or even four small can cost. Here is a combination where leading the nine works poorly.

```
         ♣ J10
♣ 932          ♣ KQ764               If West leads the nine, South's eight turns into a late
         ♣ A85                         winner.  I don't have statistics on how expensive it is to
                                       lead nines and tens from three card holdings. I can offer
                                       a guess, though. I think that leading an unsupported ten
```
from 1053 or the like will cost a trick as much as 20% of the time. Leading a nine will be less costly, but it will haunt you perhaps 10% of the time. Better to lead small from these holdings.

Here is my final example of why not to lead the ten or nine from these holdings. I bet you have had this one happen to you at one time or another.

```
W      N      E      S
       1D     1S     2NT
P      3NT    P      P
P
```

```
         NORTH
         ♠ Q
         ♡ KQ87
         ◊ Q1074
         ♣ K873
```

```
WEST                 EAST                 If West leads the ten of spades, East won't be able to
♠ 1053               ♠ A9764              set up spades since South now has three stoppers. If
♡ 10432              ♡ AJ6                West leads the three, East will win and can continue the
◊ 865                ◊ AK3                suit effectively. South will go down after this defense.
♣ 1094               ♣ 65
```

```
         SOUTH
         ♠ KJ82
         ♡ 95
         ◊ J92
         ♣ AQJ2
```

A Little Quiz On Leading From 10xx or 9xx.

WEST	W	N	E	S
♠ K94		1H	P	1S
♡ Q873	P	2C	P	2NT
◊ 1063	P	P	P	
♣ QJ4				

Lead the three of diamonds. Other leads are poor. You are leading diamonds primarily because they are the unbid suit. It might tempt you to lead the ten, but that is definitely wrong. The chances are too great that it will cost you at trick.

There is only one time where you might lead the ten from this holding. Refer to the last question in the Quiz Section at the end of the book.

WEST	W	N	E	S
♠ 74		1D	1H	1NT
♡ 1095	P	2NT	P	3NT
◊ 108763	P	P	P	
♣ K82				

Lead the ten of hearts. When you have a three card holding headed by the 98x or the 109x, treat the holding as if it is a sequence. Lead the nine or ten instead of leading the low one. If you had the 1043 of hearts, you would lead the three. The 1095 combination is much stronger than the 1043 combination. True, leading the top card from the 983 or the 1093 can confuse partner a little, but the net gain to your side is worth the small ambiguity.

WEST	W	N	E	S
♠ A653		1S	P	2C
♡ 963	P	2D	P	2NT
◊ 53	P	3NT	P	P
♣ AQJ8	P			

Lead the nine of hearts. This is a moment for thinking. If you make the normal lead of the three of hearts and if your partner can get in, he may return a heart. Given the bidding and your great stuff in clubs, it isn't likely that East will think of leading a club back, which is really what you want. You are hoping for two things. You hope that leading the nine of hearts does not blow a heart trick for your side. That is certainly possible. Next you hope that the nine of hearts will awaken East to the fact that you don't care for them. You gain when East can work out the hand and defend well. I think East will have a better chance of getting it right after your lead of the nine as opposed to the three of hearts. Nothing you lead will guarantee success, but you can do something to improve your chances.

CHAPTER TEN

LEADING DOUBLETONS

The reasons you lead doubletons are varied. Unlike a singleton, you might lead a doubleton against suits for one reason or another and against notrumps for a different set of reasons.

Leading Doubletons Against a Suit Contract.

Leading doubletons has little in common with leading a singleton. Singleton leads have the potential to be instant killers. Doubletons can be effective too, but they come with many drawbacks. In order to be effective, you have to find partner with a strong holding or with the ace. If he has the ace, he has to decide whether to take it at trick one or wait for the second round of the suit.

Since leading doubletons doesn't get you many quick ruffing tricks, they aren't an effective weapon. Doubleton leads have merit but it is limited. Much of the time, leading a doubleton turns out to be an exercise in just not blowing a trick. If a ruff comes out of it, it is a bonus.

W	N	E	S
			1NT
P	2C	P	2H
P	4H	P	P
P			

WEST
♠ K432
♡ J85
◇ 85
♣ A873

Not a nice hand to lead from. Hearts and clubs are eminently wrong. Leading hearts can cost a trump trick. Leading from an ace-high suit against a suit contract is so terribly wrong that I have included an entire chapter showing why you should avoid that lead. Your choice seems to be to lead the two of spades or the eight of diamonds. Leading from broken holdings is more nervous than usual when you are leading into a strong one or two notrump opener. All in all, leading the eight of diamonds is a sensible choice. It is not a great lead. It is, hopefully, less poor than the other choices.

Times you should lead a doubleton include when partner has bid the suit. You can also lead a doubleton when the bidding indicates a certain suit be led. Don't forget that partner's silence in the bidding may suggest against that.

W	N	E	S
	1C	P	1H
P	1NT	P	2H
P	P	P	

WEST
♠ 84
♡ K92
◇ J1086
♣ J864

Leading the doubleton spade 'sounds' like an acceptable choice. Neither opponent wanted to show them. But, neither did your partner. East has an opening bid and remained silent. If he could have bid spades, he would have. I suspect that South has four spades himself. Lead the jack of diamonds.

Overall, leading doubletons is just slightly more than neutral as long as you don't lead them at the wrong time, in which case they are suicidal.

Leading Doubletons Against Notrump

This is not a good lead against notrump. If your partner has bid the suit, go for it. If your partner has made a lead-directing double during or at the end of the auction, get it out there. If partner didn't bid during the auction, you will lead a small doubleton more or less as a last resort. You might lead it if it is an unbid suit. You might lead it if the auction suggested your partner has length there. Whatever the reason, it won't be a dynamic lead except by accident.

W	N	E	S
	1D	P	1H
P	2D	P	2NT
P	3NT	P	P
P			

WEST
♠ 83
♡ 86542
◇ Q753
♣ 83

What should you lead? Hearts is a hopeless lead since declarer bid them. The next page shows a possible layout of the heart suit.

♡ Q

♡ 86542   ♡ AK10

♡ J973

East has three heart honors, which is the most you can hope for. A heart lead will make East happy for a moment, but it will not last. East will take his ace and king of hearts and continue with the ten. East will spend the rest of the hand hoping to get you in to cash some heart winners. Unlucky. You don't have an entry and even if you did, the heart suit is still not established for your side.

Leading a diamond is also senseless. North has six diamonds (usually). It is one of the suits that declarer will try to set up himself. This leaves you with the 83 of spades and the 83 of clubs. Can either of these be right? Given your weak hand, it is possible that East has twelve or thirteen or even fourteen points. If he had five spades, he would have bid them. He might have five good clubs, though, and not have felt safe about bidding them at the two level. Lead the eight of clubs. Don't have your hopes up, but at least feel you thought out the best choice. If you get lucky, East will have five good clubs and enough entries to make the lead effective.

NO ONE VULNERABLE

W	N	E	S
			1D
P	1H	P	1NT
P	3NT	P	P
P			

WEST
♠ AQ3
♡ QJ53
♢ K762
♣ 96

Once again, your choices are unhappy ones. Hearts were bid on your left and diamonds on your right. When declarer rebid one notrump, it confirmed he has four or more diamonds, so leading those is not good. Also, when South rebid one notrump, he promised (well, probably promised) two or more hearts. Leading hearts is as bad an idea as leading diamonds. (I will expand on this later.) Leading spades could work, but it could be embarrassing too. The best choice is to start the nine of clubs. You aren't leading it because you expect it to work. You are leading it because you don't want to chance other leads which are dangerous.

A Little Quiz On Leading Doubletons

WEST	W	N	E	S
♠ J83		1D	1H	1S
♡ 63	P	1NT	P	2S
◇ QJ8	P	P	P	
♣ QJ863				

Lead the six of hearts. Whenever you get a bid from your partner, especially an overcall, it is a good idea to lead his suit. Your clubs are attractive and on other days might be the right lead. But not after partner has bid a suit.

WEST	W	N	E	S
♠ K52		1C	P	1S
♡ 87	P	2S	P	P
◇ AJ74	P			
♣ QJ82				

Lead the eight of hearts. North bid your best suit, clubs, and diamonds are not leadable. A pity that partner couldn't bid. Since there is no reason not to lead a heart and since there is good reason not to lead any of the other suits, the heart is led by process of elimination.

WEST	W	N	E	S
♠ J10				1NT
♡ Q73	P	3NT	P	P
◇ Q872	P			
♣ J873				

Lead the jack of spades. This lead combines the boring qualities of a doubleton lead with the dynamic qualities of a sequence lead. In part, you lead spades because the other suits are poor choices, but since you have the J10 of spades instead of the 42, you are actually pleased with this choice. In a later chapter, I will discuss why leading a minor suit on this bidding is poor in general.

WEST	W	N	E	S
♠ A875	1C	P	1D	1H
♡ K73	1S	2H	P	P
◇ 74	P			
♣ KQJ4				

Lead the king of clubs. The doubleton diamond is a poor choice given your excellent club holding. Some players tend to grab singletons and doubletons for no other reason than that they are there. East bid diamonds, but that fact does not compensate for the quality clubs. In general, you lead doubletons without much enthusiasm.

CHAPTER ELEVEN

SEQUENCE LEADS

Sequence leads are an interesting animal in the zoo of opening leads. They can be both wonderful and frustrating. The opponents bid to three notrump thusly.

W	N	E	S
	1H	P	1NT
P	2NT	P	3NT
P	P	P	

WEST
♠ KQ10
♡ Q8653
◇ J2
♣ 972

Feeling that your hearts are dead after North's heart bid, you select the king of spades. Partner may have four to the jack, which will be nice for the defense. Anyway, nothing else looks good so making a little wish for partner

to have the jack of spades is not greedy. On a really good day, the hand looks like this.

NORTH
♠ 86
♡ AKJ107
◇ KQ7
♣ AQ6

WEST	**EAST**
♠ KQ10	♠ A9532
♡ Q8653	♡ 4
◇ J2	◇ 953
♣ 972	♣ 10543

Your partner encourages you with the nine of spades. You continue with the queen and ten and East runs off the rest of the suit. Down one. Without the spade lead, a greedy declarer can take twelve tricks and an ungreedy declarer can take ten. Does this make the spade lead a winner? On this hand it does. But on the next hand? You judge.

SOUTH
♠ J74
♡ 92
◇ A10864
♣ KJ8

W	N	E	S
	1H	P	1NT
P	2NT	P	3NT
P	P	P	

NORTH
- ♠ J86
- ♡ AK742
- ♢ KQ6
- ♣ A5

WEST
- ♠ KQ10
- ♡ Q8653
- ♢ J2
- ♣ 972

EAST
- ♠ 9532
- ♡ J
- ♢ 9753
- ♣ KQJ3

SOUTH
- ♠ A74
- ♡ 109
- ♢ A1084
- ♣ 10864

Oops. In my youth, I was warned repeatedly by the club pessimist against leading the king from this holding. He told me that losing a trick to the layout on the left was the worst crime in bridge. On this layout, the king of spades is the friendliest lead West can make for South. South's eight tricks will turn into nine when South wins the ace of spades and leads toward the jack. What is the answer? Is that pessimist right? Should West never make this lead? Assuming you can accept the good with the bad, here are some thoughts on sequence leads.

Let's start with the good ones. Everyone likes to have a sequence like AKQ or KQJ10 or QJ1097 to lead from. These sequences are easy to spot and just as easy to lead. The only issue I will address here is that you must still remember to listen to the bidding before you make your opening lead. Usually, a solid sequence is the right lead. Once in awhile, you will have reason not to lead from a good sequence.

W	N	E	S
	1D	P	2C
P	2D	P	2S
P	3S	P	4S
P	P	P	

WEST
- ♠ 73
- ♡ K1083
- ♢ QJ108
- ♣ Q75

The diamond holding is solid and leading it will never cost you a trick in the diamond suit itself. But, if you consider that there is little chance you can set up a diamond trick and then use it, perhaps a different lead may be better.

                    NORTH
                    ♠ K862
                    ♡ Q74
                    ◇ AK974
                    ♣ 6

WEST   EAST   If you lead the queen of diamonds against four spades,
♠ 73   ♠ QJ4   they will make an overtrick. If you lead the three of
♡ K1083   ♡ AJ2   hearts, the unbid suit, you set four spades one trick.
◇ QJ108   ◇ 652   Feel free to draw your own conclusions. Leading from
♣ Q75   ♣ 9432   a solid sequence is usually a good idea, as long as you
                                        listen to the bidding and don't be dogmatic about the
            SOUTH   lead.
            ♠ A1095
            ♡ 965
            ◇ 3
            ♣ AKJ108

When your sequence gets weaker, your decision becomes more nerve-wracking. I guarantee
that you have experienced bad decisions like these in the following diagrams. You led the
jack of diamonds against, say four spades, and found the suit like this. A disaster!

        ◇ Q92

◇ J1076   ◇ K84   You got one trick, but if you hadn't led the suit, you
                                    might have had two. Of course, if you didn't lead the
        ◇ A53   suit, you might have gotten none if declarer could get
                                    rid of them somewhere.

        ♡ K1084

♡ QJ7   ♡ 6532   Lead the queen here and declarer can win with the ace,
                                    draw trump, and finesse the ten of hearts. The king
        ♡ A9   drops your jack and the eight is good. Bad time for the
                                    sequence lead.

        ♡ A64

♡ KQ75   ♡ 983   If you lead the king, South will take the ace and later
                                    sets up a trick with his J10. The sequence lead didn't
        ♡ J102   work here either.

A Fact Of Life

I don't know how you measure crimes, but if you fail to lead from a particular holding and failure to do so lets the opponents make their contract, it seems to me to be as culpable as leading it and giving up the contract. As you saw in the previous three diagrams, a well intentioned lead may not work for you. My advice? You must not become gun shy about trying something dynamic. If you shy away from leading from kings or if you are appalled at the thought of leading from the QJx of a suit, you are missing out on many good leads.

Let me put this to you in a different light. You can follow all the cliches and live an emotionally pure life as a defender, but you won't win. If you step out and do some of the things I suggest in this book, you will have some huge disasters, but you will have many successes. Also, you will start to win a lot more than the cautious defender who never takes a chance. As long as the things you do are correctly thought out and not flat out silly, you will be a good opening leader.

Do the best you can and see where the chips fall. For every one hundred good leads you make, there will be fifty bad ones. Bad leads happen to everyone. As long as you make more good ones than bad ones, you are ahead of the player who makes one hundred blameless leads.

Enough philosophy. Back to the discussion about leading from two card sequences such as the KQ4 or the QJ73. Is it possible to choose the opportune times to lead from lesser sequences? Yes. In general, it is possible.

If you judge that it is probably all right to lead a certain suit based on the auction, you should be happy to have a good holding in your hand to lead from. Holdings like QJ4 combine nicely with any honors your partner may have. If your partner has nothing in the suit, you rate to lose a trick. But, if your partner comes through, you gain one or more tricks. Later in the book, there is an extended discussion of leading from holdings like K1083 and Q983. These leads, just like some of your sequence leads, need partner to come through for you. If you wish, you might choose to read ahead to the chapter on leading from kings, queens, and jacks. The guidelines that apply there apply here too. Here is an example:

W	N	E	S
	1C	P	1H
P	2H	P	P
P			

You have the QJ72 of a suit and are wondering whether to lead it.

If you have the QJ72 of spades, an unbid suit, it is a decent holding to lead from.
If it is in hearts, the trump suit, it is dangerous to lead.
If it is in diamonds, the other unbid suit, it is an acceptable lead.
If it is in clubs, the suit dummy opened, you should avoid leading it.

You will find that if you are thinking of leading from the QJ72 of a suit, you will be about as happy to have it to lead from as if you have the KJ72 of the suit. If, in your mind, this is the correct suit to be leading, both of these holdings will be equally effective.

If you have a better holding like the QJ108 to lead, you are happier to lead it than when you have the QJ72. The third card in the sequence gives you a near guarantee that you will survive, even when partner has nothing in the suit.

There is one last question to ask about sequence leads. Is it always correct to lead the top card of the sequence? I suggest you do this. If you have a three card holding, such as J102 or QJ8, lead the top card. No exceptions. Lead the top card against notrump contracts and suit contracts. It is when you have a four card or longer suit that you rethink your lead. If you have four cards in the suit headed by a two card sequence such as QJ73 or KQ64, your lead will vary according to whether you are defending against a suit or notrump. The following section looks at this issue.

Are You Leading Against Notrump Or A Suit?

If you have a four card or longer suit to lead from and you have a two card sequence, lead the top of the sequence against suits and lead low against notrumps. The reason for this is that in general, you are only trying to get one or two tricks in a suit when you are defending against suit contracts whereas against notrumps, you are trying to set up an entire suit. Say this is the heart suit.

♡ K103

♡ QJ74   ♡ A862

♡ 95

In notrump, you would lead low. Declarer plays low from dummy and gets his king of hearts in a moment or two, but the defenders can run the rest of the suit when they get in. Against a suit contract, the timing for defenders is different. If West leads the four of hearts against a four spade contract, South may reflect that good defenders don't underlead aces. In this light, South plays low from dummy. East has to take the ace and the defenders have lost one of their tricks. For whatever it is worth, I asked a computer to test this theory. I gave the opening leader the QJ63 of hearts and had it look at lots of four spade contracts dealt at random. It turned out that the queen of hearts (assuming you think the suit should be led) worked better than the three. There were times when leading the suit was wrong, but that is true of just about any lead.

Interestingly enough, if you follow the rule and always lead the sequence against suit contracts, you will get a hidden benefit you haven't read about before now. You are East with the A862 of spades in the following setup. You opened one club and your partner responded one spade. You raised to two spades, but eventually, South became declarer in four hearts.

NORTH
♠ 1074

EAST
♠ A862

Against their four heart contract, your partner leads the three of spades. You win the ace and declarer plays the nine. You know from the fourth best lead that declarer has one more card in this suit. Do you know where the king of spades is? Do you know where the queen and jack are? I do. As should you. Think about it before continuing.

West has the king and South has the queen. How do I know? I know that South has one more spade. If South has the king, my partner has the QJ53. With a two card sequence, he should lead the queen. He did not. He must have the KJ53 and declarer the Q9. Such inferences can be handy.

Leads from Interior Sequences

Interior sequences (sometimes referred to as broken sequences) must not be mishandled. When I give lectures, everyone is happy to lead the jack from the J1095 of a suit or the ten from the 10984 of a suit. But give these players the same sequences with a higher honor also, and suddenly there is cause for concern.

AJ1074	Lead the jack against notrump. Do not lead this suit against a suit contract.
KJ1094	Lead the jack against any contract.
A1094	Lead the ten against notrump only. Do not lead this suit against a suit contract.
K1095	Lead the ten.
Q1098	Lead the ten.

If your opening lead is going to be from one of these holdings, do not lead the fourth best. Leading fourth best from an interior sequence can cost tricks in two ways.

The first way is that partner may not believe your lead to be fourth best. Take the KJ1094 suit for instance. Say you lead the nine of this suit against a suit contract. Your partner will not think you are leading from the KJ1094 but from the 985 or some such holding. While this is not a likely occurrence, it is an expensive one if your partner fails to follow up on your lead. Likewise, if you lead the eight from the Q1098, your partner may not appreciate your actual holding.

The second way leading fourth best from an interior sequence costs is shown in this example.

W	N	E	S
			1H
P	1S	P	2H
P	3H	P	4H
P	P	P	

NORTH
- ♠ KJ87
- ♡ K7
- ◇ J52
- ♣ K654

WEST
- ♠ 962
- ♡ Q82
- ◇ Q1096
- ♣ A93

EAST
- ♠ Q1054
- ♡ J3
- ◇ K743
- ♣ J108

SOUTH
- ♠ A3
- ♡ A109654
- ◇ A8
- ♣ Q72

North's heart raise was a thoughtful choice based on trusting South to have six hearts for his rebid. Against four hearts, West decided to lead diamonds, which was a normal choice. I suggested above that you should lead the top card from an interior sequence. Look what happens if West decides to lead fourth best. The six is led and South, doubting that West is leading from the king-queen of diamonds, plays low from dummy. East has to play the king else South can win with the eight. After playing two rounds of trumps, South leads the eight of diamonds toward dummy. West can take his queen but the jack is good now for a club discard. If West leads the correct card from his diamond sequence, the ten, declarer can't get two diamond tricks and four hearts goes down as long as West does not jump in too soon with his ace of clubs.

Expert Trick

Here is a useful exception you should know. When leading against notrump, you should lead the queen from the specific holding of KQ109 or longer. The idea is that if your partner has the jack, he is requested to play it. This is easy for partner to recognize since it will look odd to him to see your queen lead when he has the jack. He should remember your agreements and play it. It is obvious why this is a good treatment. You lead the king against one notrump and this is what you see.

W	N	E	S
			1NT
P	P	P	

NORTH
♠ 54
♡ K86
◇ Q1093
♣ 10653

WEST
♠ KQ1092
♡ 1072
◇ A7
♣ J87

On your king lead, East plays the three. Are you sure he does or does not have the jack? If he does, leading the suit again is good for the defense. If East has two little ones, a switch is right. Do you think your partner should play the jack on your king? If he has it, you would like to see it. Don't overdo this lead. Use it with discretion. You don't want to be guilty of the following:

NORTH
♠ 54
♡ K86
◇ Q1093
♣ 10653

WEST
♠ KQ1072
♡ 1072
◇ A7
♣ J87

Here, your spade suit is slightly weaker. Again, you lead the king. Again your partner plays the three. If your partner started with the jack, do you want him to play it? Let's pretend that partner has the J3 in both diagrams. In the first case, the jack from East will simplify the defense. In the second case, the jack will cost a trick. South has the A986 which will turn into a second stopper if East plays the jack at trick one. How can East tell when it is right to play the jack and when it is wrong? The answer is to play that you lead the queen from the solid KQ109 combination and the king from the KQ108 or weaker combinations. Your defense will still have some problems, but they will be fewer.

Leading An Ace Against Notrump

There is a cousin to the expert trick on the previous page. You saw that when you hold the KQ1093 of a suit against notrump, you can lead the queen to ask your partner to play the jack. You can extend this treatment to some other holdings too. Say the opponents bid to three notrump and you are on lead with this hand. Assuming you are going to lead diamonds, which one should you lead? A useful agreement is that when you have a near solid suit headed by the ace, the lead of the ace demands that partner play an honor if he has one and give count otherwise.

WEST
♠ 74
♡ 983
♢ AKJ108
♣ J83

If, on your lead of the ace, East plays the queen, you will run off the rest of the suit. If East does not have the queen, he gives count. He will play as indicated in the following list.

72   Play the seven. East is not encouraging. He is just showing you how many diamonds he has.

732   East will play the two. He is not saying he likes or dislikes the suit. The message of the two is that he has an odd number in the suit. He might have one, he might have three, and he might have five.

8743   Probably right to play the seven or the eight. You want to play a high enough card that your partner will be able to tell you have lower cards, thus indicating you have an even number. If you played the four from this holding, West might think you have a three card suit.

Q976   Drop the queen on the ace. West is not asking you if you like the suit. He is asking you to play an honor if you have one. You have one. Play it. If you play the nine, West won't interpret it to mean you like the suit. He will interpret it to mean you have two or four cards in the suit. He might switch suits on you, which won't be good.

AKQ105   You can use this opening lead method from all three of these holdings. Note,
AKJ104   just for the record, that when you have the AKQ105, you can lead the queen
AQJ106   or the ace to get partner to drop the jack for you.

Following Up After Your Sequence Lead

The following material is not strictly opening lead stuff, but it is relatively ignored in bridge literature. Here is the issue.

W	N	E	S
			1NT
P	3NT	P	P
P			

	HAND 1			HAND 2	
	NORTH			NORTH	
	♠ K75			♠ K75	
	♡ 642			♡ 642	
	◇ KQJ6			◇ KQJ6	
	♣ Q64			♣ Q64	
WEST		EAST	WEST		EAST
♠ J82		♠ Q1064	♠ J2		♠ Q1064
♡ QJ9		♡ K83	♡ QJ1097		♡ K83
◇ 743		◇ 85	◇ 743		◇ 85
♣ 10853		♣ A972	♣ 1085		♣ A972
	SOUTH			SOUTH	
	♠ A93			♠ A983	
	♡ A1075			♡ A5	
	◇ A1092			◇ A1092	
	♣ KJ			♣ KJ3	

Look at the West hands. In hand one, West sees that leading a club is not very exciting. Instead, West leads the queen of hearts, hoping to find East's suit. East likes the lead and signals with the eight to show this. West, thinking he has hit gold, continues with the jack. East comes into the picture now. East can see that his king of hearts is in the way and may unblock it on West's jack. This results in declarer getting three heart tricks.

Let's go to hand two. West has a good heart sequence so leads the queen. On this hand, West has a real suit and hopes to set it up. East likes hearts so signals with the eight. Declarer holds up on the first heart as before and West continues with the jack. You will note that from East's perspective, hands one and two are identical, right down to South's playing the five of hearts at trick one. What should East do? If West has led from a three card suit as he did on hand one, East better keep his king. If West has led from the QJ1097 as on hand two, East better get his king out of the way. Is there is way for East to tell? Yes. There is a rule that applies to this situation.

RULE –When you lead your top card from a sequence and are allowed to win the trick, you should continue with the lowest card in your sequence. For example:

KQJ7   Lead the king and if it wins, continue with the jack.

QJ105   Lead the queen and if it wins, continue with the ten.

KQ4   Lead the king and if it wins and if you choose to continue the suit, continue with the queen.

J1094   Lead the jack and continue with the nine.

Using this rule, East will know on hand one that West has lead from a short sequence. East will keep his king and will be rewarded with another heart trick later. This is not a great triumph, but it does avoid an embarrassing moment. Likewise, on hand two, West will continue with the nine of hearts. East already knows that West has the jack of hearts so the nine of hearts will inform East that the sequence is headed by the QJ109 and not the QJ(x). Three notrump will go down when East plays the king of hearts. Here is a hand from a recent bridge column where the defenders were not in sync.

NORTH
♠ Q76
♡ KQ8
◇ 86
♣ KJ1075

WEST
♠ J109
♡ 64
◇ Q1052
♣ 9642

EAST
♠ AK543
♡ J9
◇ K973
♣ A3

SOUTH
♠ 82
♡ A107532
◇ AJ4
♣ Q8

East opened one spade, South bid two hearts, and North raised to game. West led the jack of spades, which was allowed to win. West continued with the ten. East won his king and had to decide whether to try to cash the ace of spades or whether to shift to a diamond. From East's point of view, leading a diamond would be wrong if South had three spades and the AQJ of diamonds. A diamond switch would allow South to take two diamond finesses and discard the spade loser from dummy. How can East tell what to do? The answer is that on this hand, West defended poorly. West led the jack of spades, which was correct, but should have continued with the nine and not the ten.

This follows the rule that says after winning the first trick with a sequence lead, you must follow with the lowest card in your sequence at trick two. East will know West has the J109 so will switch at trick three. This gets the defenders four tricks for down one.

You may ask how East knows that West has the J109 and not the J9 doubleton. This requires a little thinking. If West has the J9 of spades, it means declarer has three to the ten. If South has three to the ten, he would cover the jack at trick one.

A Little Quiz On Sequence Leads

WEST	W	N	E	S
♠ 983	P	1C	P	1D
♡ K1095	P	1S	P	2D
◊ Q94	P	P	P	
♣ AJ4				

Lead the ten of hearts. It is easy to choose a heart since it is the only unbid suit. There is no reason not to lead hearts, so the only question is which heart to lead. The five is terribly wrong since it can cost you tricks in many ways.

WEST	W	N	E	S
♠ QJ95	P	1S	P	2H
♡ Q43	P	2NT	P	3C
◊ K976	P	3H	P	4H
♣ 104	P	P	P	

Lead the six of diamonds. Much of the time, you would lead the queen of spades. Here, North opened with one spade. This is a warning sign against leading spades. Leading diamonds may not work either, but you have less specific concern that a diamond is a poor choice.

WEST	W	N	E	S
♠ K8652				1H
♡ A3	1S	2C	P	3NT
◊ QJ7	P	P	P	
♣ 1053				

Lead the queen of diamonds. Your partner didn't raise spades so he doesn't rate to have much there. If you are lucky, East will have something in diamonds. You have a sure entry in the ace of hearts. Even though you have only three diamonds, the queen and jack are a strong start to setting up some tricks if East can contribute something.

WEST	W	N	E	S
♠ 1094		1C	P	1H
♡ QJ1052	P	1S	P	2NT
◊ K8	P	3NT	P	P
♣ J76	P			

Lead the five of hearts. You can't set up this suit unless East has a helping card like the king, ace, or nine. Leading the queen is likely to block the suit. You make this lead only because you know South has four hearts.

CHAPTER TWELVE

LEADING FROM KINGS AND LESSER HONOR HOLDINGS AGAINST SUIT CONTRACTS

When you have nice sequences to lead or when you have a tempting singleton to lead or when your partner has bid a suit, opening leads are not so tough. It is when you have indifferent holdings in all four suits and a partner who didn't bid that your opening leads become thought-provoking experiences.

The opponents bid all by themselves to four spades and you have the KJ73 of hearts. How do you feel about leading the three of hearts?

I will grant you that leading from this holding can be bad. It can be very bad. Sometimes leading away from a king is the only lead you can make which allows them to make their contract, and when you choose such a lead, you may never hear the end of it. But it can work out some of the time.

Let me show you a few hands. In all cases, you are declarer in four spades from the West seat.

WEST	EAST	
♠ Q97543	♠ A862	If North leads a trump, diamond, or a club, making
♡ A108	♡ 942	four spades will be an easy affair. You will set up the
◊ Q5	◊ KJ107	diamonds and discard the two losing hearts. With good
♣ AJ	♣ K2	luck, you will make twelve tricks. With normal luck,
		you will make eleven tricks. With bad luck you will
		make ten. Only with immeasurably wretched luck will
		you make less than ten.

How do you feel if North leads the three of hearts? Personally, I would be annoyed. South plays the queen of hearts at trick one and when the hand is over, you are down. If it occurs to you to look at North's heart holding, you will see he led from the KJ73. I ask you. Did North make a good lead or a lucky lead or was it supernatural? Whatever you think of it, it was effective.

Here are some similar layouts. In all of the following cases, West plays in four spades against the lead of the three of hearts.

WEST	EAST	
♠ Q97543	♠ A862	You are in four spades again and North leads the three
♡ AQ2	♡ 964	of hearts. South plays the ten and you win the queen. It
◇ K4	◇ J1098	seems that you have gotten a free trick. You lead a
♣ Q8	♣ AK	spade to the ace, felling the ten and jack. It's time to go

after diamonds. You lead the jack and guess to play the four from your hand. North wins with the queen. Back comes the king of hearts. You take your ace and lead the king of diamonds. North takes his ace and cashes the jack of hearts. With your later spade loser, you are down one.

Going over the hand with your friends you discover you were the only declarer to go down. Your friends got a club lead. This didn't give declarer a free heart trick, but it didn't stop four spades either. After winning the club, it was possible to establish diamonds and later to discard two hearts. Isn't this strange? Against you, the defense leads a heart away from the king. It gives you a free trick. Yet you end up going down. Even though the heart lead didn't help the defense immediately, it gave the defense a head start.

WEST	EAST	
♠ Q97543	♠ A862	Here we are in four spades again. North leads the three
♡ AQ2	♡ 964	of hearts and South puts up the ten. You get a free
◇ Q	◇ KJ84	trick with the queen. Sooner or later, you lead the
♣ AK2	♣ 107	queen of diamonds and the defenders take it. You are
		able to throw away your two of hearts and end up

making eleven tricks. Do you get a little gloat in at North's expense? Not at all. It didn't matter that North led away from the king of hearts. West got a cheap trick but it didn't make any difference since West was going to discard all of his heart losers anyway. North probably felt sad at the end of trick one, but when the hand was over, he knew he hadn't lost a trick. Hopefully South is equally enlightened and is not telling North about opening lead theories.

The point of these three example hands is that leading away from kings is not automatically a bad thing. I can construct lots of hands where leading from a king is the killing lead and I have no doubt that you can remember lots of hands where it was the only lead to give away the contract.

So who is right?

I am.

There are reasons why I am right and there are reasons why you don't agree. The reason I am right is that leading from kings has proven itself over the long haul. Weight of experience wins this one.

So why don't you agree with me? The one biggest reason you don't agree is that you have learned the hard way that leading from kings is bad. That is to say, you led from kings for awhile and got stung doing it. I am going to make two assumptions.

1.   Some of your leads from kings were poorly timed. If you lead from a king when you shouldn't, you rate to get a poor result.

2.   Some of the times where you led from a king you got a good result. Probably quite a few of the times turned out well for you. The problem is that your memory is selective and remembers only the bad results. Bridge players are people too. They want the best of all things all the time. When you lead from a king and get a good result, you accept it as your normal entitlement. When you lead from a king and get a bad result, you get the bad result, which is painful enough, and then you get reinforcement at the table when your partner points it out. Sometimes declarer pipes in that the contract was hopeless without that helpful lead. Ouch. To make matters worse, your friends always seem to ask about your bad boards during the dinner postmortems.

Is it worth trying to lead from kings or should you avoid the issue?

Face it. Leading from kings is a potent source of tricks. If you doubt this, ask the best player in your company this question.

"If I was never to lead from a king for the rest of my life, how much would my defense suffer?"

If you are uncertain what this player will say, I suggest you put this book down for a moment and get on the phone. Note that I am asking you to call the best player in your circle, not necessarily your favorite partner. If you are lucky, that person is your partner and you will already be a believer in this matter.

My opinion is that it is hard to put the answer into measurable terms. I will though, cheerfully promise you that I would feel deprived of a potent weapon.

Which Are the Best Combinations to Lead from Against Suit Contracts?

Ideally, you will be dealt nothing but AKQ and KQJ combinations to lead. I once had a dream where I was on lead with the KQJ10987654 of a suit. I led the king and declarer ducked. I led the queen and he ducked again. In my dream I led the suit nine times and declarer ducked all of them! I woke up before I was able to set up the suit.

Life at the table is different. Instead of KQJ10 suits, I see a parade of suits like these:

KJ43   You won't get rich leading from combinations like these as your only
                source of tricks, but sometimes, these are the only suits you have.

Q976

J863

K1084

Q432

10872

> # Which of these combinations would you prefer to lead from?

W	N	E	S
			1S
P	2C	P	2S
P	3S*	P	4S
P	P	P	

*South can pass

Let's assume you decide to lead a heart. Which of the six combinations above would you prefer to lead from? Would you like leading from the 10872, or would you prefer the KJ43, or would you settle for one of the in-between holdings?

When you make an opening lead, one of your goals is to set up tricks for your side. Setting up tricks requires that your side have some high cards in the suit you are leading. This means that if you lead from the 10872, you won't set up a trick unless your partner has a good holding in the suit. If partner has the jack, nothing good will happen for you. If partner has the queen, not much will happen either. If partner has the king, you may get a trick, but you may not. Even if partner has two honors like the queen and jack or the king and jack, you don't guarantee setting up a trick. And, if partner has the ace, but no other honor, all you are doing is taking a trick you were always going to get and you may be giving the declarer extra time to do what he wants.

If you are going to lead from one of these broken holdings, your lead won't work unless partner has some help. Look at it this way.

If you lead from the KJ43 and partner has the queen, you have two potential tricks. If you lead from the 10872, and partner has the queen, you have gained nothing. Worse, you may have helped declarer by leading the suit to his benefit rather than yours.

If you lead from the KJ43 and partner has the ace, you have three potential tricks. You might even be able to give partner a later ruff in this suit. If you lead from the 10872 and partner has the ace, you gain nothing.

This is the key. If you are willing to attack a suit, you are better off if you have some of the necessary honors in your own hand. The better your holding in a suit, THE LESS YOU HAVE TO WISH FOR in partner's hand. Wishing for partner to have one honor in the suit you lead is a lesser wish than wishing for him to have two or three honors. Don't be greedy.

Of the combinations on the list, I would prefer to have the KJ43 to lead from. In fact, if the bidding suggested to me that this was the suit I should lead, I would be fairly pleased to have the KJ43 to lead from. As your holding gets worse, your enthusiasm for the lead will diminish. Queens and jacks are less appealing than kings to lead from and lesser holdings are worse yet. NOTE the value of tens and nines. Q1082 is better to lead from than Q973, which is somewhat better than Q532. Short of putting a big unwieldy table here, it is hard to quantify the difference a ten or nine spot makes, but I assure you it is significant. Here is the rule for you again.

Rule - Leading Against A Suit Contract

When you are leading from a broken holding, the more honor cards you have to lead from, the better. This is because success requires less from partner. Leading from the KJ75 is superior to leading from the 10752.

Given the same high cards in a suit, it is better to lead suits with good spot cards. Leading from the Q1083 is much better than leading from the Q642.

A Comforting Reminder

Leading away from kings and queens and jacks may not always be a good idea. It is right often enough, though, that doing so should have a prominent place in your thinking. You should not refuse to lead from such holdings just because you got a bad result some time previously.

A Little Quiz On Leading From Broken Holdings

WEST	W	N	E	S
♠ J73				1S
♡ K983	P	2S	DBL	3S
◊ 82	P	P	P	
♣ J864				

Lead the three of hearts. This is clear. Here, East showed something in the unbid suits. Your heart holding is ideal. Leading from a king in a suit partner likes has a high priority.

WEST	W	N	E	S
♠ Q1073				1NT
♡ 84	P	2C	P	2H
◇ KJ43	P	3H	P	4H
♣ Q73	P	P	P	

Lead a trump. The point here is not that a trump lead is correct. The emphasis is that when South opens a strong notrump, leading from a broken holding is more dangerous than normal. Had South opened two notrump and reached four hearts on a similar auction, it would be even more dangerous to lead, say, a spade or a diamond.

WEST	W	N	E	S
♠ 6532		1S	P	2C
♡ Q1065	P	2S	P	3NT
◇ 64	P	P	P	
♣ AQ6				

It is nice when partner bids a suit, but this won't always be the case. An unbid suit isn't as appealing as one partner suggested, but it does have its charm. Lead the five of hearts. Leading a 'safe' spade or a 'safe' diamond is too passive. Timing is everything on defense. Unless you are *sure* that it is right to be passive, you should avoid it.

WEST	W	N	E	S
♠ 8				1S
♡ K432	P	2D	P	2S
◇ A75	P	3S	P	4S
♣ 97652	P	P	P	

The right lead is clearly the two of hearts. The more important question is this. How do you feel about this choice? It would be nice to have the KQJ of hearts, but you don't. You have the K432. Given that this is the hand you were dealt, you should feel that the heart lead is the only lead worth considering. It isn't a great lead, but it is much superior to the alternatives. Remember this. If you fail to attack, declarer will have time to set up some diamonds tricks. You know there is a dangerous suit in dummy. Attack while you are in to do so.

WEST	W	N	E	S
♠ Q73	P	P	1S	2H
♡ 73	2S	3H	P	4H
◇ K10985	P	P	P	
♣ QJ3				

Lead the three of spades. Do not lead the queen and do not lead another suit. You don't always lead partner's suit, but it does rate a serious look. Here, East opened the bidding with one spade, so he usually has a fair suit. Any other lead suggests a case of overthinking.

CHAPTER THIRTEEN

LEADING SINGLETONS

There are many leads which appear to be routine. Leading a singleton against a suit contract is almost automatic. Or is it? Leading a singleton can be a crushing lead but it can also rank among the worst choices imaginable. It all depends on the bidding and on what your alternatives are. The same applies to most of the other so called automatic leads. When you have the ace-king-queen of a suit, it feels right to lead one to start the defense. Would you believe that there are times when this is a terrible choice?

When Should You Lead a Singleton Against a Suit Contract?

Since this lead is one which almost automatically jumps out of a defender's hand, it is not necessary to encourage most players to lead singletons. What is needed is a little thought before you put your singleton on the table. Be honest. When you have a stiff to lead, how much thought do you give to the alternatives? Do you look at other choices or are you content to see the singleton and lead it on the theory that it is right more often than not? If you are guilty of this, you are also guilty of lazy bridge. The times you should lead a singleton are many. I agree that leading a singleton is often good, but I will resist leading one without due consideration. Here is a list of things to think about when you have a singleton.

1.   Did your partner bid the suit and if so, how much can you read into the way he bid it? Go back to chapter 4, where I discuss "Did partner bid the suit?" If you don't want to review that section, you can take it on faith that leading a suit partner has bid is usually OK.

2.   Did your LHO bid the suit? If so, leading a singleton is a reasonable thing to do.

3.   Did your LHO bid the suit and get support or the hint of support from his partner? If so, leading a singleton is not good. Leading this suit is more likely to hurt your partner's holding than to gain a ruffing trick.

This is a typical result when you lead a singleton unwisely.

W	N	E	S
			1H
P	2C	P	3C
P	3H	P	4H
P	P	P	

NORTH
♠ AJ2
♡ 1095
◇ 86
♣ AQ975

WEST
♠ Q1065
♡ Q72
◇ A9542
♣ 6

EAST
♠ K983
♡ 63
◇ Q103
♣ J432

SOUTH
♠ 74
♡ AKJ84
◇ KJ7
♣ K108

I am making this one easy for you. Instead of looking at the West hand only and having to pick an opening lead, you get to look at all four hands. Without further comment, let's see how the defense goes if West leads his singleton club. Dummy will play low and South will win the trick. South, expecting West to have a stiff club, will probably play the ace and king of hearts. With both opponents following, South will start leading clubs. West can ruff at his leisure, but declarer will have time to discard a spade and a diamond on the clubs. If South guesses diamonds correctly, he will make an overtrick. This result makes the singleton lead look shabby.

Let's try it with a more thoughtful lead. West won't lead a heart from Q72 and leading from ace-high suits is terrible in general, so West settles on a spade. This lead puts declarer in jeopardy. If he plays low from dummy, East will win and will return a diamond. South doesn't know it yet, but if he misguesses diamonds, he goes down.

NOTE that the effect of a club lead is just as bad for the defenders if East has the queen of clubs instead of the jack. In fact, it is bad for the defenders when East has no club honor at all. Just for the record, say the clubs are distributed differently. Say these are the clubs.

♣ Q9853

♣ 6   ♣ K1042

♣ AJ7

Without a club lead, East will probably get a club trick. With a club lead, East will get no club trick. In addition to East not getting a club trick, the club lead gives declarer important timing. In this layout and in the previous layout, a club lead was very expensive.

4.   Did your RHO bid the suit? Leading a stiff is bad. Basically, if your RHO has bid
       a suit or has raised his partner or has implied a fit for his partner, leading the suit
       is bad. A possible exception is when your RHO opened one club or one diamond
       on what might be a three card suit.

W	N	E	S
			1S
P	2C	P	2H
P	3H	P	4H
P	P	P	

NORTH
♠ 86
♡ AQ86
◊ 92
♣ AJ1084

WEST   EAST   How do you think the play will go if West leads the
♠ 4   ♠ KJ972   singleton spade?
♡ 753   ♡ 104
◊ Q8753   ◊ KJ6   Assuming declarer is astute enough to know it is a
♣ Q653   ♣ K92   singleton, he will know to win the spade lead and draw
                                        trumps. Later he will finesse in spades again. This
           SOUTH   gives him four hearts, three spades, two aces, and a
           ♠ AQ1053   ruff in dummy. Ten easy tricks. Let's say West leads a
           ♡ KJ92   diamond instead, the unbid suit. South will win the ace
           ◊ A104   and likely will go to dummy with a trump in order to
           ♣ 7   finesse the queen of spades. Continuing, he will play
                                        the ace of spades and will get a shock when West ruffs.
                                        If West now leads his last trump, declarer will come up
                                        a trick short.

OK. So you led a singleton and it didn't work because you didn't get your ruff. Do you
think that if you get a ruff, the lead will automatically turn out for the best? Leading a
singleton and getting a ruff out of it sounds like a good way to conduct a defense.

Make up your mind and then go to the next page.

W	N	E	S
			1C
P	1D	P	1S
P	2S	P	4S
P	P	P	

NORTH
♠ K763
♡ Q2
◇ 9743
♣ Q72

WEST
♠ 984
♡ A1075
◇ QJ1082
♣ 4

EAST
♠ J5
♡ J864
◇ K65
♣ A1096

SOUTH
♠ AQ102
♡ K93
◇ A
♣ KJ853

Try it in four spades with the stiff club lead. East wins the ace and gives West a ruff. West cashes the ace of hearts, which gets the defense off to a fast start. It adds up to a blazing burst of energy which is followed by a slow finish. South wins the second heart, draws trump, and claims. Let's see how it works if West avoids leading declarer's club suit and instead leads his diamond sequence. South will take his ace and is likely to draw trumps. After doing so, he will attack clubs. East wins the queen with the ace and continues diamonds. South, seeing a possible overtrick, ruffs and tries the king of clubs. Ouch. West shows out. The defense can't be stopped from taking the ace of hearts and two more diamonds and the contract fails by one trick. Odd comparison. If West gets a club ruff, the contract makes. If West does not get a ruff, the contract goes down one.

The theme here is that when you lead a stiff in declarer's known side suit, you are solving his problems in that suit. Even if you do get a ruff, you usually lose so much timing that you end up with a net loss.

5.   Is the singleton an unbid suit? Look elsewhere first, but if nothing else seems right, leading it is probably a good idea.

6.   Did partner bid another suit? If so, leading partner's suit might be better than leading a singleton.

7.   Do you have an honor combination to lead? A very rough generalization is that it is better to lead high card combinations than to lead singletons. For instance:

W	N	E	S
			1S
2H	3S	P	4S
P	P	P	

WEST
♠ A65
♡ KQJ107
◇ 3
♣ K984

Do you lead the king of hearts or the three of diamonds? I can give you a guideline for this situation. Assume the bidding did not give you any hints about what to lead. When you have a choice of leading a sequence and setting up tricks as opposed to leading a singleton in hopes of getting a ruff, you should lean towards leading the sequence. There are many factors which will influence your choice. The two major factors are these.

A. The stronger the sequence, the more you should tend to lead it. By this, I mean you are happier to lead from the KQJ than the KQ9. Likewise, you are happier to lead from the KQ10 than the QJ9. When your sequence is as weak as the QJ76, I would say that the two leads are about tied in terms of value.

B. The longer your suit, the less chance you have of setting up tricks by leading a sequence. Leading from the KQJ alone will gain you more tricks against a suit contract than leading from the KQJ7 or the KQJ64 or the KQJ764. I judge that the honor lead is better until your suit is five and a half cards long, at which point it is about a tie. Keep in mind that if your partner has raised the suit, the odds change toward the singleton.

8. How good a hand do you have? If you have a huge hand and can tell that partner won't have an entry, leading a singleton can be a waste of time. Look at the hand above. Your good high cards tell you that partner is broke. Leading the king of hearts is a standout choice. Leading your diamond will help declarer with the diamond suit and may cause you to lose heart tricks if declarer has time to get rid of them.

9. A strong reason for considering a singleton is that you have a sure trump entry. If you lead a singleton when you have two or three little trumps, there is a danger that declarer will win the lead, draw trumps, and run off the suit you led.

10. One powerful warning sign against leading a singleton is possession of four or more trumps. Imagine the times you declared a hand and discovered that one of your opponents had four trumps. It can be a painful discovery. With four trump in your hand, consider other leads before settling on the stiff. The example following shows how devastating it can be for declarer when an opponent has four trumps.

SOUTH DEALS
NO ONE VULNERABLE

W	N	E	S
			1S
P	1NT*	P	2C
P	3S	P	4S
P	P	P	

*Forcing

A defender who has
four trumps has a
nasty little surprise
for declarer.

NORTH
♠ KJ4
♡ KQJ8
♢ 753
♣ Q97

WEST   EAST
♠ 7652   ♠ 10
♡ 5   ♡ A96432
♢ KJ86   ♢ Q1094
♣ A863   ♣ 52

SOUTH
♠ AQ983
♡ 107
♢ A2
♣ KJ104

North-South bid to four spades without interference. What should West lead? Each suit would get votes, some of them misguided. Look at the effect of various leads from the West hand.

If West leads a trump, South will draw trumps and knock out the ace of clubs. Whatever the defense returns, South has time to take the clubs and then set up a heart trick.

If West leads his singleton heart, East will win and can give West a ruff. Whatever West returns, South can win and draw the trumps. The hearts will get rid of South's diamond loser. The only remaining loser will be the ace of clubs.

If West leads clubs, South will be in control, regardless of which club West leads. In fact, a club lead is atrocious and is not worth considering. I note the result of a club lead in the interests of completeness.

West should note his four spades and realize that they are a big defensive asset. If West leads from his king of diamonds, declarer can't make four spades. He can draw trumps and attack clubs or hearts. Say he attacks clubs. The defenders will take the ace of clubs, cash a diamond, and continue diamonds. Declarer will ruff with his last trump and when he attempts to set up his last trick in hearts, the defenders will have a diamond for the setting trick. It is scary how potent the 7652 of spades are on this hand. Since I have the pen and can make up hands to suit my point, you have every right to complain that a diamond lead does not have to work. I agree. In some areas of bridge, points can be proven. I can probably prove to you that bidding six spades missing the AKQ of spades is bad. In other areas, proof is harder to establish. This is the case here. Given that I can't prove that a diamond lead is best on this hand, accept that experience has shown that it is better than the alternatives.

11.   This is a classic error. If they voluntarily bid to a slam, don't lead a singleton if you have an ace in your hand unless partner bid the suit. Surely, unless the opponents are mad, your partner won't be getting in to give you a ruff.

Should You Lead a Singleton In an Unbid Suit Against Notrump?

Sooner or later, this thought will occur to you. The bidding will go 1NT - 3NT, or something like it, and you will have this thing to lead from:

WEST
♠ 8732
♡ 9
♢ 10763
♣ J763

You think to yourself that the opponents have between twenty-five and thirty points, which means your partner has as many as fourteen. Hm. Lots of entries over there. Wonder if he has a heart suit. If he does, and if he can get in a few times, we may be able to set three notrump. I will lead the nine of hearts. Is there anything wrong with this thinking?

Yes. There is lots wrong. The nice thing about this issue is that it is provable. Let's say you are thinking about leading the nine of hearts. What are you hoping for? You are hoping partner has good hearts and some entries. Will you be happy if partner has five hearts to the KJ? Give him the KJ853, five hearts with a nice heart spot tossed in. Does this make the nine of hearts a good lead?

For a moment, let's put you in the South seat. You are in three notrump. What suits do you attack? The answer is that you attack the suits where you have the most length. If you have four hearts to the A762 opposite the Q104, you might play on hearts yourself. Might you ever play the ace and another heart? Here is the entire heart suit.

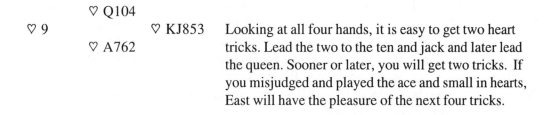

♡ Q104

♡ 9   ♡ KJ853   Looking at all four hands, it is easy to get two heart
         ♡ A762   tricks. Lead the two to the ten and jack and later lead
                                          the queen. Sooner or later, you will get two tricks. If
                                          you misjudged and played the ace and small in hearts,
                                          East will have the pleasure of the next four tricks.

```
        ♡ Q104
♡ 9              ♡ KJ853
        ♡ A762
```

Here are some additional thoughts for you to consider if you are seriously thinking about leading the singleton nine of hearts. The bidding went one notrump by South and three notrump by North. North seems not to have a four card major. It is almost a certainty that you are leading into South's four card heart suit. He might even have five. Most players open one notrump routinely with a five card minor and quite a few do it with a five card major. Even if you get lucky and find your partner with six hearts, it is still possible for declarer to have four of them, which means you are faced with an uphill struggle. My advice is never to lead a singleton against notrump unless partner has bid the suit or has doubled for the lead.

Here is another example. You will note that the result is the same.

```
        ♠ A95
♠ 3             ♠ Q10762
        ♠ KJ84
```

Spades is the unbid suit and West leads the three. East will play the queen and declarer the king. At some time in the play, South may lead the four, intending to finesse dummy's nine. But, seeing West show out, South just goes up with the ace and returns the nine. This gets declarer four winners. If declarer was left to his own devices, he might play the four to the ace and finesse the jack. Seeing the bad break, he will change his attack. Still, if East can get in twice, he will be in a position to return the queen of spades, setting up two tricks, and will cash them as soon as he gets in again. Curious. When West leads the suit, declarer gets four painless tricks. When declarer leads the suit, he gets only three tricks and he loses important timing. All of this is typical and expected. Lead something else and avoid the problem.

A Little Quiz On Leading Singletons

WEST	W	N	E	S
♠ K72				1S
♡ 3	P	1NT	P	2S
◇ J10873	P	P	P	
♣ Q653				

Never let it be said that leading singletons is bad. They are often excellent leads. This is the case here. The right lead is the three of hearts. West has a trump entry and his weak hand overall suggests that East will have some entries to give West heart ruffs. My suggestion is that you mentally get your singleton ready and then think if there is a reason not to lead it. Be honest here. If you see a reason to lead something else, you should do so. If you have doubt, leading the singleton is probably OK since when it works, it works very well.

124

WEST	W	N	E	S
♠ AK73		1C	P	1H
♡ 873	P	2H	P	P
◇ 2	P			
♣ 109763				

Lead the king of spades. Sequences have a higher priority than singletons. Say you lead the king of spades and see that a diamond switch looks good. You can still make the switch. If you lead the two of diamonds and the dummy makes your lead look bad, you are stuck with it.

WEST	W	N	E	S
♠ 8764		1C	P	1H
♡ J973	P	1S	P	1NT
◇ 6	P	P	P	
♣ KQ62				

Do not lead the six of diamonds. In a later chapter, I will show you why the heart three is the best lead. You may not feel like making that lead now and wish to choose another suit. The one promise I make you here is that the diamond lead is the worst of the lot.

WEST	W	N	E	S
♠ J65				1C
♡ Q10865	P	1H	P	1S
◇ KJ53	P	3S	P	4S
♣ 2	P	P	P	

The best lead for you is the three of diamonds. It will fail you some of the time, but making this lead will mean you have avoided a common trap. The popular lead with this hand is the two of clubs. This violates one of the strongest lead guidelines you have, which says you should not lead a singleton into the person who has bid or raised the suit.

WEST	W	N	E	S
♠ Q				1H
♡ 1084	P	1S	2D	2H
◇ QJ875	3D	3H	4D	4H
♣ 10964	P	P	P	

Having decided not to bid five diamonds, (no one was vulnerable), you have to choose between the queen of spades and the queen of diamonds. With so many diamonds, there is no chance of getting two tricks there. The queen of spades is a reasonable choice. There are other reasons why the spade lead is OK. North bid them, but South did not raise them. A second reason is that if East has the ace of spades, you may get a ruff and then be able to get him in for a second ruff. You do not often lead a singleton instead of partner's suit. You need a good reason to do so.

WEST	W	N	E	S
♠ KQ106				2NT
♡ 432	P	3C	P	3H
◇ QJ1065	P	4H	P	P
♣ 4	P			

I would choose the king of spades or the queen of diamonds or even a trump. All of these leads rate to be better than the singleton club lead. One major reason is that leading a singleton into a two notrump bidder is not a good habit. You rate to finesse your partner out of something and very rarely get a ruff for your efforts. You have a slight additional hint from the bidding in that East didn't double three clubs.

WEST	W	N	E	S
♠ 985				2C
♡ 3	P	2D	P	2S
◇ J87653	P	3S	P	4NT
♣ 932	P	5D	P	7S
	P	P	P	

If you consider that South used Blackwood and then bid seven spades, your side doesn't have an ace unless South can't count to four. Assuming they have all the aces, you won't get a heart ruff by leading the singleton heart. Since no ruff is forthcoming, you should look for a safe lead. With three little trumps, it is reasonable to lead a trump. The lead to avoid is the non-productive heart lead. If East has the queen or jack, your lead may ruin a potential trick in his hand.

WEST				
♠ 63				
♡ KJ108753	W	N	E	S
◇ 3	3H	P	P	3S
♣ Q87	P	4S	P	P
	P			

With no one vulnerable, you started with three hearts and found yourself outgunned. Your opening lead is pretty easy. Start with the three of diamonds. There is an interesting expert trick you should know about here. It is summed up in the following rule.

Rule

If an opponent preempts and does not lead his suit, he probably has a singleton in the suit he is leading. If he does lead his suit, it is likely that he does not have a singleton to lead. He could, of course, have a singleton trump, but he would not be leading that. This insight is often helpful to you when your LHO preempts and you end up as declarer.

CHAPTER FOURTEEN

LEADING TRUMP
OR
NOT LEADING TRUMP

When I started to play bridge, I used to go to the Bridge Week Regional at the Ambassador Hotel in Los Angeles. Not knowing who was who in those days, I asked who I should kibitz and was directed to watch someone named Lew Mathe. Didn't know the name for beans. I learned it quickly. The time I spent watching Lew was an experience. I could write pages on Lew's approach to bridge, but will limit myself to the rule he taught me about leading trump.

His partner had led a trump and it was not the right lead on this particular hand. Lew explained to his partner that leading trump was not permitted. "There is one and only one time that leading trump is correct."

His partner apparently did not know the one and only one time exception and asked what it was. I wish you could hear Lew's answer and how he delivered it.

"When it is right!"

Your first reaction might be that this was a flippant answer. It wasn't. Lew was expressing that he wanted his partner to think. What he meant was that his partner was not allowed to lead a trump unless he saw a reason to do so. He hated hearing partner say, "I didn't know what to lead, so I led a trump."

Some players are too lazy to think, and they lead a trump for the reason that they don't feel like working out the best lead. Lew wanted his partners to lead trumps only when it was right to lead them.

The next time you find yourself reaching for a trump, ask yourself if you are doing so because you know it is a good lead or because you are confused. Uninformed trump leads are usually bad leads. When you lead a trump, you put declarer in to do what he wants. If he has enough tricks to make his contract, you shouldn't be leading trumps. You should be taking your tricks.

When *Should* You Lead Trump?

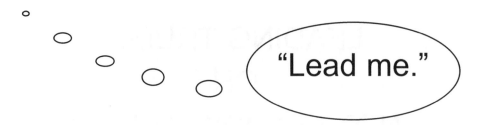

"Lead me."

You have been on lead against many auctions where at the end of the bidding, you heard this little voice crying out for you to "Lead me". That is the voice of a trump waiting for its moment. It may be that you heard the voice but did not recognize what it was saying. Usually, if you didn't get the hint and led something else, you got a bad result, at which point you came to notice that a trump lead would have been a wonderful choice. Is it possible to tell when a trump lead is called for and when not? What makes this so?

Dummy Has a Ruffing Value

When you lead a trump, you usually have a good reason to. There should be something about your hand and the bidding that tells you a trump lead is good. The most likely reason for leading trumps is when declarer has shown two suits and you fear he is going to get ruffs in dummy. Here are some auctions to show this thinking.

N	S
	1H
1S	2C
P	

This auction strongly suggests a trump lead. South has hearts and clubs. North would give a preference to hearts on almost any excuse. Playing in a minor suit is seldom done if a major suit is at all playable. Here are two possible hands for North.

#1	#2
♠ KJ876	♠ J8653
♡ 7	♡ 73
◇ K763	◇ K2
♣ J63	♣ QJ43

On hand one, North passed two clubs. This is an expression that he prefers clubs to hearts. Even though North did not say "clubs" out loud, his pass was a powerful admission that he has club support. As an aside, note that North did not rebid spades or introduce diamonds. Both bids are horrible. When your partner opens in a suit and rebids another suit, the chances are great that he has one or none of your suit. It is good bridge for North to pass two clubs, getting to a known seven card fit, and avoid getting in trouble. Here is a complete hand diagram using the first example dummy. Without bothering to look at South's hand or the East-West hands, it is clear that a trump lead may be the best defense. The following diagram shows a possible setup using hand diagram one from the previous page.

```
                NORTH
                ♠ KJ876
                ♡ 7
                ◊ K763
                ♣ J63

WEST                    EAST
♠ A9                    ♠ Q10543
♡ J98                   ♡ K1042
◊ Q952                  ◊ J10
♣ Q852                  ♣ A9

                SOUTH
                ♠ 2
                ♡ AQ653
                ◊ A84
                ♣ K1074
```

West, if he thinks about it, will realize that a club lead is a good idea. It is relatively easy to conclude. Spades are silly. Why try for a ruff when you have four trumps yourself? Hearts are declarer's best suit. Leading them is awful. If you lead hearts, it suggests you were asleep during the first round of the bidding. Leading a diamond is possible. No serious fault to leading them. But because the auction so strongly suggests a trump lead, I prefer that. With a club lead and a club continuation from East, South will end up one trick short, even if he finesses the queen of hearts. With a diamond lead, declarer can make by rising with the king of diamonds, finessing in hearts and ruffing hearts in dummy. It may look odd for West to lead a trump from four to the queen. Given the bidding, however, it is a good choice. The result on this hand is not far from being typical.

Leading Trump When the Opponents Have a Preference Auction

When your LHO gives a preference, you should consider leading a trump. Be aware, though, that some preferences are not really preferences. Matchpoint greed causes some preference bids that don't deserve a trump lead. You can't always tell what is going on, but there are some hints available. Take the next auction.

N	S
	1H
1S	2C
2H	P

Here, North returned to two hearts. How strongly does this auction call for a trump lead?

N	S
	1H
1S	2C
2H	P

Here is the auction again along with a hand that North might have for his preference to two hearts.

NORTH
♠ Q984
♡ J7
◇ AJ74
♣ 1054

This North hand shows an important point about bidding. North did not pass two clubs. With three clubs and just two hearts, he went back to hearts. It is important to realize that when responder goes back to two of a major, he is not confirming a real preference. He may be making a greedy bid hoping that the major suit will produce a better score. This means that when they have a preference auction, you should not automatically lead trumps. This especially applies when your opponents are using a forcing notrump response to a major suit. See the following example.

N	S
	1S
1NT*	2C
2S	P

*Forcing

The one notrump bid is a forcing bid. If you do not play in tournaments, you won't have to worry about this sequence. This scientific auction almost warns against a trump lead. Responder seldom has three spades and often has just two. The forcing notrump method does some strange things to the bidding. When responder bids his forcing notrump, opener is required to bid again. If opener has another suit to bid, he does so. Some of the time, opener has no other four card suit to show and instead has to bid a three card minor suit. Because opener may have a three card minor suit, responder goes to great lengths to go back to opener's major. I have seen people give a preference to two spades with two spades and FIVE clubs. As you can see, a trump lead isn't necessary to stop club ruffs in dummy. Against auctions like this one, you should look for something else to lead besides a trump.

N	S
	1S
1NT*	2H
2S	P

*Forcing

When opener rebids two hearts, he promises a real four card or longer suit. North doesn't run back to spades as quickly as he does when opener rebids a minor. A trump lead against this specific preference auction can be right.

How strong is North's preference in the following auction? Out of curiosity, do you think that West should have bid three hearts over three diamonds? West does have eight high card points and the ten of hearts for a bonus. Is all this worth a further bid?

W	N	E	S
		1H	1S
2H	P	P	3D
P	P	P	

WEST

♠ K1074
♡ J104
◇ 862
♣ KJ4

First, the answer to the bidding question. West should pass three diamonds. It is usually wrong to bid to the three level unless you have four trumps or else an incredible maximum.

As for the opening lead, this sequence by North showed a preference for diamonds. It is possible that the opponents are in big trouble. Once in awhile, South competes as he does here and finds North with a crummy hand. It is understandable that you wouldn't double three diamonds, but given that North will often come down with a stiff spade and two or three diamonds only, you ought to get a trump on the table. If they have a thin fit, you may beat three diamonds quite a bit.

NOTE. Just because you think they have ruffing values in dummy is not automatically a reason to lead trump. If you can see that your side has no winners in declarer's second suit, you should not lead trumps. If, however, you have a good holding in declarer's second suit, you should consider a trump lead as you did on the last hand above.

N	S
	1S
1NT	2H
2S	P

WEST

♠ 98
♡ 86542
◇ KQ98
♣ K2

The auction suggests a trump lead, but your heart holding tells you otherwise. You have no late heart winners to protect and your length tells you that whatever partner has is going to fall soon, if in fact he has anything at all. Lead the king of diamonds instead. Lead trumps when you see a reason and lead something else otherwise.

If your hearts were better, you should give thought to leading a trump. This situation is shown on the next page.

```
    N    S
         1S
  1NT   2H
  2S     P
```

WEST
♠ 98
♡ KQ98
◊ 86542
♣ K2

The auction is the same as before, but your hand is different. You have three potential heart tricks if declarer can't ruff them in dummy. Between your hand and the bidding, the facts all point at a trump lead. Lead the nine of spades. Remember the rule. Lead trumps when you see a reason for doing so.

WEST
♠ 98
♡ 7
◊ K10732
♣ K8732

Against the same auction as above, you chose to pass it out in two spades. A wise decision. If North hasn't much in either of the majors, he rates to have a fist full of the minors. You did good to defend with this hand. You still have to find the right lead. Either clubs or diamonds could be right, but there is a reason to start a spade. You don't have heart winners to protect, but your partner may have them. Leading a trump is a thoughtful lead. A side benefit is that declarer may wish to ruff hearts in dummy. He may play the ace and king of hearts intending to ruff further hearts in dummy. You will surprise him when you ruff first.

Of passing interest is that you would never lead a heart. Do not lead singletons or doubletons into the person who has bid or raised a suit that his partner has bid.

WEST
♠ 953
♡ AK109
◊ KJ10
♣ 762

Lead a trump. Keep away from those high hearts. If you can get the trumps off dummy, you may end up with four heart tricks. If you lead a high heart to take a look, it rates to cost you two tricks. Declarer gets to ruff a heart in dummy plus, if he has the QJ of hearts, he can now set up a high card trick in hearts.

When you are wondering whether to lead a trump, think about what you yourself might have for a given auction. You may be able to decide when a trump lead is good and when it is terrible. Here is an example of a little known bidding trick that you can use. You should be equally aware of what to do when your opponents pull it on you.

Your partner opens one 15-17 point notrump and you have the following indecent hand.

YOUR HAND	What, if anything, do you bid with this hand when your partner opens
♠ 7653	one notrump? The answer is two clubs. Bid Stayman and ask for a
♡ 10943	major suit. If partner has a major, he will bid it and you will pass. This
♢ 10654	is obviously a big improvement over playing in one notrump. If partner
♣ 8	doesn't have a major to bid, he will bid two diamonds. Again, you pass.

This time you are less sure of the fit because partner might have a
bunch of clubs and just two diamonds. In the long run though, this won't happen. Usually
partner will have a four card major or at least three diamonds. It is possible, remember, for
partner to have five diamonds, which will be wonderful.

Looking at this zero point Stayman hand, one thing leaps out at you. You have short
clubs. You have to have just one club to ensure you have enough support to pass
whatever partner bids. You can't bid Stayman with ♠ 3 ♡ 9764 ◇ Q874 ♣ J743
because partner will bid spades more often than not.

OK. Let's go back to the opening leader's problem after hearing this auction.

W	N	E	S	
			1NT	Whether South bids two of a major or two diamonds,
P	2C	P	?	your hand should wander down to the trump suit and
P	P	P		stay there until one of them sticks to your fingers. I

won't tell you that you MUST lead a trump, but I will
tell you that the part of your hand with the trumps is
the first place you should look. Say that South rebids
two hearts and that becomes the contract.

WEST	Even though leading from the J1053 of hearts does not feel normal, the
♠ Q83	auction so strongly suggests a heart lead that I would choose the three of
♡ J1053	hearts. The club queen is futile, given the bidding. Dummy will have a stiff
◇ K4	club much of the time. The only thing a club lead does is to give declarer a
♣ QJ104	head start on getting club ruffs in dummy.

When the Opponents Have Enough Strength To Show Their Hands

When opponents have weak hands, they sometimes give preferences on some hands that
don't really have trump support. This is not true when the opponents are bidding strongly.
On auctions where the opponents have game strength, their preferences tend to be real. A
strong hand does not have to give a preference if it does not want to. There are other
things to do.

N	S
	1S
2C	2D
2S	?

If their auction starts this way, the two spade bidder usually has three card support. Standard bidders use this sequence to show an eleven point spade raise and Two Over One bidders use this sequence to show a game forcing spade raise.

The longer the auction, the more you learn about their fit. Some preferences come late in the bidding and do not promise real support.

N	S
	1S
2D	2S
2NT	3H
3S	?

North is showing a doubleton spade. He could have two hearts but he is likely to have three. If you are wondering whether to lead trumps, look to your heart suit to see if you have any honors worth protecting.

WEST
♠ 974
♡ A1094
♢ 84
♣ Q763

With two or three potential heart winners, leading trump is thoughtful. If your hearts were worse, you would lead a club. Conversely, if your clubs were headed by the QJ108, it would be OK to lead them. With North suggesting a lukewarm preference for spades, a trump lead is not going to be imperative.

When Your Partner Passes Your Takeout Double

When you make a takeout double of a one level bid and partner passes, you should lead a trump. This lead was discussed earlier in the section on leads when partner passes your takeout double.

WEST	EAST
♠ 7	♠ KJ1098
♡ KJ86	♡ A5
♢ AKJ4	♢ Q107
♣ K983	♣ Q102

This is the hand shown earlier. South opens one spade and West doubles for takeout. When East passes for penalty, West should lead the seven of spades.

Expert Trick

There is a powerful case for leading a trump when your partner doubles the opponents at the two level in a fit auction. For instance.

W	N	E	S
		1D	1S
2C	2S	DBL	P
P	P		

WEST

♠ 2

♡ Q82

◇ Q83

♣ AK10764

Your partner heard your two club bid and says he can set two spades. If you trust partner, you can pass the double. Lead the two of spades. This situation was also discussed earlier in the section where partner doubled the final contract. The combined hands should look more or less like this.

WEST	EAST
♠ 2	♠ AJ109
♡ Q82	♡ KJ65
◇ Q83	◇ AJ72
♣ AK10764	♣ 5

With this layout, your side is not likely to have a game. You should get three hundred with a spade lead, though, which will be excellent if all you can make is a partscore. The way to maximize your result is for West to lead the two of spades. If West leads anything else, there is some risk that declarer will get to ruff something in dummy, which will cost your side one of your setting tricks.

After a Conventional Bid By the Opponents

W	N	E	S	
1D	2D*	P	2H	*MICHAELS

W	N	E	S	
1S	2NT*	P	3D	*UNUSUAL

These two sequences start many competitive auctions. Your side opens and the next player shows a two suited hand. If South shows no interest in North's suits, it is likely that a trump lead is good for you. Here is why.

After 1D - 2D - P, South has to bid a major. He sometimes has to bid a two card suit. Give South this hand. ♠ 82 ♡ 105 ◇ KQ72 ♣ K8763. South will probably bid two hearts. In the play, he will surely try to ruff a spade or two in his hand. If the defenders look ahead and lead trumps to stop this, declarer won't get any ruffs.

The same is true when North bids an unusual two notrump and South bids three of a minor. It is a good strategy for South to bid a lot of either minor on any excuse just to make life hard for the other side. When South bids just three clubs or diamonds, there is a fair chance that he has a poor hand and he may also have a poor fit. A trump lead or a trump switch is often the right defense.

```
                NORTH
                ♠ 2
                ♡ K2
                ◊ AJ876
                ♣ K10764
```

```
WEST                    EAST
♠ AKJ54                 ♠ 107
♡ A65                   ♡ J1043
◊ Q93                   ◊ K1054
♣ 98                    ♣ QJ5

                SOUTH
                ♠ Q9863
                ♡ Q987
                ◊ 2
                ♣ A32
```

If West leads a spade and switches to a club, South will win the ace of clubs and will play the ace of diamonds followed by a diamond ruff. After a spade ruff in dummy, South ruffs another diamond in his hand. After this start, three clubs will make. If West starts a trump, declarer can win and play two diamonds, but he can't get back to dummy in time to ruff another diamond.

A lightweight suggestion is this. If the opponents use one of these conventions and responder seems unhappy, consider leading a trump. If responder gets excited, a trump is not likely to be right unless you KNOW it is right.

W	N	E	S
1S	2NT	P	4D
P	5D	P	P
P			

```
WEST
♠ KQ853
♡ AQJ
◊ 85
♣ 1084
```

South has a good diamond fit and North has enough to go on to game. East's silence is also something to worry about. He appears to be broke. The one thing I would not lead here is a trump. The following hand shows why.

NORTH
♠ 4
♡ 53
◇ AJ973
♣ AKJ97

WEST	EAST
♠ KQ853	♠ A102
♡ AQJ	♡ 10862
◇ 85	◇ 102
♣ 1084	♣ 6532

SOUTH
♠ J976
♡ K974
◇ KQ64
♣ Q

I can't see any lead other than the king of spades. If you worry yourself silly, you might talk yourself into a heart lead, but no amount of introspection should convince you to lead a trump. With the king of spades lead, five diamonds goes down one if East overtakes the spade and returns a heart. Without this defense, declarer has time to take twelve tricks. The king of spades isn't guaranteed to set five diamonds, but it is a better shot than leading a trump.

An Excuse for Nervous Players

Sooner or later, you will find a hand where a trump lead is right, not because you can find a reason to lead one, but because the other leads are terrible. It is allowable to lead a trump on the excuse that you don't know what to lead, but only after you look at all of the alternatives.

W	N	E	S
	1D	P	1H
P	2H	P	3H
P	P	P	

WEST
♠ KJ2
♡ 53
◇ QJ32
♣ A962

Spades aren't right for leading and diamonds, with North bidding them, are distinctly dangerous. Clubs, by definition, are not leadable. Lead a heart. Had North's opening bid been one club instead of one diamond, the queen of diamonds would be correct.

Do not carry this excuse too far. When you are thinking of leading a trump for lack of anything else, you should consider it a challenge to find an alternate lead first.

NORTH DEALS
NORTH-SOUTH VULNERABLE

W	N	E	S
	1D	P	1S
P	1NT	P	4S
P	P	P	

NORTH
♠ J7
♡ KQ74
◇ AQJ4
♣ J74

WEST
♠ 1062
♡ J65
◇ 8532
♣ A92

EAST
♠ Q3
♡ A1093
◇ 1097
♣ K1065

SOUTH
♠ AK9854
♡ 82
◇ K6
♣ Q83

If West leads a heart, the defense will get a heart, two clubs if they switch in time, and a late spade trick. Hearts is not an outstanding lead, but it is at least an unbid suit. Down one.

West hasn't much good to choose from. But that is no excuse for giving up. What if West decides that a trump is best? South will assume West does not have the queen of spades and will play low from dummy. (After all, who leads from the queen of trumps?) East's queen is a goner now and declarer will take an easy eleven tricks. The trump lead costs your side a trick in trumps and a trick in timing. Mr. Mathe would not be pleased.

When Not To Lead Trumps

There are times where leading trumps is terrible. I guess that if you lead trumps every time the opponents get to a suit contract, you will be very right perhaps 20% of the time. It won't matter what you lead on perhaps 30% of these hands and it will be wrong about half of the time. Remember Lew Mathe's advice. "Lead trumps when it is right." To achieve this, you have to pay attention. Tossing a trump on the table will be wrong too often if you do it randomly. Fortunately, there are some guidelines for when a trump lead is bad.

1. Don't lead a singleton trump. Even if you feel that leading a singleton trump is a good idea, the common effect of the lead is to ruin whatever partner has in trumps. The chances of the singleton lead being good enough to make up for the damage to partner's holding is slight. Since leading a stiff trump could be right by accident, I will put the rule to you in a different way. I said earlier that you could lead a trump if you looked at all other leads and genuinely decided that they were all dangerous. If you look at the other suits and decide to lead a trump and you now discover that you have just one of them, go back and research the other suits until

you find something else to lead. Saying you can't find a good lead is not an excuse for leading a singleton trump.

I rate the average cost to you when you lead a stiff trump is about one half of a trick. Remember. If you have a singleton trump, your partner rates to have three or four of them. If he has, say, three to the queen, your lead will turn a potential trick into a definite aggravation for your partner. Here are some likely layouts showing the futility of leading a singleton trump.

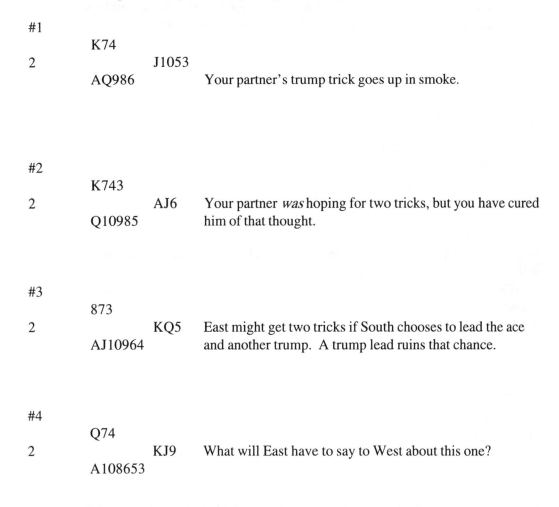

#1

    K74

2   J1053

    AQ986   Your partner's trump trick goes up in smoke.

#2

    K743

2   AJ6   Your partner *was* hoping for two tricks, but you have cured

    Q10985   him of that thought.

#3

    873

2   KQ5   East might get two tricks if South chooses to lead the ace

    AJ10964   and another trump. A trump lead ruins that chance.

#4

    Q74

2   KJ9   What will East have to say to West about this one?

    A108653

Are there exceptions to this rule? Yes, there are. There are two times where leading a trump is mandatory, regardless of how many you have. Both of these have been discussed earlier. Remember them. Lead a trump, even if it is a singleton trump, in both of these cases. The first is when you double a one bid and partner passes it out (discussed in WHEN PARTNER PASSES YOUR TAKEOUT DOUBLE). The second situation is discussed in the section DID YOUR PARTNER DOUBLE THE FINAL CONTRACT. These two topics can be found in items 7 and 8 in Chapter 3.

2. Don't lead a trump when you have four of them. This rule is breakable, but rarely so. When you have four trumps, you have a defensive asset that declarer will hate to find out about. When you are on lead with four trumps, put ruffs on a back burner. Think first about developing your high card tricks. Perhaps you can set up a suit and force declarer to ruff. If you can make declarer ruff a few times, you may end up with more trumps than him.

When you have four trumps, it is fine to lead a singleton in a suit bid by partner. Your goal is not to get ruffs but to set up some tricks. Leading singletons in suits the opponents have bid is a bad idea and even leading a singleton in an unbid suit is not automatic when you have four trumps.

W	N	E	S
	1S	P	1NT*
P	2C	P	2D
P	P	P	

*Forcing

WEST
♠ 9
♡ J10985
◊ Q852
♣ A83

You have four good trumps. Lead the jack of hearts. Leading the nine of spades is too awful for words.

W	N	E	S
			1H
P	1S	P	2D
P	2H	P	P
P			

WEST
♠ 2
♡ Q875
◊ Q95
♣ K10854

This is an auction that comes up daily. RHO opens hearts, bids diamonds, and gets a preference back to hearts. Do not lead spades. The strongest asset you have is the Q875 of hearts. Use them wisely. Lead the five of clubs.

140

NORTH
♠ Q10876
♡ 102
♢ J72
♣ AJ6

WEST   EAST
♠ 2   ♠ AJ954
♡ Q875   ♡ J6
♢ Q95   ♢ A6
♣ K10854   ♣ Q972

            SOUTH
            ♠ K3
            ♡ AK943
            ♢ K10843
            ♣ 3

The play can go in many ways. Try this one. South wins the ace of clubs in dummy and finesses the ten of diamonds. West wins the queen and leads another club, ruffed by South. South leads a diamond to the jack, won by East. Another club is played and South ruffs. If South plays a diamond, East will ruff it. If declarer cashes the two top hearts he can then cash a diamond, but West has the rest of the tricks now. Declarer ends up down two. Not terribly well played, but typical. How will declarer play if West goes after a spade ruff? East will win the ace and presumably will give West his treasured ruff. West can switch to clubs, but it will be too late. Declarer has time to lose two diamonds and one more heart and will come to eight tricks. Quite a difference.

W	N	E	S
	1D	1S	2H
P	3H	P	P
P			

WEST
♠ 4
♡ J753
♢ QJ104
♣ Q874

Lead your stiff spade. Leading partner's suit is normal on most auctions. I confess to you that leading the spade here is not all that appetizing since I have a trump trick coming in sooner or later. If my clubs were headed by the QJ108, I would consider leading them instead of a spade. The main point here is that when you have four trumps, getting ruffs on defense is less important than normal.

3.   Don't lead a trump if it endangers a potential trump trick. This is a logical rule. There are some holdings that are specifically dangerous for you to lead from. Two or three cards to the ten or jack may look safe, but they are not. The next pages shows some combinations where an innocent trump lead hurts your side's trump holding. It was dangerous to lead a singleton trump. That is not the only time a trump lead can hurt you.

#1

	KJ64		
1073		Q2	In case one, South was probably going to play the suit by leading the ace and then finessing the jack. After your lead, he will play low from dummy and East's queen will get slaughtered.
	A985		

#2

	Q84		
1073		K2	In case two, your side might have gotten a trick if declarer misguessed the trump suit. After a trump lead, South will never lose a trick.
	AJ965		

#3

	K92		
J64		Q7	The third case is a full disaster. Without a trump lead, you were going to get a trump trick. With a trump lead, South will play low from dummy and take East's queen with the ace. Now, South can finesse against West's jack and will lose no trump tricks at all.
	A10853		

#4

	Q82		
J64		K9	If you thought the previous trump lead worked out poorly, grab a seat and hold on for this one. If West does not lead a trump, it is possible that declarer will lose two tricks. A reasonable play would be for him to lead the three to the queen, losing to the king, followed later by leading toward his hand and finessing the ten. West produces the jack for two trump losers. If West leads a trump, dummy plays low and East has a wrenching decision. Say he plays low. South wins with the ten, plays the ace and suddenly has no losers at all. Or, if East plays the king, South can win and lead the ten back. Whether West covers or not, there are no trump tricks for the defenders.
	A10753		

I noted that leading doubleton tens and jacks of trump is also dangerous. It is so dangerous that it is worth avoiding unless you absolutely positively for sure know that a trump lead is necessary. You better be on firm ground when you make that lead. Here are the usual nightmare examples.

#1

103

J74

K85

AQ962

If you lead the ten, dummy covers with the jack and ergo, no trump trick for your side.

#2

J2

1083

Q76

AK954

If you lead the jack, a sure winner goes down the drain. South takes the first trick in his hand and goes to dummy to finesse against East's queen. True, declarer might think West is fooling around with the QJ doubleton and play the two top trumps from his hand. If declarer does this, you will have dodged the proverbial bullet, but you won't have gained anything and you will definitely have lost a trick on those occasions where declarer guesses correctly.

"Sorry about that, partner.

Perhaps I had a better lead."

#3

J4

K72

A106

Q9853

Here is yet another attempt by a defender to lose a trick. If West does not lead a trump, declarer has two sure losers. If West leads the jack, declarer will guess right some of the time and that will cost you. NOTE that leading the little card from these holdings never gains and often will cost you something.

#4

92

Q73

K104

AJ865

Even a doubleton nine spot can cost you a trump trick if you lead it. Without a trump lead, the defense has a sure trump trick. If West leads the nine, dummy will cover with the queen. East covers with the king and South takes his ace. Now, East's ten can be picked up with a finesse and the defenders come out with no trump trick for their efforts.

4.   Don't lead a trump if their bidding suggests strength and tricks.

This one is tricky. Here is the general idea. If the opponents have bid strongly and seem to have tricks and your hand suggests that nothing bad is going to happen to declarer, you should attack and try for your tricks before they get away. Here is a typical example.

W	N	E	S
	1D	P	1S
P	3S	P	4D
P	4S	P	P
P			

This is a strong auction. North's rebid showed sixteen to eighteen support points for spades and South's four diamond bid was a hint towards a slam. North didn't like his hand for slam purposes, but you can tell that they have the values for ten tricks. I promise you that a trump lead will cost you in the long run. The value of being on lead is something you should treasure. If you lead a trump, you give the lead to their side. On the sequence shown, I would not lead a trump. Categorically. I would check my clubs and hearts and look for a lead there. If, during my search for an opening lead, I found a singleton diamond, I would be reluctant to lead it. I *might* lead a diamond if I had four of them since I might be able to give partner a diamond ruff either now or later. The auction above applies to the four lead problems following.

WEST
♠ 87
♡ Q753
♢ 952
♣ A1074

Rightly or wrongly, I lead the three of hearts. The auction tells me they have enough tricks if we don't get ours fast. The reason I lead a heart instead of a club is that leading from aces is almost automatically not done. Much more about that later. Here is a scenario you have seen many times. The bidding goes as above and you must lead with the hand here. Note the differences between an aggressive heart lead and a passive spade lead.

NORTH
♠ AKJ4
♡ AJ
♢ Q10873
♣ 96

WEST	EAST
♠ 87	♠ 63
♡ Q753	♡ K964
♢ 952	♢ KJ4
♣ A1074	♣ Q832

With a spade lead, South wins and attacks diamonds. He will need to ruff one diamond in his hand to set up the suit, but after that he will be able to discard his heart losers. Along the way, a club guess will determine if he makes four or five.

SOUTH
♠ Q10952
♡ 1082
♢ A6
♣ KJ5

With a heart lead, South is in trouble. If he takes his ace and plays as above, East will win the second round of diamonds and cash the king of hearts. The club switch forces South to guess correctly to make ten tricks. A bad guess and he is down.

144

WEST	
♠	94
♡	KQ7
◇	9763
♣	Q974

Lead the king of hearts. When the auction suggests that you lead a certain suit or suits, it is nice to have a sequence to lead from. In the auction from the previous page, the opponents bid spades and diamonds. It is logical that you look to the unbid suits for a good lead. The Q974 of clubs is not a bad holding to lead from, but the KQ7 of hearts is too tempting since it builds up one trick for sure and puts us in contention to take two or three tricks.

WEST	
♠	A3
♡	J83
◇	9763
♣	A763

Lead a diamond. You hope to get in with the ace of spades and give partner a diamond ruff. If East has three spades, you will be able to get in with the ace of clubs and give partner a second ruff. Nice lead if it works. If you had the KQ7 of hearts, such as on the previous hand, you would have a choice of leads. I would opt for the king of hearts.

WEST	
♠	753
♡	Q73
◇	QJ97
♣	Q73

With diamonds tied up, you know they won't have a running source of tricks. You should not lead a diamond, given both opponents have bid them. What you should lead is less clear. Both clubs and hearts could be right and they could both be wrong. *Because I have their diamonds so well stopped*, I can be talked into leading a trump, even though it is contrary to my instincts.

Additional Strong Auctions Which Suggest a Source of Tricks for Declarer

Other sequences which suggest they have good values plus good suits are the following.

W	N	E	S
	1S	P	2H
P	4H	P	P
P			

Dummy has a five card spade suit to work on. Your hand will give you a hint as to whether dummy's spade suit can be set up for tricks.

W	N	E	S
	1D	P	1S
P	3D	P	3H
P	3S	P	4S
P	P	P	

Dummy has a super diamond suit waiting to come into its own. Against this auction, I would look at my clubs first. Leading a trump would not occur to me. Declarer is going to try to draw trump and then run the diamonds. Leading a spade helps declarer do one of the things he most wishes to have done.

W	N	E	S
			1H
P	2D	P	3D
P	4H	P	P
P			

This is a common auction. Opener bids a major suit and raises his partner's two over one response. When they get to game in the major, you know they have a fit and you know they have a side suit to supply tricks. You must attack against this kind of bidding. Leading a club or a spade sounds right and probably is.

Strong Sequences Which May Or May Not Include a Source of Tricks for Declarer

Some sequences tell you they have game points but do not suggest an obvious worry about a running suit. Here are some of them.

W	N	E	S
			1NT
P	2C	P	2H
P	4H	P	P
P			

You know dummy has four hearts and ten or more points. You have no idea that there is a running side suit anywhere.

W	N	E	S
			1S
P	1NT	P	3S
P	4S	P	P
P			

Hard to say. South is strong, but North may be pushing. You know very little about their hands other than that they have a good trump suit.

W	N	E	S
			2C
P	2D	P	2H
P	3H	P	4H
P	P	P	

Again, you know little about their hands other than that they have lots of points. South has a game forcing two bid and North shows six points with heart support. North may have a 3-3-4-3 hand with six random points or he may have a good five card suit on the side and nothing else. Who knows? What they have is a mystery. Since South's bidding was uninformative other than that he has wonderful hearts and a huge hand, you have little to go on. On the other hand, you are probably not going to beat four hearts with any lead, so you needn't feel too bad about your uncertainties.

Recap

     A.   If they have a strong auction.

     B.   If they have a fit.

     C.   If they have a KNOWN good suit for tricks.

If all three of these three things exist, you have to be extremely aggressive on lead. No passive leads and no trump leads.

A Little Quiz On Trump Leads

WEST	W	N	E	S
♠ AJ876				1H
♡ Q86	1S	P	2S	3D
◇ 875	P	P	P	
♣ A8				

Lead a trump. South showed hearts and diamonds. North's pass says he prefers diamonds to hearts. He might have a huge preference. A trump lead is clearly right here. Many demerits if you lead the ace of spades or the ace of clubs. More on this soon.

WEST	W	N	E	S
♠ 83				1NT
♡ Q96	P	2C	P	2S
◇ AJ82	P	3S	P	P
♣ Q754	P			

Lead the three of spades. The auction itself does not call for a trump lead, but your hand has no reasonable opening lead other than a trump. Leading into a strong one notrump bid or a two notrump bid is hard because you know declarer has a lot of high cards, which diminishes the chances that your partner will have some help for you. Leading from a queen can be a good choice on a different sequence. But not on this one.

WEST	W	N	E	S
♠ QJ87				1C
♡ AK7	DBL	P	P	P
◇ KJ654				
♣ Q				

This is a reminder for you. Of all the times where you should lead trumps, this is the best known. You made a takeout double and your partner passed, saying he wanted to defend. Lead the queen of clubs and help partner draw trumps. He will be pleased you have the queen and he will be especially pleased to see it at trick one.

WEST	W	N	E	S
♠ J5				1S
♡ 86532	P	2H	P	2S
◇ QJ6	P	4S	P	P
♣ K83	P			

Lead the queen of diamonds. This is the best lead by a mile. Curiously, the next best lead is the three of clubs, leading away from the king. Leading a heart is bad because declarer rates to use the suit as soon as he gets done with trumps. Leading a heart gives up the needed time to set up your tricks. Finally, if there was ever a bad time for a trump lead, this is it. Your trump holding is dangerous. If partner has a spade honor, you may have a trump trick if you don't lead one. If you do lead one, you risk blowing a trump trick, plus you surrender the timing of the hand to declarer.

WEST	W	N	E	S
♠ K2			1S	2C
♡ AQ753	2H	3C	P	P
◇ KJ7	DBL	P	P	P
♣ 742				

Lead the two of clubs. Congratulations on finding a double. Doubling without a trump trick is usually not good. Here, though, you have an opening bid and your side doesn't have a fit. Whatever tricks they have rate to be in clubs, with perhaps a high card trick somewhere. If you don't lead a club, dummy may get to ruff something. Leading a club makes sure that the only tricks they get are the ones they are entitled to.

WEST	W	N	E	S
♠ 72				3S
♡ KJ32	P	P	P	
◇ A976				
♣ Q82				

You will have days like this. All the leads are risky. One lead in particular that I hate is a trump lead. A three spade bid shows a good suit, but it does not have to be solid. You may be helping declarer draw trumps. Also, there is no reason to suspect dummy is ruffing anything. Far better to lead a heart and hope that you are setting up tricks for your side. One added inducement for this lead is that a preemptor usually does not have many high cards on the side. There is less than the normal chance that dummy will have the ace of hearts and declarer the queen. There is a good chance that dummy will have the ace and queen, but that is OK since declarer can always take that finesse if he wants to. But that is all pessimistic thinking. Be positive and hope that partner has one of the missing heart honors. If so, you are off to a good start. Believe me. Opening leads are not easy. Believe me again when I say that being optimistic (and sensible) is a better approach than being cowardly and not so sensible.

CHAPTER FIFTEEN

LEADING ACES AND UNDERLEADING ACES AGAINST SUIT CONTRACTS

I have alluded to leading aces and underleading aces in various places in the earlier chapters. Do you remember my opinion of these leads?

There are times when you can't find a nice lead. On inspecting your hand, you note you have the A874 of an unbid suit. Do you think it might be right to lead this ace? You might have two quick winners if you take them right away. Or maybe if you don't take it right now, it will get away. After all, if you take your ace, you won't lose it. Not only that, you get to see the dummy before deciding what to do next. It could be a good idea to lead the ace, couldn't it?

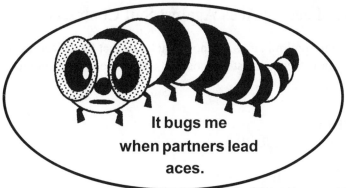

It bugs me when partners lead aces.

I give a lot of lectures on bridge. One of the things I talk about is leading aces against a suit contract. Or, worse yet, underleading them. I talk for an hour about why you should not lead suits headed by the ace. Then, while everyone answers a list of questions on opening leads, I walk around the room and look over their shoulders. Inevitably, I find a player who moments prior refused to lead away from a king yet with a clear conscience is now tossing an ace out there at trick one.

Why is it that so many players insist on making the worst imaginable lead over and over and over? I think that once in the past, a player failed to lead an ace and the result was that the opponents made their contract. As was the case when a defender led away from a king and got a crummy result, a fear crept in. Lead away from a king and give up a free trick. Fail to lead an ace and lose it. Both of these events are painful and memorable. What is overlooked is that the cure is much worse than the problem. You can give up leading from kings and stop leading aces, which will solve one problem, but it will create a bigger one. Your opponents will make more contracts than ever against you.

Let me tell you something about opening leads. I have played bridge for over thirty-five years, which works out to over half a million hands, give or take a hundred thousand or two. I have been on opening lead well over one hundred thousand times.

Have I ever made a bad lead? You betcha! Want to hear a few stories about my opening leads? Take my word for it. I have made some of the worst leads imaginable. Did they cost? Yes, they did. Does this tell me that I should give up making opening leads?

That would cure me of making bad leads, but it would create some time problems since we would never get from the bidding to the play.

One of the themes of this book is that your opening leads won't always be wonderful. The best they can be is reasonably good. To that end, I am giving you some guidelines which will help you do two things. You will make fewer bad leads and you will make more good ones. You will note that if you take everything in this book to heart and if you add on thirty years of experience, your leads will still not be perfect.

On Not Leading Aces Against Suit Contracts

So much for preliminaries. By now you know that I hate leading aces and I abhor underleading them against suit contracts. Here are some examples.

SOUTH DEALS
NO ONE VULNERABLE

W	N	E	S
			1S
P	1NT	2H	P
P	2S	P	P
P			

WEST   What should West lead? East did overcall two hearts so that suit should
♠ 7652   catch your eye. Is that enough reason to lead the ace of hearts? My
♡ A85   experience says that even with partner overcalling the suit, leading the
◇ J1092   ace is a losing proposition. Here is a possible setup.
♣ 96

NORTH
- ♠ J10
- ♡ J4
- ◇ A63
- ♣ Q87542

WEST
- ♠ 7652
- ♡ A85
- ◇ J1092
- ♣ 96

EAST
- ♠ K4
- ♡ K10963
- ◇ Q85
- ♣ AKJ

SOUTH
- ♠ AQ983
- ♡ Q72
- ◇ K74
- ♣ 103

West is on lead against two spades after a typical competitive auction where North did a little pushing. Should West lead his partner's suit or should he lead something else? Let's see what happens with a heart lead. If West leads the ace of hearts and continues the suit, East will take the king. At this point, it doesn't matter what East does. The king of spades is onside so declarer can finesse in spades, draw trumps, and will end up with eight tricks. What happens if West leads something besides hearts? Say he leads the jack of diamonds. South will probably try to set up a heart trick or get a heart ruff in dummy. It won't work. If South leads to dummy's jack, East takes the king and returns a trump. South finesses to dummy's jack and leads another heart. South's queen is taken by West and another spade lead leaves South with six losers. I know. You are thinking that I made up this hand to prove a point. I did not. The result on this hand is typical of what happens when you lead an ace. Here, partner bid the suit and it wasn't a hot lead. Leading aces of unbid suits is less of a bargain.

SOUTH DEALS
NO ONE VULNERABLE

W	N	E	S
			1S
P	2S	P	4S
P	P	P	

WEST
- ♠ J7
- ♡ A96
- ◇ J8652
- ♣ K53

How do you feel about leading the ace of hearts? Ask yourself this question. In the long run, how much does leading the ace of hearts gain for me? Does it gain half a trick on the average? Perhaps more? Or, if you think it is not a good lead, how much does leading the ace of hearts cost? Does it cost half a trick or might it be more expensive than that?

```
                    NORTH
                    ♠ 8432
                    ♡ Q103
                    ◊ A94
                    ♣ J87
```

```
WEST                      EAST
♠ J7                      ♠ 65
♡ A96                     ♡ J752
◊ J8652                   ◊ Q107
♣ K53                     ♣ A642
```

```
                    SOUTH
                    ♠ AKQ109
                    ♡ K84
                    ◊ K3
                    ♣ Q109
```

At the majority of the tables, West led a boring fourth best diamond. Declarer won, drew trump, and led clubs. Eventually, the hand came down to playing the hearts for one loser. South lead a heart to the king, losing to West's ace and later lost a trick to East's jack. Down one. At most of the tables, there was a short discussion about whether they should be in game or a partscore. Since four spades depended more or less on a finesse for the heart jack, the hand was dismissed to random luck.

Things were different at one table. West, not pleased with his choices of opening leads, decided to lead the ace of hearts. The rational was the usual. "Perhaps I will have a better idea of how to defend after I see the dummy." West won the trick and after intense scrutiny, discovered that he was no better off than he was when the hand started. West finally decided to lead another heart and the play was over. Unlucky? Not in my opinion. The only luck on this hand was that South was fortunate to have West on lead.

What should West lead? I agree with West that the hand has no good lead. If I held this hand, I would view all leads as uncomfortable.

1.   A trump lead is dangerous. If East has a trump honor, a trump lead risks losing a defensive trump winner. On a scale of zero to one hundred on how happy I am to lead a trump here, it rates about ten points. Hardly dynamic.

2.   Leading a diamond from five to the jack is uninspired, but it does achieve some degree of neutrality. There is something to be said for a neutral lead when the alternatives are poor. I rate it at about 45 points on the scale.

3.   Leading a club is possible too. Earlier, I suggested that leading from a king can be an excellent choice, but doing so requires a reason other than that you have a king. There is no hint in the bidding that a club is the right suit to lead. It can work out, though, so I give it a 35 on the scale.

4.   How about the ace of hearts? The result on this hand is typical enough that I can let you form your own conclusion. I give it an 8 since there are some times where it is right. These times will be accidents, though. There is no logic to tell you the ace of hearts is best.

5.   Finally, there is the six of hearts. What about that? Awful. That is the kindest word I can come up with. Leading an ace against a suit contract is bad. Leading away from an ace is worse. I give it a generous 4 on the lead scale.

The reason it gets anything at all is in awed deference to the fact that it can work, albeit for no predictable reason. Here is a layout which makes it a winner.

```
              NORTH
              ♠ K62
              ♡ K8542
              ◊ 94
              ♣ J82

WEST                     EAST
♠ J7                     ♠ 83
♡ A96                    ♡ Q107
◊ J8652                  ◊ 1073
♣ K53                    ♣ A10964

              SOUTH
              ♠ AQ10954
              ♡ J3
              ◊ AKQ
              ♣ Q7
```

With the six of hearts lead, South will think that West may have underled the queen of hearts, but not the ace. He will duck in dummy only to see East produce the queen. South will be down one. When South finds out that West underled the ace of hearts, there will be a moment of psychological triumph for West. As I said, leading from the A96 of hearts can work, but it is so rare that it is outside my realm of consciousness to try it. For those who insist that underleading an ace is good bridge, you can use this hand as an example. The other 96% of the time, it will be neutral or bad. Much more on this in a page or two. Underleading aces against a suit contract is such a bad habit that it deserves and gets its own section.

SOUTH DEALS
NO ONE VULNERABLE

W	N	E	S
			1S
P	2S	P	4S
P	P	P	

WEST
♠ J7
♡ A96
◊ J8652
♣ K53

Here is the West hand and auction again for reference. There are some points worth noting here. The first thing you must recognize is that there is no good lead. This is an ordinary hand, but it is also a difficult hand. You will notice that the best lead rated only 45 points. This is not uncommon. There will be many occasions where you must choose from poor choices. You have to accept this fact. On some hands, there will be no good leads to make. Remember my statement earlier about having made thousands of bad leads? Hands like this one are the reason. If you had to lead from this hand a hundred times, you would make the winning lead less than half of the time.

SOUTH DEALS
NO ONE VULNERABLE

W	N	E	S
			1S
P	2S	P	4S
P	P	P	

WEST
♠ J7
♡ A96
◇ J8652
♣ K53

The second point is the low esteem I hold for leading ace-high suits. Looking at the leads on this hand, you will see that leading the heart suit rates worse than anything else. Leading the ace got eight points and underleading it got four. It is rare that leading or underleading an ace rates to be a wise idea. I can almost guarantee you that if you *never* lead an ace or underlead an ace against a suit contract, your leads will be better for it. This is a fact. Learn it. When I am on lead against a suit contract, the first thing I do is eliminate any suit headed by the ace. Even if partner has bid the suit, I look elsewhere first. Somewhere in the hand, there must be a better lead. If, after honest consideration, I can't find another lead, I will look tentatively at an ace-high suit. But before I lead this suit, I will still reconsider the alternatives. Things like this can not be proven except through experience. I promise that my experiences are in agreement with all of my regular partners' experiences. Not leading suits headed by the ace is such a strong guideline that if you adopt it and never look for exceptions, you will eliminate a terrible habit from your inventory. If you are already innocent of this habit, I congratulate you and hope you never change your mind.

I will, in the extended quiz section, show some hands where you might choose to lead or underlead an ace. If partner has bid the suit strongly, or if the bidding tells you to lead it, you might lead that suit. But, as you will see, these situations are the exception.

SOUTH DEALS
NO ONE VULNERABLE

W	N	E	S
			1H
P	2H	P	4H
P	P	P	

WEST
♠ Q7652
♡ 832
◇ A3
♣ Q106

What should you led against four hearts? Should you lead a spade away from the queen, a trump, the ace of diamonds, or the six of clubs? Let me give you a piece of inside information you aren't privy to at the table. East has the king of diamonds. Armed with that knowledge, what do you lead? Is the ace of diamonds a good lead now that you know where the king of diamonds is? Here is the complete hand.

```
        NORTH
        ♠ J83
        ♡ KJ64
        ◊ Q742
        ♣ 87
```

```
WEST              EAST
♠ Q7652           ♠ K109
♡ 832             ♡ 7
◊ A3              ◊ K1098
♣ Q106            ♣ J5432

        SOUTH
        ♠ A4
        ♡ AQ1095
        ◊ J65
        ♣ AK9
```

Look just at the North-South hands for a moment. How do you like your contract? It is playable, but it is not beautiful. You have a spade loser, two diamond losers, and a big headache avoiding a third diamond loser. Your chances of losing just two diamonds are not good. Possible, but not good. If you played in four hearts and ended up losing one spade and three diamonds, no one would say you were a terrible player.

What is your opinion of four hearts if West leads the ace of diamonds? That is good since it solves your problems in the diamond suit. The bad news is that West leads another diamond to East's king. Back comes a third diamond which West ruffs. The end of the world? Not at all. This defense, while effective at the start, does not work. The defenders get the first three tricks, but in getting them, they have established a fourth round diamond winner which can be used to discard the spade loser. Even when leading an ace seems to have been good, it wasn't.

On Not Underleading Aces Against a Suit Contract

Do you think I was unreasonably hard on leading aces against a suit contract? If you do, you should not bother reading the next few pages. As terrible as leading an ace is, underleading an ace against a suit contract shows a new magnitude of bad judgment. There are many reasons why.

1.   An opponent may have a stiff king.

2.   You may give declarer a trick with his king that he could not otherwise get.

3.   Even if your partner has the king, underleading your ace may not GAIN you a trick.

4.   Your partner may have the king but not know to play it. I will show you an example of this in a moment.

5.   Even when you get lucky and find dummy with the king and your partner with the queen, your lead may not GAIN you a trick.

6.   Even when you get lucky and find dummy with the king and your partner with the queen, your partner may not know to play it.

7.   You may have a better lead.

8.   When you lead away from the ace and it costs your side a trick, it is often your partner who looks silly. This is a bad way to treat your partners.

Here are some examples of what can happen when you underlead an ace against a suit contract. You are East in the following settings. Your partner leads the five of diamonds against two spades.

W	N	E	S
			1C
P	1H	P	1S
P	2S	P	P
P			

NORTH
◊ K103

WEST		EAST
◊ 5		◊ Q94

West leads the five and dummy plays the three. Which diamond should East play? Make up your mind and read on.

If West has led from the J865, as in the first diagram, East must play the nine. South will win the ace and will somehow have to deal with a potential diamond loser. If East plays the queen, South will win the ace, but now can finesse dummy's ten of diamonds and end up losing no diamonds. It is necessary for East to play the nine of diamonds at trick one.

In the second diagram, West has chosen to lead from the ace. In this situation, East must go up with the queen. If East plays the nine, South will win the jack and now, if he judges what to do, will lose only one diamond trick to the ace. If you follow my advice and never lead low from an ace versus a suit contract, your partner will never misguess what to do in this situation. He will be very happy to know that he can count on you not to have the ace and will defend accordingly.

♡ Q103

♡ A96   ♡ J752   This is the heart suit from a few hands ago. West led the
                              ace and that was the end of the heart tricks for the defense.
         ♡ K84   If West had chosen to lead the six instead, that also would
                              have murdered the defenders' second trick in hearts.
                              Substituting one bad lead for another is not an
                              improvement.

Even when you lead from the ace and find partner with the king, you may not gain
anything. For instance.

W	N	E	S
	1C	P	1S
P	2S	P	3C
P	3S	P	4S
P	P	P	

NORTH
♠ K976
♡ AKJ
◇ Q96
♣ 1092

WEST   EAST   With any kind of defense, as we would like to call it,
♠ Q4   ♠ J82   South has five potential losers if spades divide three-
♡ 1065   ♡ Q832   two and more losers if they divide poorly. With a little
◇ A832   ◇ K104   imagination, the defense can make a contest out of it.
♣ J763   ♣ 854   Let's see what happens if West leads a heart. It is
                                really the only sensible lead given the hand. Spades are
         SOUTH   dangerous, diamonds are barred, and the bidding warns
         ♠ A1053   against a club lead. Then, having decided to lead a
         ♡ 974   heart, West must lead the five. Leading the ten from
         ◇ J75   this holding is bad for many reasons. Go back and
         ♣ AKQ   review Chapter Eleven if you are not convinced.

With the heart lead, South has to struggle with his
contract. At some point, he will finesse in hearts and
when that loses, will probably finesse West for the ten
of diamonds. When East produces it, South is down
two. This defense and the ensuing result ought to
please most bridge players. Some prefer to do it the
hard way, as shown on the next page.

W	N	E	S
	1C	P	1S
P	2S	P	3C
P	3S	P	4S
P	P	P	

NORTH
♠ K976
♡ AKJ
◇ Q96
♣ 1092

WEST
♠ Q4
♡ 1065
◇ A832
♣ J763

EAST
♠ J82
♡ Q832
◇ K104
♣ 854

SOUTH
♠ A1053
♡ 974
◇ J75
♣ AKQ

The defense on the previous page was unimaginative. Let's try it again with a cunning two of diamonds lead. Declarer plays low from dummy and East, thinking that West is probably leading from the jack, plays the ten, hoping that declarer will have to win with the ace. No. This time, declarer wins with the jack. One trick lost by the defenders. Can they lose another? Give them a chance. It requires some thinking by South to make four spades, but he can do it. One way is to return a diamond. The idea is to lose the two obvious diamond losers and then hope to endplay someone in the end game. Say, for instance, that the defenders take their diamonds and lead a club. South plays the two top spades, the three top clubs, and leads a spade to East's jack. Fini! It was not easy, but the defenders did it. I wonder what East is thinking at trick ten when he realizes the effect of West's lead.

The following is my favorite example of what not to do on opening lead. I have published it in more than one place. If it is new to you, enjoy it. If not, be reminded and don't do what West did.

NORTH
♠ QJ83

Before looking at the hand on the next page, answer this question. You are in a heart contract. You have the QJ83 of spades in dummy and the singleton ten in your hand. How many spade tricks can you get out of this combination? How many spade tricks do you have to lose along the way?

SOUTH
♠ 10

I will bet you did not envision the result that occurred at the table.

SOUTH DEALS
EAST-WEST VULNERABLE

W	N	E	S
			1H
DBL	2H	2S	4H
P	P	P	

NORTH
♠ QJ83
♡ QJ86
◇ 82
♣ 765

WEST
♠ A76
♡ 3
◇ J9763
♣ AQJ2

EAST
♠ K9542
♡ 5
◇ Q1054
♣ 1084

SOUTH
♠ 10
♡ AK109742
◇ AK
♣ K93

The play held more than passing interest. West started with the six of spades. Dummy played the three and East cogitated. As you can see, the defenders can take the first four tricks if they do the right things. But they didn't. Thinking that South probably had the singleton ace of spades and West the 1076, East played low on the opening lead. South won with the ten. South took two diamond tricks and led a heart to dummy, drawing all the trumps. When the five of clubs was led from dummy, East failed to play the ten, so declarer played the three, losing to West's jack. West, sure that the spade ace was going to cash (he thought declarer had the king), played it. South ruffed it, went to dummy with a trump, and led the queen of spades. Poor East. East covered, but it didn't matter. South ruffed and went to dummy with the third round of trumps. One club went on the jack of spades and declarer conceded the last club. Making eleven tricks. Want to hear the postmortem?

A Little Quiz On Leading Or Underleading Aces Against Suit Contracts

WEST
♠ 87632
♡ 43
◇ KJ3
♣ A95

W	N	E	S
		3C	3H
5C	5H	P	P
P			

Lead the ace of clubs. I did not say never to lead aces. This is one of the times where leading an ace is called for. East has bid the suit strongly. Also, there is an urgency to get the club trick if you have one. Finally, it is not likely that leading the ace will set up a trick for their side given your partner's promised strong suit.

WEST	W	N	E	S
♠ 873				1C
♡ AJ95	P	1D	P	1S
◇ 106	P	2S	P	4S
♣ Q975	P	P	P	

Lead a trump. In the section on trump leads, I made the statement that you should lead a trump when you know it is right. If you aren't sure that a trump is right, you may lead one if you have fairly rejected all other leads. Here, a trump lead is sensible. South may wish to ruff clubs in dummy. The ten of diamonds has some merit, but a trump lead is acceptable. Following is something for you to think about.

A RULE

Whimsical ace leads are worse than whimsical trump leads.

Leading the ace of hearts on the above hand just because hearts is the unbid suit is poor reasoning. You already know what I think of thoughtless trump leads. As bad as they are, thoughtless ace leads are worse.

NORTH-SOUTH VULNERABLE

WEST	W	N	E	S
♠ 8			1H	1S
♡ A9762	4H	4S	5H	P
◇ J4	P	5S	P	P
♣ 86532	P			

Lead the ace of hearts. The combination of East bidding hearts plus having them at the five level makes it a reasonable lead. Perhaps, after seeing the dummy, you will know the best shift. Note that your side can't possibly take two heart tricks so leading the ace won't jeopardize a heart trick.

NO ONE VULNERABLE

WEST	W	N	E	S
♠ 73	1C	P	1H	1S
♡ AJ10	2H	2S	3H	3S
◇ QJ5	P	P	P	
♣ KQ872				

A trump, the king of clubs, or even the queen of diamonds can be right. The heart ace is not right. It might work out, but it is not a good lead. East's bidding does not promise the king of hearts. Leading the ace will set up a heart trick for South more times than you like.

Did I imply in the heading for this quiz that it might be right to underlead an ace against a suit contract? It might be, but it is too far fetched to look for those times. My firm advice is that you never make that lead.

CHAPTER SIXTEEN

WHEN SHOULD YOU LEAD DOUBLETON ACES, KINGS, QUEENS, AND JACKS AGAINST A SUIT CONTRACT?

This question is a popular one. The possibility of getting a ruff seems to enervate many players into trying one of these leads. Is the chance of success worth the effort?

For starters, if you lead a doubleton ace or king, your chances of getting a ruff are much better than your chances of getting a ruff when you lead from a lesser holding. If you lead from the Ax, all you need from partner is the king to make the lead work. If you lead from the Kx, you will get a ruff if partner has the ace and you may get moving toward a ruff if partner has the queen.

At the other extreme, if you lead the doubleton 83 of a suit, you need a very good holding from partner to earn a ruff.

There is a catch in this, though. If you lead from the doubleton 83, you are less likely to get a ruff, but you are also not too likely to blow a trick by leading the suit. Conversely, if you lead from the ace or king doubleton, you have fair chances of getting a good result, but you run a serious danger of losing a trick when the lead turns out poorly. Here is a philosophical question for you. You are on lead with the West hand against two hearts.

W	N	E	S
			1H
P	1NT	P	2H
P	P	P	

WEST
♠ 10983
♡ J83
◇ K2
♣ A982

What is West's best lead against two hearts?

Let's say you choose for one reason or another to lead the king of diamonds. Will your partnership be able to live comfortably for the rest of the session if these turn out to be the four hands?

NORTH
♠ J652
♡ Q
♢ QJ1086
♣ J54

WEST
♠ 10983
♡ J83
♢ K2
♣ A982

EAST
♠ AQ74
♡ 1076
♢ 753
♣ KQ10

If you get innovative and lead the king of diamonds, declarer will take eleven tricks while you and you partner signal to each other how many tricks you could have taken with a different lead.

SOUTH
♠ K
♡ AK9542
♢ A94
♣ 763

If you make the mundane lead of the ten of spades, you can actually set two hearts. East takes the ace of spades and switches to the king of clubs. West says he likes them so East continues with the queen and ten. West, by now, knows where the high cards are so he leads his last club. If dummy ruffs with the queen or if East is allowed to ruff with his ten, declarer will have one heart loser. The later diamond loser will be the setting trick. Eleven tricks or seven tricks?

I am content not to make leads like the one here. When leading doubleton kings on speculation works, it's nice. When leading them fails, the trauma on the partnership is right there, and it stays for a long time.

Following are some thoughts on leading doubleton honors.

Leading a Doubleton Ace

I have already stated that leading a doubleton ace is a bad lead in general. At least when you do lead an ace, you get a trick out of it. Also, if the dummy shows you that this was the wrong lead, you are still in to find a switch. Still, it is usually not worth leading.

Here are some specifics.

A.   If partner has bid the suit, it is OK to lead a doubleton ace. But. Before automatically taking it out of your hand, you must look at alternatives. Remember too that on some sequences, your partner does not promise much in the suit. Leading a doubleton ace is a much better idea when partner opens the bidding or overcalls in the suit than on most other auctions.

W	N	E	S
1C	DBL	1H	1S
2C	2S	P	P
P			

WEST

♠ J107
♡ A6
◇ J3
♣ AK10764

Here is a sequence where partner has bid a suit. He could have the KJ1073 but he could also have five to the jack. Even worse is possible. If I did not have a clear choice, the ace of hearts would appeal. On this hand, I have a fine lead in the king of clubs. There is no way I will talk myself out of that lead. Leading doubleton aces is rarely a first choice.

B.   If it is an unbid suit, you can consider the lead of a doubleton ace, but it is less appealing than when partner has bid the suit. There is an important point worth mentioning here. If you have a weak hand, there is a chance that your partner will have some high cards. Your lead has a decent chance of finding partner with a needed high card to make your lead work. If you have a good hand, the chances of finding partner with an important card are diminished. You should reconsider your lead if you can tell that partner won't contribute anything.

C.   If the opponents have bid the suit, leading a doubleton ace is a bad idea. Even if you get a ruff, you are going to set up some tricks for them and they may gain from that in the long run. In the discussion on leading aces there is a hand which shows this.

Leading a Doubleton King

This is also to be avoided. It has a chance of working, but the cost of failure is too high to make this a habit. When leading a doubleton king, the hand has to pass certain tests.

A.   If partner bid the suit, leading it is OK although as usual, you should look at the alternatives first. RULE: Any time you are thinking of leading a doubleton, you should look at other leads too. Very seldom is leading a doubleton of any size really high on the list. The times where the lead stands out are always when partner bid the suit or has shown something in the suit. Perhaps he made a vulnerable overcall or made a takeout double showing values in the suit you are thinking of leading.

B.   Unbid suits are not ideal. A reminder: this is true no matter what doubleton you are leading. The weaker your hand, the better your chances of finding partner with a helping card. The stronger your hand, the less chance that partner will have something useful for you.

C.   Like other doubleton leads, it is not good to lead doubleton kings if the opponents have bid the suit. Some exceptions may be made if partner bids notrump along the way, thus promising strength in the suit, but still use caution.

Leading a Doubleton Queen

This is dangerous unless partner has bid the suit. There are too many combinations where leading a doubleton queen fails. Here is a case of a poorly timed lead.

	K973	
Q5		A1082
	J64	

If you lead the queen, dummy covers and East will probably win with the ace. Thinking you have the jack, he will return the suit. Declarer will play low from his hand and win in dummy. Your lead gives the opponent two tricks in the suit! If left to his own devices, declarer may get one trick, but he may also get none. He will never get two. Look at it this way. You led a doubleton queen, you found partner with a nice holding in the suit, and the lead worked as badly as imaginable. Don't bother telling me that East should play low on the king. If he did that and West happened to have the QJ of the suit, the ensuing discussion would be brutal.

	A87	
Q5		K1064
	J932	

Another unnerving result. If West leads the queen, dummy takes the ace and later leads toward the jack for a second trick. South might get three tricks out of this if he guesses the suit correctly. If West had resisted the lead, South would have to work hard to get a second trick in this suit.

	1082	
Q5		A943
	KJ76	

This is no better. If declarer has to play this suit himself, he often ends up with just one winner. Two tricks out of this suit is possible, but never three. When West leads the queen, however, declarer is not put out to get three winners. Avoid this lead unless your partner has bid the suit.

W	N	E	S
1C	P	1D	1S
P	2S	P	P
P			

WEST

♠ A8
♡ KJ104
◊ Q7
♣ QJ982

Lead the queen of clubs. If the clubs were a weaker, say QJ653, you might lead partner's suit. The point is that on this sequence, East's diamond bid does not mean much in terms of suit quality. Change the bidding a little to the following and your lead will change.

W	N	E	S
1C	DBL	1D	1S
P	P	2D	2S
P	P	P	

On the hand above, you can lead the queen of diamonds. Opposite a bid and rebid suit, the Q7 of diamonds is worth leading. East's one diamond bid didn't promise much in diamonds, but his two diamond bid did. East could have passed one spade. If he had crummy diamonds, he would have passed or bid something else.

The following is a hand from personal experience. Fortunately, I was declaring the hand. This hand came from a World Championship. I won't say which one since I doubt the opponents wish to have this hand recreated in print.

NORTH SOUTH VULNERABLE

W	N	E	S
		1NT	2D
P	P	DBL	RDBL
P	P	P	

WEST

♠ Q2
♡ K106
◊ 9432
♣ 8532

South's two diamonds was a natural bid. Your opponents were using antediluvian bidding methods at the time. Today, you have to search high and low to find a tournament player who still bids this way.

You will notice that I didn't tell you what East's double meant. West was uncertain at the time so I am giving you the same information he had. In other words, you have to guess.

What should West lead?

I will admit that the correct lead depends somewhat on what you think East's double means. There was obvious confusion which you will see in a moment. If you choose the queen of spades, your score for this hand is ....(I will tell you in a second). Here is the complete hand.

```
                NORTH
                ♠ 1053
                ♡ Q8753
                ◇ 5
                ♣ KJ109

WEST                    EAST
♠ Q2                    ♠ A98
♡ K106                  ♡ AJ94
◇ 9432                  ◇ J6
♣ 8532                  ♣ AQ64

                SOUTH
                ♠ KJ764
                ♡ 2
                ◇ AKQ1087
                ♣ 7
```

The good news is that the scoring was a little different when this hand was played. Two diamonds doubled and redoubled was worth 1510 when it made two overtricks. Today it would be worth 1560! A less enthusiastic lead would have resulted in down one for plus 400 points if the defenders were careful. An improvement. There is an important aside here worth mentioning. East meant his double to be for takeout. When South redoubled, West must bid if he does not want to defend against two diamonds. Here, West should have bid three clubs or perhaps two hearts. Either is better than what happened. West's pass, as far as East was concerned, said that defending two diamonds redoubled was a good idea. It wasn't.

Leading a Doubleton Jack

All the bad things I said about leading doubleton queens hold true here. A doubleton jack is a little bit less dangerous than leading a doubleton queen, but that is a slight complement indeed. For the most part, you lead doubleton jacks only when partner has bid the suit constructively or has made a takeout double suggesting the suit.

A Little Quiz On Leading Doubleton Honors Against Suit Contracts

WEST	W	N	E	S
♠ Q7		1C	1S	2H
♡ Q87	P	3H	P	4H
◊ J10852	P	P	P	
♣ 1075				

Lead the queen of spades. When partner volunteers a suit, leading it is a good idea. Here, East overcalled one spade. He could have passed so he will usually have a decent suit. Leading the jack of diamonds shows disrespect for partner's bid.

WEST	W	N	E	S
♠ 1087			1H	1S
♡ 873	P	2S	P	4S
◊ 108653	P	P	P	
♣ K3				

Lead the three of hearts. Do not lead the king of clubs. When your partner opens the bidding with a suit, you need a strong reason not to lead it. Leading the king of clubs is very dangerous.

WEST	W	N	E	S
♠ 1087				1D
♡ 873	P	1H	P	1S
◊ 108653	P	2S	P	3S
♣ K3	P	4S	P	P
	P			

Lead the king of clubs. This is the same hand as above but the auction is much different. Here, the opponents bid the other three suits and did not show or hint at club strength. Since your partner should have about thirteen high card points, it is fair to hope for something good in clubs. Lead the king of clubs and await partner's signal. Let us hope it is encouraging.

WEST	W	N	E	S
♠ 1087				1NT
♡ 873	P	2C	P	2H
◊ 108653	P	P	P	
♣ K3				

Lead a trump. Do not lead the king of clubs. There are two reasons for this. The first is that South opened one notrump and will probably have something good in clubs. The second reason is that East did not double two clubs. If he had really good clubs, he could have doubled. Yes, East may have the ace of clubs on this auction, but the odds suggest otherwise.

WEST	W	N	E	S
♠ 876		1D	P	1S
♡ Q7	P	2S	P	3S
◇ A84	P	P	P	
♣ Q6532				

Lead the three of clubs. Leading doubleton honors is a poor habit unless partner has bid the suit. The doubleton queen of hearts here is not wise given you have no specific reason to lead the suit.

WEST	W	N	E	S
♠ 97		1D	DBL	1S
♡ Q7	P	2S	P	P
◇ Q10764	P			
♣ J762				

East's takeout double suggests strength in hearts. You can lead the queen of hearts here. It is not a wonderful choice, and if you chose the two of clubs instead, that is not bad. Either lead is acceptable. Had East not doubled, the queen of hearts would be poor.

WEST	W	N	E	S
♠ K63		1D	P	1H
♡ J103	P	1NT	P	2H
◇ A6	P	P	P	
♣ 107643				

This hand is more of an exercise in avoiding a bad lead. Either spades or clubs could work and I would choose from one of them. A heart won't do anything good for you but it might not cost a trick if you are lucky. The one lead to avoid for sure is the ace of diamonds. You lead a doubleton ace when you have a reason to do so. When there is a reason NOT to lead a doubleton ace, you should listen. North opened one diamond which is about as strong a reason as you can have for not leading the suit.

WEST	W	N	E	S
♠ Q96				1C
♡ A72	P	1H	P	1S
◇ J6	P	3S	P	4S
♣ 108753	P	P	P	

Lead the jack of diamonds. Other leads don't appeal and diamonds are at least an unbid suit. An understanding East will have a good holding for you.

168

LEADING AGAINST A SUIT CONTRACT WHEN THE OPPONENTS HAVE BID THE SUITS YOU WANT TO LEAD

For this section, assume your partner has not bid. When you are on defense against a suit contract and have to find an opening lead, it is relatively rare that you will lead a suit bid by the opponents. There is a reason for this. Unless you have a solid sequence to lead, there is a chance that leading a suit will give the opponents a free finesse or will give declarer time to set up tricks. Remember, if you have K1075 of an unbid suit, it is reasonable to lead it against a suit contract since you can hope for partner to have some help for you. If you have the K1075 of a suit the opponents have bid, you should not lead it except as a last resort. The chances of finding partner with a helping card are less than normal. Very often, an unbid suit will be the best choice even when you don't have much in the suit to lead from.

Even when you have some great holding in a suit they have bid, leading it may concede tempo. This hand came up in a regional open pairs. What would you lead?

W	N	E	S
	1H	P	1S
P	2C	P	4S
P	P	P	

WEST
♠ 752
♡ QJ108
◇ QJ64
♣ AJ

Do you lead the solid heart sequence or do you prefer another lead? If another lead, why?

W	N	E	S
	1H	P	1S
P	2C	P	4S
P	P	P	

    NORTH
    ♠ 8
    ♡ AK763
    ◊ A83
    ♣ K1084

WEST	EAST
♠ 752	♠ J3
♡ QJ108	♡ 942
◊ QJ64	◊ K75
♣ AJ	♣ Q7652

    SOUTH
    ♠ AKQ10964
    ♡ 5
    ◊ 1092
    ♣ 93

This innocuous hand doesn't look like much but it does have an important theme. With a heart lead, declarer wins the ace and ruffs a heart in his hand. Now he draws trumps. Eventually, South must lead a club to the king so does so. When West turns out to have the ace of clubs, South has enough entries to ruff another heart. This sets up the fifth heart, which gives South a total of twelve tricks. Had West led a diamond, the unbid suit, declarer gets only eleven tricks since he can't set up the hearts in time to use them.

A nasty quirk of fortune or was it predictable? I can't say for sure that this kind of thing will always happen to you, but in my experience, leading one of the opponents' suits has a way of haunting me. With diamonds being unbid, the queen of diamonds has much more potential for you than the queen of hearts, dummy's known five card suit.

Another example.

W	N	E	S
	1H	P	1S
P	2S	P	3S
P	4S	P	P
P			

WEST
♠ 92
♡ AK98
◊ A98
♣ J1072

The obvious lead is the ace of hearts. Isn't it always right to lead from an ace-king high suit against a suit contract? It is in all the tables of opening leads, right up there near the top. Unfortunately, you don't win at bridge by following tables. You win by referring to tables, but with some judgment mixed in. Leading from an AK high suit may be on the top of most lists, but those lists don't include the warning that some AK suits are not the same as other AK suits. Here is the hand that caused this problem.

NORTH
- ♠ AJ85
- ♡ QJ1076
- ♢ 2
- ♣ A54

WEST	EAST
♠ 92	♠ 76
♡ AK98	♡ 54
♢ A98	♢ QJ6543
♣ J1072	♣ Q93

SOUTH
- ♠ KQ1043
- ♡ 32
- ♢ K107
- ♣ K86

If West leads the ace of hearts, South will have time to draw trumps and set up the hearts for discards. Making ten easy tricks. If West is more thoughtful about his lead and finds the jack of clubs, the defenders will come out of it with four tricks. South can set up hearts, as before, but the defenders have a head start. They have time to set up a club trick which will be enough for down one.

There are some times where you can reasonably lead a suit bid by the opponents, but it will usually not be from an honor combination. It is OK to lead a singleton or perhaps a doubleton of a suit bid on your left. There are some warning signs which I discussed in the sections on leading singletons and doubletons earlier, but as long as you are aware of the dangers, it is OK to lead singletons or doubletons in suits bid on your left.

A MAJOR DIFFERENCE exists between defense against suits and against notrumps. Against a suit contract, you should virtually never lead a suit bid on your right unless it is just patently obvious that you should do so. Against notrump, there will be times where your best lead by far is a suit that has been bid by your right hand opponent. I will develop this curious thought in the discussion of leads against notrumps.

A Little Quiz on Leads When They Have Bid Your Suits

WEST	W	N	E	S
♠ J652				1C
♡ Q62	P	1H	P	1S
♢ AJ6	P	2S	P	P
♣ Q62	P			

An unlovely hand to lead from. Diamonds feel right from the bidding, but the AJ6 is not leadable. You have to look elsewhere. I suggest the two of hearts. Trumps are dangerous with your holding and this leaves you with a choice of leading hearts or clubs. Leading through dummy is an OK thing to do in general. Note that North showed a seven or eight point hand so it is not likely that his hearts are really great. Be prepared for this lead to stink. It may happen. Most likely, you will see that the other leads weren't much better.

WEST	W	N	E	S
♠ J62		1H	P	1NT
♡ QJ83	P	2C	P	2D
◊ 96	P	P	P	
♣ KJ53				

Lead the queen of hearts. This is another unpleasant hand to lead from. When you have no good lead and when partner didn't bid, and when the opponents have bid all of your good suits, it is going to be unpleasant. You know that East has some points since you have a weak hand and the opponents have not shown a lot. East probably does not have good spades. He rates to have about ten points and if they included good spades, you would have heard about them. The J62 of spades is not a good holding in this circumstance. Diamonds are automatically rejected since there is no reason to expect a ruffing value in dummy. Also, if dummy has just one diamond, declarer will have some problems with the suit. Why help him by leading one for him? The reason I choose the heart lead is not that I expect anything good to happen. It is that I hope it does not give anything away. Since South did not preference to two hearts, it is likely that he has just one heart. If so, I don't have to fear dummy having the AK10xx. South won't be able to win the heart and later finesse the ten. A club lead is not as safe. South may have two or three clubs on this bidding. Leading one can be expensive if East has no club honor. Really, the entire goal with this lead is to not feel like a dunce after the first trick is over with.

172

CHAPTER EIGHTEEN

LEADING AGAINST NOTRUMP WHEN THE OPPONENTS HAVE BID YOUR SUITS

Sometimes you will find yourself on lead against an auction where all four suits have been bid. This can make it difficult to choose your opening lead.

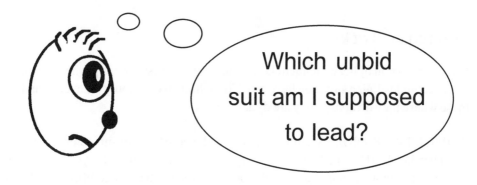

Which unbid suit am I supposed to lead?

W	N	E	S
			1D
P	1S	P	2C
P	2H	P	2NT
P	3NT	P	P
P			

WEST
♠ KJ65
♡ J64
◇ Q93
♣ 964

Don't bother figuring out what to lead. Just realize how uncomfortable your choices are when the opponents bid all four suits.

Sometimes the opponents haven't bid all the suits on their way to a notrump contract, but when you go to make your opening lead, you see that the only suits you have worth leading are the ones they have bid. For example.

W	N	E	S
	1D	P	1H
P	1S	P	1NT
P	P	P	

WEST
♠ Q1062
♡ J1083
◇ K1064
♣ 3

This time, North-South have bid just three suits, but they just happen to be the suits you have. Your opening lead is going to be difficult.

Two Expert Tricks

I can offer two insights which will help your leads against notrump when you are considering leading a suit they have bid. These hints won't apply on every hand but on those where they do apply, they are dynamite.

EXPERT TRICK ONE: When you are on lead against a notrump contract, holdings such as QJ1053 or KQ1072 or J10965 are very nice to have. Normally, you lead the top card in this suit without giving it a second thought. This is usually a good choice. There is a time, though, when the routine lead is not the best lead.

When you have a good sequence to lead from, but the suit has been bid by an opponent, you must consider whether their bidding the suit might not force you to look elsewhere. You may find a better lead, but in spite of the suit being bid, you may still choose to lead it. My first expert trick is this. If you have a suit headed by a three card sequence, you should consider leading fourth best and not the top of your sequence. The reason is that you can tell from the bidding that your partner will not have length in the suit. He can have a high card, but it may be singleton or doubleton. If you lead the high card from your sequence, the suit can get blocked, and even though you get lucky and find partner with good help for your lead, you won't be able to untangle the suit.

NOTE that an opponent does not have to bid a suit to show he has four cards. Some auctions exist where a four card suit can be shown without the suit actually being bid. Here is an example of this.

W	N	E	S
			1NT
P	2C	P	2H
P	3NT	P	P
P			

WEST
♠ QJ1063
♡ J82
◊ 83
♣ A94

South opens a sixteen to eighteen point one notrump. North bids Stayman, asking for a major, and South shows he has hearts. This does not interest North, who goes to three notrump. What do you lead? Before leading, ask yourself what North's bidding was all about.

The correct opening lead is the six of spades. Seem odd? The reason is this. North asked for a major and didn't like South's answer. You know for sure that North has four spades and was hoping to find a spade fit. The fact that North has four spades means that your partner has one or two. It is right to lead spades since they are so good, but it is wrong to lead the normal top of a sequence. Lead the six and hope that your partner can produce the ace, king, or nine. Let's say you lead the queen and find partner with the king. That is good news, but it will be bad news if the king is singleton. Likewise for the ace or the nine. Here is the complete hand. It shows you what can happen when you ignore the warning signs.

NORTH
♠ A754
♡ Q5
◊ KJ62
♣ 1075

WEST
♠ QJ1063
♡ J82
◊ 83
♣ A94

EAST
♠ K9
♡ 10764
◊ Q1097
♣ 632

SOUTH
♠ 82
♡ AK93
◊ A54
♣ KQJ8

West leads the queen of spades and declarer decides to hold up, playing the four from dummy. What should East do? If East is a thoughtful defender, he will play the king and return the nine. This is good play, but it isn't good enough. West will already be regretting his lead. If West plays low on the nine, declarer will let East have the trick. Unfortunately, East can't continue spades so declarer will have time to knock out the ace of clubs. South will have nine tricks and the time to get them. You will note that West can not afford to overtake the nine with the ten. If he does that, North's seven will turn into a second spade stopper.

Amazing stuff for the kibitzers. Frustrating stuff for the defenders. West leads the queen of spades, gets lucky enough to find East with the king and the nine, and the suit is still impossible to set up. Ouch.

The solution? Try the effect of leading the fourth best spade. West leads the six and declarer properly plays low from dummy. East wins the king and returns the nine as before. This time, though, West can afford to overtake with the ten and the spades can be established before West's ace of clubs is removed. Three notrump goes down one after the thoughtful six of spades lead.

Remembering the Auction

Let's say you have the QJ1063 of hearts. If you choose to lead them, which card should you lead? If you choose not to lead them, why not? Here are the three main situations.

1.   If the opponents get to a notrump contract and no one has bid hearts, make your normal lead of the queen. *It is correct to lead the top card of your sequence except when the opponents' bidding tells you not to.*

2.   If the opponents get to a notrump contract and one of the opponents has shown a four card holding, consider leading the six.

Assuming you choose to lead a heart, you would lead the six from the QJ1063 against these sequences.

W	N	E	S
	1D	P	1H
P	2D	P	2NT
P	P	P	

South is likely to have just four hearts. Lead the six of hearts.

W	N	E	S
	1C	P	1D
P	1H	P	1NT
P	P	P	

Lead the six of hearts. You know from the bidding that North has exactly four hearts.

W	N	E	S
			1C
P	1H	P	1NT
P	P	P	

You can't be sure whether North has four hearts or five, but it is acceptable to hope he has four. Lead the six of hearts and hope partner has at least the nine for you.

W	N	E	S
			1NT
P	2C	P	2S
P	2NT	P	P
P			

Ask the opponents if North promises four hearts. If he does, you should lead the six of hearts. This Stayman sequence is informative. If the two notrump bid does not promise four hearts, you should lead the queen. Remember. You lead the queen unless you KNOW that one or the other of your opponents has a four card holding. You are entitled to listen and take advantage of any information that comes your way.

W	N	E	S
			1NT
P	2C	P	2S
P	3NT	P	P
P			

Lead the six of hearts. This time North guarantees four hearts. He would not bother with Stayman if he wasn't interested in a major.

3.   If the opponents get to a notrump contract and one of the opponents has shown a good holding in the suit OR if the suit has been bid and raised, lead something else. You should not lead a heart from the QJ1063 on these auctions.

W	N	E	S
	1H	P	2D
P	2NT	P	3NT
P	P	P	

If North-South are playing five card majors, you know the hearts are not going to be productive. Almost surely you should look for a better lead.

W	N	E	S
	1S	P	2H
P	2S	P	3NT
P	P	P	

South should have a five card heart suit for his two over one response. I would not lead the suit against this bidding.

W	N	E	S
	1D	P	1H
P	2H	P	2NT
P	3NT	P	P
P			

It sounds like South has four hearts and North has raised with three. Leading a heart against this auction from your QJ1063 is sure disaster. Hold on to them and wait for your tricks.

If you have the patience of a log and the memory of an elephant, you may want to remember this next situation. It is the kind of thing that you wait years for.

W	N	E	S
	1H	P	2D
P	2H	P	3NT
P	P	P	

WEST
♠ 872
♡ QJ1094
◊ KJ7
♣ J4

Even though hearts have been bid and rebid, it looks like they are your best source of tricks. A neutral spade lead might be best, but the hearts, headed by a four card sequence, do tempt. Try leading the four of hearts. Your partner might have the eight. Or South might misplay the suit. Perhaps this is the heart setup.

    ♡ AK865
♡ QJ1094   ♡ 72
       ♡ 3

If you lead the four, declarer has to be specifically insightful enough to play the eight. He is more likely to play low from dummy or to win with the ace or king. Say he decides to play low, definitely the correct play on many hands. Your partner will play the seven and when he finally realizes he has won the trick, he may work out to return the suit. If you get in twice with your diamonds, you will set three notrump. If you make the routine lead of the queen you will establish two heart tricks, but only two. Really, leading the four of hearts is an effective ploy that deserves to work. Incidentally, the diagram above is hardly the only one where leading a small heart works for you. There are lots of others where the four of hearts is the winning lead.

The guidelines here apply to normal sequences and to interior sequences. Against a notrump contract, all of these holdings should lead fourth best if one of the opponents has shown four cards in the suit.

AJ1053

A10954

KJ1043

K10943

QJ1053

Q10943

J10964

AK1064

KQJ43

It is hard to bring yourself to lead low from the last two combinations, but assuming you choose the right time to do so, the fourth best may be the winning lead.

178

One of the hardest holdings for a defender to lead low from is the KQJ43 combination. If the opponents don't bid the suit, leading the king is correct, but if they have either bid the suit or implied the suit, leading low can be right.

W	N	E	S
			1D
P	1H	P	2C
P	2D	P	2NT
P	P	P	

NORTH
- ♠ Q653
- ♡ 9876
- ◊ QJ5
- ♣ J4

WEST
- ♠ J842
- ♡ KQJ43
- ◊ 93
- ♣ 106

How would you feel if you led the king of hearts and found partner with the A5 doubleton? The good news is that he has the ace, but the bad news is that you can only take three heart tricks. East can play the ace and return the suit, but because your side had to spend two high heart honors on the first trick you can not run the suit.

Here is another special case. It may seem to you like I am showing a lot of rare situations, but they do happen and when they occur, there is no margin for error. Also, as you can see from the examples, the cost of failure is high. The time spent on these odd cases is well used since learning some of them will help you when other related cases appear.

W	N	E	S
1S	DBL	P	3NT
P	P	P	

WEST
- ♠ A10763
- ♡ AQJ94
- ◊ Q8
- ♣ 4

You restrained from bidding hearts, which was probably wise under the circumstances. This doesn't mean you won't lead them. How should you attack in hearts? Should you lead the queen? Should you lead low? What is best?

♡ K876

♡ AQJ94   ♡ 3   This is a curious combination. The winning lead is the ace.
    ♡ 1052   If North has four to the king and South the doubleton or
                                    tripleton ten, you will lead the queen next to establish the
                                      suit. In the diagram on the left, you led the ace and now see
                                      the K876 in dummy. You know the ten, wherever it is, will
                                      be squashed when you continue the queen.

♡ 10876

♡ AQJ94   ♡ 53   If dummy comes down with four to the ten, you will know
    ♡ K2   that the best continuation is to lead low and hope that South
                                        has the doubleton king. If you lead the queen and find the
                                        situation as shown here, declarer will win the king and still
                                        have a stopper. NOTE that if you did not have the nine of
                                        hearts, the ace of hearts lead wouldn't have the same merit.

You have to be a believer and you have to have courage to make some of the leads shown
in this section. Here is the operative philosophy you must follow.

*It is better to lose one trick when you lead fourth best from a sequence
and it does not work than to lead the top card and lose three or four
tricks when the suit blocks.*

Important Reminder Notes

1.   The previous discussion applies when you have a three card sequence. If you are
        fortunate enough to have a four card sequence like the QJ1095, go ahead and
        make your normal lead.

2.   The previous discussion applies when you are leading against notrump. If you are
        on lead against a suit contract, you will tend to avoid suits they have bid. If you
        must lead one of the opponents' suits against a trump contract, you should lead
        your normal card. Leading fourth best from sequences is done only against
        notrump contracts.

The second expert trick, just like the first expert trick, is used to help you with leads
against notrump. This is as important a trick as you will ever find. I urge you to read the
following discussion and then reread it. Leading against notrump with hands where all
your leadable suits have been bid is difficult. If you are going to be effective with your
opening leads, you must know how to see through the bidding to find the best lead.

Two Important Auctions

	Auction One		
W	N	E	S
			1D
P	1H	P	1NT
P	P	P	

	Auction Two		
W	N	E	S
	1C	P	1H
P	1S	P	1NT
P	P	P	

In Auction One, your RHO opened a suit and rebid one notrump over one heart. In this case, it is the dummy who bid hearts.

In Auction Two, the opponents bid three suits on their way to one notrump. In this case, it is declarer who bid hearts.

There are important differences between these two auctions which you must be aware of. They may look similar, but they are not. The differences in the bidding warn you of certain traps to avoid and certain good things that most players have never heard of.

1. On the first auction, it is dangerous to lead hearts, the suit dummy bid.

2. On the second auction, it is often correct to lead hearts, the suit declarer bid.

3. On both auctions, you tend not to lead from broken holdings when dummy is the one who bid the suit. On Auction One, it is *extremely* dangerous to lead from a broken heart holding such as K1073 and on Auction Two, it is *moderately* dangerous to lead from broken holdings in clubs and spades.

Auction #1

N	S
	1D
1H	1NT
P	

Do not lead a heart from holdings such as KJ53. Dummy has four of them and declarer has two or three of them. Dummy will often have something like the Q985. He might have five of them. It is possible that dummy has five hearts and declarer three. When this happens, your partner will have just one. You will not gain anything by attacking the heart suit on this kind of bidding.

EXPERT TIP TWO: When your right hand opponent opens one of a suit and rebids one notrump, and ends up declaring in notrump, *do not lead from broken holdings in a suit bid by dummy.*

Here is an all-too-typical situation. The following diagrams show the heart suit as it might be after the 1D - 1H - 1NT auction from above. In all of these cases, West has a nice heart holding to lead from. With no information, a heart lead would be fine. On the auction here, leading hearts is flat out dangerous. The problem is that dummy is going to have some length sitting over you. Whatever spots dummy has will haunt you for the rest of the hand.

#1

♡ K853

♡ Q10642   ♡ A9

♡ J7

Your partner has the ace of hearts which is as useful as you can hope for. Still, if you are going to set up heart tricks, you will have to give declarer two heart tricks first.

#2

♡ Q983

♡ KJ762   ♡ A4

♡ 105

The same thing happens here. If West leads a heart, East takes his ace and returns the suit. If West wishes to set up a long heart, he has to give dummy two tricks first. The defense may not have time to do all of this.

#3

♡ J9632

♡ KQ107   ♡ 5

♡ A84

Leading this suit is suicide for the defenders. The king of hearts lead gives declarer four heart tricks. Listen to the bidding and avoid leading dummy's suit on this sequence.

#4

♡ AJ83

♡ K10764   ♡ 92

♡ Q5

If West ignores the warning signs and leads the six, South will take East's nine with the queen. At South's leisure, he can take two more tricks whenever he wants to. In the meantime, West has gained nothing, has lost at least one trick, has conceded timing to declarer, and adding insult to injury, has to hang on to his hearts for the rest of the hand in order to keep declarer from taking four tricks in the suit.

What If They Have Bid Three Suits?

Auction #2

N	S	
1C	1H	This auction looks much like auction #1. Don't let the similarities fool
1S	1NT	you into thinking they are the same thing. They are not. There are some
P		mean differences. The next discussion shows how they differ.

Here is a nasty question for you. The bidding has gone as shown above. You are on lead with the West hand. You will note that the opponents have bid three suits before South ends in one notrump. You will also note that the suits they bid are the ones you have. Your choice, therefore, is to lead one of the suits they bid or to lead your singleton. This hand is one of my favorites. I have given it to quite a few players, some of them experts. It surprises me how many find the wrong lead. Perhaps you will do better.

WEST	Listening to the auction, you will remember that diamonds is the unbid suit so
♠ Q1076	your first inclination should be to look at your diamonds. In this case, you
♡ Q1076	find you have a disappointing singleton two of diamonds and four cards in
◇ 2	each of the other three suits. Leading the unbid suit is often reasonable, but it
♣ Q1076	is not so reasonable that you should lead a singleton. You will do better by
	leading something else.

In case you aren't enjoying this hand, let me give you some encouragement. There is, between the spades, hearts, and clubs, a choice which is magnitudes better than the others. One of these three suits is quite good to lead from. In fact, if you know the expert trick that applies, you will be happy to have this problem. All you need to do is figure out which of the bid suits is the winner.

You have the Q1076 of spades. If you lead the six of spades, you are making a time honored lead by leading through the bidder. The same logic might be used to justify a club lead. Tradition has it that leading through strength is a good thing to do. In actual fact, tradition falls flat on its face here. There are times when leading INTO the person who bid a suit is better than leading THROUGH the person who bid it. This is best shown by example. Assume the suit shown here is hearts and that the opponents have bid the suit. You are West with the Q1076 of hearts and are thinking of leading them.

Note the difference in the effectiveness of a heart lead against these two sequences.

W	N	E	S
			1D
P	1H	P	1NT
P	P	P	

W	N	E	S
	1C	P	1H
P	1S	P	1NT
P	P	P	

```
              ♡ A983                        ♡ K4
    ♡ Q1076            ♡ J52      ♡ Q1076            ♡ J52
              ♡ K4                          ♡ A983
```

You are West. In the diagram on the left, hearts were bid by North. You lead the six of hearts. How well does this work for you? Dummy plays the eight and East the jack. South wins the king and goes about his business. Sooner or later, your side continues hearts. Say you lead the queen, losing to dummy's ace. This sets up a trick for you but that is all. You will end up with one trick and declarer will end up with three. Leading the suit bid on your left works poorly, just as described in the previous pages.

In the second diagram, hearts were bid by South. The opponents' heart suit is the same as in the first diagram except that the length in hearts is now in declarer's hand. You lead the six of hearts into the bidder. This time, the play goes better for you. Dummy plays the four and East the jack. South wins the ace and proceeds. When your side gets in, you can lead another heart, felling dummy's king. West now has two tricks to cash.

It is important to see what happened here. When you led dummy's suit, the high spot cards in dummy gave you fits. The reason is that dummy's high spot cards are OVER your spot cards. In the second diagram, you had success because your high spot cards were OVER declarer's high spot cards. Your intermediate cards are placed to take advantage of their positional strength. You can formulate two important rules here.

RULE #1 - When your left hand opponent opens one of a suit and the opponents bid three suits leading to your RHO bidding one notrump, their weak spot is often going to be the one suit that declarer bid.

RULE #2 - When your right hand opponent opens and rebids one notrump, leading dummy's suit usually works out very badly.

Here is another example showing the difference between leading a suit bid by dummy and a suit bid by declarer. The discrepancies are more brutal than usual. Just for the record, I don't have to stay up nights thinking about these situations. They pop up every day at the table. If I want examples, I just play a day of bridge and pick out the best.

$\heartsuit$ K1085

$\heartsuit$ J974 $\quad$ $\heartsuit$ Q32 $\qquad$ $\heartsuit$ J974 $\quad$ $\heartsuit$ Q32

$\heartsuit$ A6 $\qquad\qquad\qquad\qquad$ $\heartsuit$ K1085

N	S
	1C
1H	1NT
P	

The diagram on the left shows the situation where you lead dummy's suit. If you lead the four of hearts through the dummy, the play will go thusly. Dummy will play the five, and East, the queen. South will win with the ace. Now, if and when declarer feels like it, he can finesse the ten of hearts for two more tricks. If he wishes, he can finesse the eight and leave the K10 sitting there over your J9. Leading a heart in this setup gives declarer three sure tricks and denies your side even one trick. This is a powerful example. It typifies what can happen when you lead from a broken suit through the person who bid it. This example emphasizes the rule I showed you earlier.

RULE - When your right hand opponent opens one of a suit and rebids one notrump, and ends up declaring in notrump, do not lead from broken holdings in dummy's suit.

N	S
1C	1H
1S	1NT
P	

This is the auction used in the second of the above diagrams. If West leads the four of hearts, leading into the heart bidder, the play goes favorably for the defense. East's queen forces South's king. When the defenders get in, a further heart knocks out the ace. As soon as East gets in, he will lead his last heart and West will take two tricks. In this diagram, the heart lead works like a charm. The difference is huge and it is predictable.

Alert

N	S
	1C
1S	1NT
P	

On this sequence, South usually has two or three spades. Rebidding one notrump with a singleton in partner's suit is rarely done. For this reason, leading spades is a bad choice as discussed in this chapter. Do not confuse this auction with the other auction I have been talking about.

N	S
1C	1H
1S	1NT
P	

On this sequence, I talked about why leading a heart, into the bidder, was often the right defense. Leading hearts can be right, but leading clubs or spades is not quite as bad as leading spades was on the previous auction. The reason is that on the auction on the left, responder may have been forced to bid one notrump when he didn't much care for it. South could have the following hand:

SOUTH	South bids one heart in response to one club but when North rebids one
♠ 4	spade, South is unhappy. He can't pass one spade, can't rebid this poor a
♡ Q8763	heart suit, can't bid diamonds with just seven points, and hates to go back to
◇ KQ1084	clubs with just two. One notrump is the only remaining bid.
♣ 95	

As you can see from this South hand, a heart lead may be good for the defenders. But it is also true that a spade or a club lead can work. The unbid suit would be playing into declarer's secret weapon. The big point here is that when the opponents bid three suits on their way to one notrump, leading one of dummy's suits should not be as quickly rejected as when they bid only two suits before getting to one notrump. Curious.

These two auctions are very important. They deserved to be discussed in detail. For many players these thoughts are totally new. In my classes, I face great reluctance at first. Then the doubts begin to fade and I get reports that someone got a good result by leading into the suit declarer bid. Or someone sheepishly admits they led from the J10763 of dumm's suit when they shouldn't have and got a stinky result.

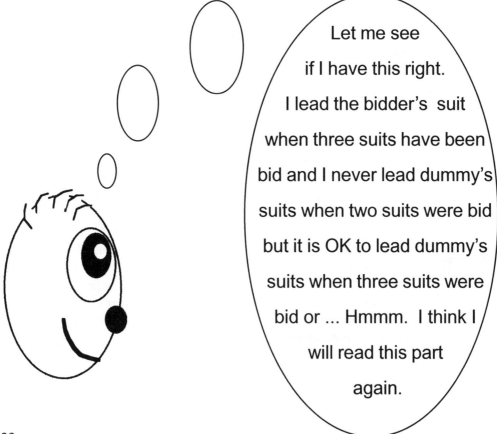

Let me see if I have this right. I lead the bidder's suit when three suits have been bid and I never lead dummy's suits when two suits were bid but it is OK to lead dummy's suits when three suits were bid or ... Hmmm. I think I will read this part again.

IMPORTANT DISTINCTIONS

READ ME!

The last few pages talked about auctions where the opponents bid a suit and you wondered if you should lead it against a notrump contract. The material above referred to one of the two common sequences shown. There are other auctions which can get the opponents to notrump which may or may not hint at a certain lead. For comparison, here are some other auctions to think about.

W	N	E	S
	1C	P	1H
P	2C	P	2NT
P	P	P	

This sequence does suggest a heart lead. North frequently has a stiff heart and South sometimes has four poor ones. South's hand may look like one of the following hands.

SOUTH
♠ KJ73
♡ AJ73
♢ Q83
♣ 93

If this is the South hand, and if dummy has a stiff heart, this suit could be a weak spot for declarer. It is logical for many reasons that a heart is a good lead for the defenders. South said he had four or more hearts, but he also said he has about eleven high card points. If South has stoppers in the two unbid suits, spades and diamonds, there won't be too much left in hearts.

SOUTH
♠ KQ95
♡ 10743
♢ AQ4
♣ 73

This is another possible South hand. I don't say that South's hearts will always be this weak, but it is possible. South would, in fact, bid one heart with this and would rebid two notrump over two clubs.

SOUTH
♠ Q983
♡ AK105
♢ Q632
♣ 9

Even if South has good hearts as he does here, a heart lead may be his weak spot. If dummy has a stiff two of hearts, a heart lead will be constructive for the defenders plus it will not be helping declarer set up spade or diamond tricks. Again, no promises, just thoughts.

W	N	E	S
			1D
P	1S	P	2C
P	2D	P	2NT
P	P	P	

This sequence is different. This time, it is likely that the best suit for you to attack is dummy's spade suit. Declarer should have five diamonds and four clubs but there is nothing in the bidding to suggest dummy has a singleton club. Hearts, the unbid suit, could be right but spades are a candidate. They should not automatically be rejected. Here is a likely scenario.

NORTH
♠ J9653
♡ Q93
◇ 1075
♣ K4

SOUTH
♠ A
♡ AJ8
◇ KQ983
♣ Q1083

This combination of hands is par for the North-South bidding. North showed spades and gave a preference to diamonds. South has extra points and makes a game try of two notrump, rejected by North. Look at the South hand. He has diamonds and clubs and he also has the hearts he needs to give him a heart stopper. What is left is just one spade. A spade lead may be good for the defense. At the least, it does not help him. There is a big difference between auctions where notrump is bid at the one level and auctions that go round and round before notrump is finally introduced.

W	N	E	S
			1D
P	1S	P	2C
P	2H	P	2NT
P	3NT	P	P
P			

WEST
♠ Q75
♡ Q83
◇ J875
♣ Q93

It would be nice if East had doubled two hearts for the lead. Had he done so, you would be reaching for a heart. Given partner did not double two hearts, the auction does not tell you what to lead. Looking at this mess, you will probably be unhappy about your opening lead. I claim that you can improve your leads on many hands by listening to the bidding, but not all. This hand is a reminder that perfection is a pleasant fantasy. I will tell you what I would lead with this hand, but it won't prove much. My choice is a spade on the theory that if South had three spades, he would give a preference to spades. South, therefore, rates to have one or two spades. Since he will have one much of the time, I accept that a spade can work. But I am not enthusiastic about this. This is the kind of hand where you discover the winning lead during the postmortem. Then, having done so, you strain to figure out why the winning lead was findable. Often, even in the light of seeing all four hands, I can't find a reason that I should have done the right thing. In my opinion, the right lead on many hands is just a guess, as happens in the hand here.

W	N	E	S
			1D
P	1S	P	2H
P	3D	P	3NT
P	P	P	

You saw this situation elsewhere in this book. When opener reverses and then settles on three notrump, dummy's suit is a prime candidate for the opening lead. Declarer has diamonds, hearts, and a club stopper. It is possible that he has a singleton spade.

Is It Ever Right To Lead a Three Card Suit Into the Bidder?

In addition to leading a suit bid by RHO from four card holdings, you can also consider leading their suit when you have a good three card sequence. This is something you must do with care since if you choose a bad moment, the lead won't work.

N	S
1C	1H
1S	1NT
P	

This auction was discussed earlier. It was noted that South has a weak hand and is also likely to have only four hearts. In addition to leading hearts from holdings like Q984, it is often right to lead them from holdings like J108, QJ9, or even a lesser holding like 1098. Honor sequences work well here when you get lucky and find your partner with four cards to an honor. This choice won't happen often, but it will be worth a thought on some hands where the best lead is uncertain.

Here is a diagram of the heart suit as you would like to find it. South has the four hearts he promised with his heart bid and in this case actually has good high cards in the suit as well.

```
              ♡ J6
♡ 1097                 ♡ K842
              ♡ AQ53
```

The ten is covered with the jack and king. South wins the ace and goes about his business. The defense is now in a position to set up two heart tricks. Say, hypothetically, that East gets in and leads a heart.

South will probably hold up. West will win the seven and continue the nine. East now has the good eight of hearts. Two things remain for the lead to be successful. East has to get in, and he has to remember that the eight is good.

Now I admit that this is a lot of work. Setting up the two heart tricks wasn't easy. For this reason, you won't often find such a lead as this. But, when your alternatives are poor, realizing the potential for this lead and acting on it can get you some nice results.

Here are some guidelines to help you determine whether or not leading into the bidder is a good idea against notrump.

1.   If it is likely that declarer's suit is just four cards long, it is a possible lead.

W	N	E	S
	1D	P	1H
P	1S	P	1NT
P	2NT	P	P
P			

South is likely to have four hearts only. I guess it will happen about 60% of the time. If you are thinking of leading into their heart suit, this is a good auction for it.

W	N	E	S
	1D	P	1S
P	2C	P	2D
P	2H	P	2NT
P	3NT	P	P
P			

Here, South bid spades and then gave a preference to diamonds. When North continued with two hearts, South bid notrump. This is a good time for a spade lead. South is likely to have four spades and dummy is likely to have just one or two.

W	N	E	S
			1NT
P	2C	P	2H
P	2NT	P	P
P			

South will usually have four hearts for this sequence. You might give some thought to leading one. The trouble is that South has a good hand and may have good hearts. Be cautious about leading into the bidder on strong auctions. See the next comment.

W	N	E	S
	1D	P	1S
P	2H	P	2NT
P	3NT	P	P
P			

Look seriously at leading spades. South's spades can be as weak as the 5432. He was forced to bid by opener's reverse so may have bid two notrump as a least-of-evils bid. Many players play that responder has to rebid a five card suit if he has one when opener reverses to two hearts. On this sequence, I expect a spade is the right lead most of the time. Only if your lead is clear-cut should you lead something else. The unbid suit, clubs? Not too likely. South can have a hand like the following.

SOUTH
♠ Q732
♡ Q5
◊ 85
♣ KJ875

Would you not respond one spade and then bid two notrump on the second round? Believe me, if I had this hand, I would bid two notrump and would be very nervous if the opening leader led a small spade.

W	N	E	S
	1H	P	1S
P	3D	P	3NT
P	P	P	

North's jump shift forced South to do something. South tends to bid notrump when he has the unbid suit stopped. He may be hoping that his spade bid will scare the opponents off the suit for a moment or two. South might have ♠ 97653 ♡ 8 ◊ J73 ♣ AQ64. A spade lead could be the killer for the defense.

2. The strength of declarer's hand is significant. If declarer has shown a weak hand, leading one of his suits may work.

W	N	E	S
	1C	P	1H
P	1S	P	1NT
P	2NT	P	P
P			

This sequence tells you that South may have four hearts, but it also tells you that South has a minimum hand. South has some points in diamonds so is likely to have little in hearts. This auction was discussed earlier in this chapter. Here, the focus is on the fact that South is weak and therefore unlikely to have good hearts along with the diamond stopper he promises.

3. The stronger declarer's bidding, the less likely you will want to lead one of declarer's suits. If declarer opens one or two notrump and shows spades on the way to three notrump, it is true that he has just four cards in spades (usually), but he is likely to have good ones. Look elsewhere.

4. The better the spots you have in the suit, the better your chances are of setting it up. Holdings like ♠ A1083 ♡ K1074 ◊ Q1082 ♣ J1074 are worth a trick or two more than holdings like ♠ A753 ♡ K632 ◊ Q652 ♣ J432. Do not overlook the spot cards.

N	S
1D	1S
2D	2NT
3NT	

WEST
♠ A7654
♡ QJ8
◊ 43
♣ 972

Lead the queen of hearts. You are not going to be able to set up the spades and use them. The player holding this hand led the five of spades and even though he found partner with the KJ8, the lead was a disaster. This was the full hand.

N	S
1D	1S
2D	2NT
3NT	

This is the entire hand from the preceding page.

NORTH
♠ 3
♡ 1075
◊ AKJ1076
♣ KQ8

WEST	EAST
♠ A7654	♠ KJ8
♡ QJ8	♡ K942
◊ 43	◊ Q95
♣ 972	♣ 653

SOUTH
♠ Q1092
♡ A63
◊ 82
♣ AJ104

After a spade lead, East won the king and returned the jack. After this start, South has nine tricks and can't be defeated. East could have returned a heart instead of a spade, but that is hindsight. More to the point, West should have led a heart himself. South must take the diamond finesse and ends up with only seven tricks. Keep your eyes on those spot cards. If West's spades had been headed by the A10954 or A10874, the lead would be reasonable. Remember, South bid the suit, so you know that he will have those annoying spot cards that you don't have.

5. If you are leading a suit declarer has bid, it works best if you have four cards in the suit and it is not bad if you have five. If you have more cards, your partner won't have many himself.

A Short Quiz

N	S
1D	1H
1S	1NT
P	

♠ 75
♡ J974
◊ QJ73
♣ K43

Lead the four of hearts. All indications suggest this is the right lead. You have the right kind of heart suit to lead into the bidder. If you are uncertain this is a good lead, reread the section above. Be leery of clubs. You can draw better inferences about missing major suits than you can about missing minor suits.

WEST

♠ 874
♡ Q5432
◇ AJ6
♣ Q7

Lead the eight of spades. This lead is arrived at by process of elimination. The hearts are poor since you have bad spots. If you had the ten or nine of hearts, they would be right. Leading a doubleton queen of an unbid minor does not appeal. Basically, you are hoping not to make a bad lead when you select the eight of spades. You are not hoping to find a dynamic start.

WEST

♠ Q763
♡ KJ2
◇ K4
♣ 10764

Lead the four of clubs. This is the unbid suit, after all, so it is acceptable in that regard. True, declarer may have clubs well stopped, but he doesn't have to have them bottled up. Do not lead a spade from this weak holding after North's spade bid.

N	S
	1D
1S	1NT
P	

WEST

♠ Q1074
♡ QJ3
◇ K9653
♣ K

Lead the queen of hearts. Be sure you realize the difference between this sequence and the first one in this quiz. Here, there is no reason to doubt South's diamond bid. A player who opens the bidding and rebids one notrump can be counted on in general to have a decent suit. Leading a diamond might work, but leading a spade (dummy's suit) is usually terrible on this sequence. It is a good sequence to be familiar with.

WEST

♠ K10763
♡ 875
◇ Q8
♣ A94

Lead the eight of hearts. You are trying to start the defense safely. Spades are still terrible, a decent five card suit notwithstanding.

WEST

♠ 64
♡ 9864
◇ KQ93
♣ Q106

Lead the nine of hearts. It might be an OK lead and it should not turn out badly. This is a hand which has no great lead but has several bad ones. A spade is poor since South rates to have a spade or two and a diamond is wrong since South rates to have a good suit. The heart isn't exciting but neither is it likely to be a disaster.

WEST	N	S
♠ Q8763	1S	2H
♡ Q105	3D	3NT
◇ K74	P	
♣ 93		

I do not know what to lead. North opened one spade showing a five card suit so this suit doesn't look encouraging. Leading hearts into the bidder is out of the question here. South responded two hearts and that usually shows a five card suit. No future there. Diamonds are no bargain either. I would settle on the nine of clubs, but it is because I have no idea what to do otherwise. The other three suits have warning signs that should not be ignored. It is possible that when the hand is over you will see, for example, that East has the KJ9 of spades or the Q10983 of diamonds in which case one of these suits will be effective. These things are possible, but there is no reason to suggest they exist on this hand unless you are into E.S.P.

WEST	N	S
♠ 986	1D	1H
♡ K87542	1S	1NT
◇ Q9	P	
♣ KJ		

This is a hand that arrives at the best lead by process of elimination. Hearts is a good choice against this bidding but certain factors must exist. You need good spots in the suit when you are leading into the bidder. This hand has terrible spots. Leading hearts will be like jumping into a pool of cold pudding and trying to make it to the other side. It will be a battle. Even if East provides you with something good like the AJ or the QJ, you will take forever setting up hearts and getting in to use them. The doubleton queen of diamonds is totally unappealing and the KJ of clubs is scary. Clubs might be South's best suit. The only lead that doesn't turn my stomach is the nine of spades. Ideally, East will have four of them. You are rooting for him to have something like the KJ74 or the Q1073. If either of these holdings occur, you are in business. As stated before, when the opponents bid three suits on the way to one notrump, leading declarer's suit can be very good. Leading either of dummy's suits can work, if you do so wisely.

WEST	N	S
♠ Q6	1C	1D
♡ 87542	1H	1NT
◇ AJ4	P	
♣ K83		

A great many hands do not come with comfortable leads. This is another such. I have been conservative about including lots of hands like this one. You have to know how to deal with hands like this, so here is one more for your consideration. Looking at this collection, you first search for a good lead. The only five card suit was bid by your LHO, but it is a poor suit. Still, the other suits are not worth leading. If you think the queen of spades is a good choice, remember that East did not bid them over one club. If East has five of them, they will be poor. If East has four spades, it means the opponents have seven of them, and they will benefit from your lead more than you will. If you look at the auction, you will see that North can have four spades. North can have a 4-4-1-4 hand or a 4-4-2-3 hand. Not unlikely. The best lead with this hand is once again a least-of-evils lead. Try a heart. I would lead the eight so as to alert partner that I don't have high honors in the suit. East can probably tell from his hand and the dummy that I have heart length, so he should work out what is happening.

194

CHAPTER NINETEEN

WHEN YOUR OPENING LEAD AGAINST NOTRUMP IS NOT OBVIOUS

This topic was visited, sort of, in the last chapter. The opponents' bidding your suits is not the only reason for going beyond the obvious when choosing a lead. There are other reasons. One common reason for not leading your suit is when you have a bad hand and don't think you will be able to get in to take your tricks after setting them up.

W	N	E	S
			1NT
P	3NT	P	P
P			

WEST
♠ 763
♡ 93
◇ J8753
♣ 964

If you lead a diamond, you will require a good diamond holding from partner to help you set up the suit. If your partner has, say, the Q94, you can set up the suit, but you won't be able to use the suit since you have no entry.

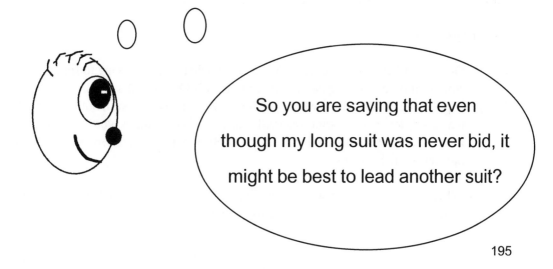

So you are saying that even though my long suit was never bid, it might be best to lead another suit?

```
              NORTH
              ♠ K52
              ♡ 1052
              ◊ A106
              ♣ A1073

WEST                EAST              If West starts with the five of diamonds, South will win
♠ 763               ♠ A108            East's queen and finesse in clubs to East's king. East
♡ 93                ♡ QJ864           will return a diamond. South has eight tricks and after
◊ J8753             ◊ Q42             leading a spade to the king, has ten sure winners. In
♣ 964               ♣ K2              fact, with the spades dividing, South will take eleven
                                      tricks.
              SOUTH
              ♠ QJ94
              ♡ AK7
              ◊ K9
              ♣ QJ85
```

West will have two good diamonds but will not be able to use them. He will have to discard them near the end of the hand. Very sad.

Go back to West's opening lead. Had West taken the view that leading diamonds was not going to be good, he might have tried leading either hearts or spades. It is hard to say which is better. On this hand, a heart lead would actually set three notrump. East has five hearts and eventually will get three heart tricks, the king of clubs, and the ace of spades. This is three tricks better than what happens when West leads the five of diamonds.

If West guesses to lead a spade, South will come to lots of tricks, but he will make one fewer than when West led a diamond.

When West has a poor hand, it is often wise to give up leading a suit that can't be set up and try to find a suit in partner's hand. As you can see from the above example, finding partner's suit isn't always easy. But the effort is worth it.

This brings up two guidelines.

1.   DO NOT LEAD AN UNBID SINGLETON when you are trying to find partner's suit. That is stretching a good thing too far. It is OK to lead a doubleton or a tripleton against notrump when you don't like your longest suit, but it is not OK to lead a singleton. This point was made earlier. It is true and is worth repeating. Leading singletons in unbid suits against notrump just because you hope to find partner is terrible bridge.

2.   When you are choosing between leading an unbid minor suit and an unbid major suit, the major suit is usually the correct choice.

196

When the bidding goes 1NT - 3NT, you know that
North has many of his cards in the minor suits. How do
you know that? If North had a major suit, he would bid
Stayman and look for a fit. North did not bid Stayman
so rates to have at least seven and maybe more cards in
the minors. When you are on lead, you can use this
information.

W	N	E	S
			1NT
P	2NT	P	3NT
P	P	P	

WEST

♠ J82
♡ 983
◊ J972
♣ Q96

If your opponents bid 1NT - 2NT - 3NT, you should worry that dummy will
have length in the minor suits. Either minor could be dangerous. The
following hand is an example of a possible North hand. You would not like
to lead a diamond and see the following situation.

NORTH

♠ K3
♡ J64
◊ Q1086
♣ K1054

WEST

♠ J82
♡ 983
◊ J972
♣ Q96

This is a possible North hand. It has invitational points and it
does not have a major suit. Not surprisingly, it does have clubs
and diamonds. It does not always have both minors, but it will
have both of them often enough that leading the two of diamonds
or the six of clubs will work poorly. If I held the West hand and
had chosen to lead a diamond and this dummy came down, I
would feel very distressed with my choice. My vote is for the
nine of hearts.

Be sure you listen to the auction. If you have the same hand and hear this auction instead,
your lead should change.

W	N	E	S
			1NT
P	2C	P	2H
P	2NT	P	3NT
P	P	P	

South has shown hearts and North has shown spades.
You should go ahead with your fourth best diamond.
Here is a possible hand for North to hold.

NORTH
♠ Q1096
♡ K106
◊ K3
♣ J542

WEST
♠ J82
♡ 983
◊ J972
♣ Q96

Whether or not a diamond works, it is clear that leading from three little hearts will not be effective. When your RHO opens one notrump and you end up on lead against two or three notrump, you must pay attention to what responder bid on the way to the final contract.

Here is another example of an opening lead when you have two suits to choose from.

W	N	E	S
			1NT
P	2NT	P	3NT
P	P	P	

WEST
♠ Q1073
♡ 43
◊ A98
♣ Q1073

You have two decent suits to lead. Should you start with a spade or a club? The answer is that a spade is best. It is best by about two to one. North didn't look for a major and that implies he has one or both minors.

When the opponents have bid to three notrump without mentioning a suit, you should go to some lengths not to lead a minor. Don't make this thought a religion, but do make it a consideration.

W	N	E	S
			1NT
P	3NT	P	P
P			

WEST
♠ Q1075
♡ 65
◊ A8
♣ Q10754

I think this hand shows how far you should go to lead a major suit. On this auction, a spade lead is just about as good as a club. If you replace the ten of clubs with the two, I would vote for a spade for sure.

WEST	
♠ Q75	With a pretty good club suit and NO other realistic choice, you should go
♡ 65	ahead with the five of clubs. You don't love to lead a minor suit against this
◊ A82	sequence, but it is not an automatically bad thing to do. It is true that North's
♣ Q10754	raise to three notrump implies minor suit strength, but it is also possible that

he has long diamonds and does not have much in clubs. Opening leads are a frustrating science because a lead that works well one day may stink up the room on another. Today, for example, your partner may have the KJ2 of clubs, in which case you have made a 'well judged' lead. On another day, your partner may have the 3 of clubs and the K10984 of spades, in which case you should be reading someone else's book on opening leads.

In cases where you are not going to lead your long suit, you should be very pleased to find yourself with a short suit headed by a sequence. Holdings like J104 and 1096 are ideal leads in notrump. If you get lucky enough to find partner's suit, these holdings combine well with honors in partner's hand.

W	N	E	S
			1NT
P	2NT	P	3NT
P	P	P	

NORTH
♠ Q8
♡ A76
◊ K1073
♣ 9864

WEST	EAST
♠ J104	♠ K975
♡ 843	♡ Q952
◊ 98642	◊ Q5
♣ 73	♣ AK2

SOUTH
♠ A632
♡ KJ10
◊ AJ
♣ QJ105

If West leads his long suit, diamonds, declarer will make nine or ten tricks depending on how he guesses hearts.

If West leads the jack of spades, declarer will go down, losing three spades and two clubs.

If West ignores the spade sequence and tries a heart instead from three small, declarer will make nine or ten tricks according to how he guesses diamonds.

NOTE that you should lead a three card sequence only if it is an unbid suit or if your partner has bid it. When the auction tells you that one of the opponents has a four card holding in this suit, leading from a three card sequence is usually poor.

W	N	E	S
			1D
P	1S	P	1NT
P	3NT	P	P
P			

WEST
♠ J104
♡ 863
◇ AJ76
♣ K82

This is a tough problem. East might have some clubs. He could have decent hearts. Both of the unbid suits are possible. The point of this problem is that leading a spade is not a good idea. North has four of them, which will hurt your chances of setting them up. Here is a possible setup.

NORTH
♠ Q972

WEST
♠ J104

EAST
♠ K85

SOUTH
♠ A63

If West leads the jack of spades, South wins the ace and then finesses dummy's nine. East gets his king but declarer has three tricks. If West does not lead spades, South, if he attacks this suit, can get two tricks but must lose two in the process.

CHAPTER TWENTY

LEADS VERSUS SLAMS

Leading against a slam is a scary proposition. The opponents have bid a slam and presumably have a lot of points and tricks. If they have a weak spot, you have to find it right away. Against game contracts, you may get off to a poor lead and still recover. Against a slam contract, it is likely that you have to get off on the right lead or else.

If you are lucky, you will have one of the following to help you find a lead against a slam.

1.   An ace-king to lead.

2.   A strong sequence.

3.   A singleton in an unbid suit.

4.   A partner who has bid a suit for you.

5.   A partner who has raised one of your suits.

6.   A partner who has made a lead directing double.

When you have a good holding to lead from or when you get information from your partner, leads against slams aren't so tough. It is when the opponents have the bidding to themselves and you have nothing obvious to lead that you need to think.

There are many aspects of leads against slams that require thought. Here are two of the tougher ones.

1.   LEADING AN ACE.

2.   LEADING FROM A KING.

How do you feel about doing either of these things against a slam?

Earlier in this book, I spent an entire chapter railing against players who lead aces. I suggested it was a fast route to mediocrity. My advice against slams is that leading an ace is worth thinking about.

Also earlier in this book, I devoted an entire chapter advising that leading away from kings (and lesser honors too) was not a bad thing at all as long as you did it when the auction suggested the suit be led. Many players hate to lead from kings against a partscore or a game. How do you think they feel about leading away from a king against a slam? Just imagine the depression they would feel if they led away from a king and allowed declarer to win a cheap trick with the queen. Is my recommendation going to be that you should not lead from an honor, which will calm many hearts, or am I going to recommend you do lead from kings, which will surely set some nerves on edge?

THE ANSWER IS that as long as you listen to the auction and believe that they are weak in a specific suit, leading from a king is an outstanding chance. Comes with risk, of course, but it is the right lead often enough that you must go through with it.

Here is a story hand.

The bidding was typical of distributional hands. South could not find out what he wanted to know so he took a chance.

W	N	E	S
	1NT	P	3H
P	4H	P	6H
P	P	P	

NORTH
♠ QJ8
♡ K86
◇ AKQ8
♣ J92

SOUTH
♠ 1074
♡ AQJ10954
◇ —
♣ A106

The bidding could have gone in other ways, but this is the one chosen by this particular North and South.

As you have noted by now, the slam has two spade losers. Bad luck. But not bad luck if the defenders lead something else. With any other lead, South can throw the spades away on the diamonds and will make the slam by taking two club finesses. The club honors were divided, so without a spade lead, the slam was making.

What did West have in spades? Let's say he had the A652. If this was his holding, he would have to lead the ace to set the slam. Let's say West had the K652 of spades. Now, if he is going to set the slam, he has to lead a spade away from the king.

Pretend you are West and that you had the K652 of spades and didn't lead one. The slam makes and your partner is showing you his ace of spades and telling you that a spade lead would have set the slam. Do you thank him for his insight and respond that you don't lead from kings against slams or do you mull it over and wonder whether it might have been a good lead?

Pretend you are East and that you have the A93 of spades. Your partner has led a diamond against six hearts and declarer made the slam. You discover at the end that your partner has the king of spades and you note that if he had led a spade, you would have beaten the slam. Do you sympathize or do you wave your ace at partner or do you mull about the lead and wonder if a spade was really the best thing for partner to have led?

This hand proves nothing except to demonstrate that the only winning defense may require that the opening leader lead an ace, or on a different layout, lead away from a king.

What Slam Are They In?

Are they in a grand slam or a small slam? If they are in a grand slam, the objective is usually to avoid giving away a trick on opening lead. Hopefully, you can trust the opponents' bidding and assume they have all the aces, so you don't have to worry yourself that partner has an ace and that you have to find the right lead.

If they are in a small slam, your side has totally different goals. Instead of playing it safe with a passive lead, you often have to attack and set up a trick to cash when you get in later. Possibly you may have to cash an ace on opening lead.

The following discussion is devoted to leads against small slams. In the real world, there are very few grand slams and most of them will make or go down regardless of the opening lead.

When Is It Right To Lead An Ace Against a Slam?

This is the number one question I get asked about when talking about leads versus slams. I could write about this topic for ages and never prove anything. Leading against slams is never as easy as leading against lower contracts. Against game and partscore contracts, it is so wrong in general to lead aces that you can put that consideration aside and deal with whatever is left over. Against a small slam, leading an ace becomes an honest temptation, and you have to include it in your thoughts. Just all the more stuff to think about.

Here is one quick generality that you can live with comfortably. If the opponents reach six notrump, you should not lead an ace. One of the reasons for leading an ace against a suit contract is that you fear declarer will discard his loser in that suit and then give you a trick in another suit. In a notrump contract, declarer can't do that. If your side can gain the lead somehow against six notrump, any ace you have at the start will be cashable.

It is when you are defending against a suit slam that you have to think about taking your ace. Since, in the long run, you will not lead an ace more often than you will, I will show situations where you should not lead an ace.

Auctions That Tell You Not To Cash an Ace Against a Slam

Leading an ace when an opponent has bid the suit.

If either opponent has bid a suit prior to looking for a slam, it is usually wrong to lead that suit. It may be a suit that declarer will need tricks in and if so, your lead of the ace will simplify his problem immediately. This is what you want to avoid.

W	N	E	S
			1H
P	2C	P	2D
P	3H	P	3S
P	4NT	P	5H
P	6H	P	P
P			

WEST

♠ Q864
♡ 874
♢ A1074
♣ 63

Should you lead the ace of diamonds? The answer is a clear no. South has diamonds and there is nothing in the bidding to tell you that he can throw all of them away.

204

Here are three diamond combinations that declarer may have to deal with.

#1	#2	#3
◇ 83	◇ 83	◇ 83
◇ KJ96	◇ K9652	◇ KQ65

In diagram one, South will lead a diamond from dummy and try to guess whether to play the king or the jack. If you have already taken the ace of diamonds, he will have no difficulty with this suit.

In diagram two, South will lead a diamond toward his king and will lose either one or two tricks depending on where the ace is. If West led the ace on opening lead, declarer's slam will be easy when it should have been impossible.

In diagram three, it looks like it does not matter whether West takes the ace of diamonds. This may or may not be true. If South needs two diamond tricks in order to discard a loser from dummy, his work will be smoothed out by the lead of the ace of diamonds.

What should West lead? I don't know. I know what I would lead, but I do not know it is right. My choice is the four of spades. Perhaps partner has the king. South cue-bid the suit, but he does not need both spade honors to do so.

Leading an ace when it is an unbid suit.

If you have an ace in an unbid suit, you can consider leading it. There are two subtle factors to think about.

1.   If your ace high suit is headed by the A10x or the AJxx or the AQxx, you don't want to be quick to lead it. There is a chance that you will get two tricks in the suit if you wait for declarer to lead it.

2.   If your ace high suit is two or three cards long, there is a good chance that declarer has a couple of cards in the suit. If he is unable to discard his cards in that suit, he will have to lead the suit himself at some time. If he has a guess in the suit, he will get it wrong some of the time. If, however, you have five or more cards in your ace high suit, it becomes more reasonable to lead the ace for fear that not taking it will cause it to disappear. If you have four cards in your ace high suit, you can flip a coin and do what fate suggests.

NOTE that all of this is predicated on not having any strong information to suggest otherwise. If your partner bids a suit and you have the ace, leading it is probably OK.

So much for not leading an ace. Everyone likes permission to lead aces so following is a list of times that leading an ace against a slam is a good idea.

But first, my usual caution. DO NOT WORK TOO HARD trying to make these guidelines justify leading an ace against a slam. Leading aces can be good, but because many players have an obsession with this lead, I want caution to be the word rather than automation. Not you nor I nor the vocal opinion giver on your block will do the right thing more than 60% of the time.

1. If your partner has bid a suit strongly or has raised you strongly, leading the ace is a good idea. If your partner has raised your suit relatively quietly, think about leading the ace, but consider another lead first. If partner has bid a suit under duress, think about another lead. For instance, if you make a takeout double and your partner bids a suit, he is not showing anything in the suit other than four cards. If your partner bids a suit in such circumstances, it is almost the same as if he had not bid at all.

2. Leading an ace is right when you think your partner can ruff the next round. This can happen when the opponents paint a picture for you. For example:

W	N	E	S
			1S
P	2C	P	2NT
P	3S	P	4S
P	4NT	P	5H
P	6S	P	P
P			

WEST
♠ 54
♡ QJ65
♦ 63
♣ A9762

Leading the ace of clubs is thoughtful. It goes against the general rule that says don't lead a suit they have bid. Their auction helped you, though. It suggests that North has clubs and South seems to have a balanced hand with two or three clubs. East can have a stiff club so leading the ace and another is a good attempt.

NO ONE VULNERABLE

W	N	E	S
		4H	4S
P	4NT	P	5H
P	6S	P	P
P			

WEST

♠ 7
♡ 32
♢ AJ97642
♣ J73

East has a distributional hand with a long heart suit. Might his distribution not include a singleton diamond? Lead the ace of diamonds. This does not have to work, but I like the effort. Here is the hand you are rooting for.

NORTH

♠ K1082
♡ 8
♢ K10
♣ AQ10852

WEST	**EAST**
♠ 7	♠ 94
♡ 32	♡ KQJ107654
♢ AJ97642	♢ 3
♣ J73	♣ 96

SOUTH

♠ AQJ653
♡ A9
♢ Q85
♣ K4

The ace of diamonds lead is, in fact, the only way to set six spades. Here are two unrelated questions. Would you open four hearts with the East hand? (I would.) And, if you were declarer, would you drop the queen of diamonds at trick one without giving it conscious thought? (You should.) I once saw a defender lead an ace in such a situation and switch to another suit at trick two when declarer falsecarded with the queen.

3. If the opponents have bid strongly and do not have a misfit, is often best to lead an ace in an unbid suit. If the opponents bid a slam and I have an ace in an unbid suit, I will give leading the suit some consideration. The auction on the next page shows such a situation. North-South bid strongly to six hearts and you have the ace of diamonds, an unbid suit. You also have a singleton club. Which will it be?

W	N	E	S
	1C	P	1H
P	3C	P	3H
P	4H	P	4NT
P	5H	P	6H
P	P	P	

WEST

♠ 97652

♡ 105

◇ A9742

♣ 3

Diamonds is an unbid suit. Lead the ace. You hope to take two tricks here in a hurry. An extra incentive for this lead is that the auction tells you they have lots of potential tricks. One lead to avoid is the stiff club. Against a slam, leading a singleton is OK unless you have an ace. When you have an ace, leading a singleton is a virtual no-no unless it is in a suit partner bid.

Leading the stiff club on this hand would be tantamount to saying that you are hoping for a club ruff. In order to get that, you have to get partner in to give you a ruff. If all this happens, you will set them two tricks. Isn't this a little optimistic? Better to lead the ace of diamonds. On a good day, you will be able to take two diamond tricks when the opponents have bid badly. It does happen.

Let me give you some comfort here. Leading aces against a slam is an emotionally easy thing to do. The fear of letting a slam make for failure to cash an ace is strong. Another fearsome thing is to lead an ace and find that you have given away the slam. Clearly, when you have an ace against a slam, whatever you do can have extreme consequences. Try following the guidelines given here. They won't always get you the best result, but they will get you consistently better than average results. When your choice works, you can take the credit. When it doesn't work, you can give me the blame. It won't bother me at all. I make enough bad leads that taking the blame for one more disaster won't faze me at all.

When Is It Right To Lead Away From a King and Other Honor Holdings?

Loosely speaking, leading from kings and queens in unbid suits is a good idea. If your partner has bid the suit, it is a better idea. You want to set up a trick so that when you gain the lead, you have a winner to cash. If you spend your time leading a trump or leading from three or four small cards, your leads will have the same effect on your defense as a sleeping pill on your attention span.

Attacking leads against a slam are not always best, but they are best more times than you think.

W	N	E	S
	1H	P	2D
P	3D	P	4NT
P	5D	P	6D
P	P	P	

WEST

♠ K1032
♡ A75
◇ 92
♣ 9862

The correct lead, at least in theory, is clear cut. You can arrive at it by process of elimination. The ace of hearts is as bad a lead as you can make. You will be helping declarer set up his heart suit for discards. Taking the ace of hearts is a good way to get on to the next hand.

Leading a trump is equally awful. It is a lead you might arrive at if there was not a good lead available, but in this case there is a good lead.

A club lead offers no chance to set up a trick barring a miracle.

Which brings us to a spade lead. If you lead a spade, you give yourself the potential to set up a spade trick. When you get in with your ace of hearts, you may have a spade trick, which will be down one. What does a spade lead require for success? All you need is for partner to have the queen of spades. Isn't this a relatively innocuous wish? Here is a normal setup.

NORTH

♠ 976
♡ KJ863
◇ AJ4
♣ KJ

WEST

♠ K1032
♡ A75
◇ 92
♣ 9862

EAST

♠ Q854
♡ 1094
◇ 5
♣ Q7543

If you lead a spade, six diamonds goes down. If you lead anything else, they make. Compare this hand with the one following. It should look familiar.

SOUTH

♠ AJ
♡ Q2
◇ KQ108763
♣ A10

W	N	E	S
	1H	P	2D
P	3D	P	4NT
P	5D	P	6D
P	P	P	

NORTH
♠ 976
♡ KJ863
◊ AJ4
♣ KJ

WEST
♠ K1032
♡ A75
◊ 92
♣ 9862

EAST
♠ J854
♡ 1094
◊ 5
♣ Q7543

SOUTH
♠ AQ
♡ Q2
◊ KQ108763
♣ A10

The bidding is the same, the lead is the same, but the result isn't. South wins the opening lead and claims. For a second, you may feel that you gave the slam away with your opening lead, but a quick look shows that the contract was cold with any lead. You did the best you could and on a good day might have found the killing lead. Such is life. Such is bridge.

CHAPTER TWENTY ONE

SOME SPECIAL LEAD SITUATIONS

In spite of my trying to give you ideas about opening leads, there is always something that falls out of the normal realm of discussion. This last chapter will cover some special auctions that don't fit the usual mold. Here are the situations covered in this chapter.

1   The opponents preempted.

2.   The auction was very competitive.

3   The opponents bid carefully and informatively and stopped at the five level.

The Opponents Have Preempted To the Two Or Three Level.

When the opponents have preempted, and the preemptor is playing the hand, your defense will be pretty good after the opening lead is made since you will have lots of inferences to draw about declarer's hand. The difficult part is getting the defense off to a good lead.

W	N	E	S
			3S
P	P	P	

WEST

♠ K32
♡ Q8762
◊ 2
♣ AJ62

The singleton diamond sticks out. You can be very optimistic about this lead. Declarer does not rate to have much in any of the side suits so you don't rate to compromise partner's holding in diamonds. If North had bid diamonds and South raised them, you would not lead the stiff diamond because doing so might crush partner's Q83 or some such holding. On this bidding, leading the diamond makes perfect sense.

WEST	Lead the two of hearts. Leading from a broken holding like this is a fair lead
♠ 983	in general. Here, it is better than normal since you are entitled to hope for
♡ KJ62	your partner to produce a useful high card in hearts. A diamond lead requires
◊ Q872	partner to have extra good diamonds for the lead to be effective. Do not lead
♣ A5	the ace of clubs. True, you have a fair chance to find partner with good

clubs, but leading the ace also runs the risk of setting up club tricks for their side. As to leading a trump, that is horrible. An important rule for you to remember is that you should never lead a trump when your RHO has bid the suit all by himself without any hint of support from partner. If you lead a spade, you may find dummy is void and your partner with the Qxx, AJx, KJx, or an assortment of other holdings that are not interested in seeing a trump lead. The trump lead may destroy a trump trick for you, but even if it does not, it concedes vital timing to their side.

WEST	Lead the queen of clubs. Sequence leads combine well with honors in
♠ Q82	partner's hand. The heart suit, while not a bad choice against this auction, is
♡ KJ32	not as good as the club lead. Sequence leads rate right up there on the list of
◊ 1064	good things to lead. As long as you are leading an unbid suit or a suit partner
♣ QJ8	has bid, holdings like the QJ8 are wonderful. Of course, if your LHO has bid

clubs along the way, you would choose a diamond or a heart instead.

The Opponents Open With a Four Or Five Level Preempt.

If your RHO opens with a four or five level preempt, you have more to think about. For starters, you know that RHO has a serious trump suit. Players open three hearts, for instance, with six card suits now and then. They do not open four hearts or five clubs with six card suits. Equally important, you don't know much about LHO's hand. If your RHO bids three spades and LHO passes, you can draw an inference that he doesn't have a good hand with support for partner. If your RHO opens with four spades, your LHO can pass with a pretty good hand.

Curiously, when your RHO opens with a four or five level preempt, leading aces has some merit. Cashing your winners before they go away takes on importance that it did not have at lower levels.

NO ONE VULNERABLE

W	N	E	S
			4S
P	P	P	

WEST
♠ K32
♡ Q8762
◇ 2
♣ AJ62

These next two hands are the same ones you had in the previous paragraphs where your RHO opened three spades. Here, he opened four spades which makes a difference to your opening lead. On this hand, leading the stiff diamond is still a good shot. You know that you will get in with the king of spades and will have a second chance to switch if you need to.

WEST
♠ 983
♡ KJ62
◇ Q872
♣ A5

After an opening four spade bid, you might think about leading the ace of clubs. The heart suit is just attractive enough that I would lead those. If the hearts were the KQ62, leading them would be automatic. It is on hands like the next one that leading aces against high level preempts becomes the proper lead.

WEST
♠ Q82
♡ Q732
◇ A64
♣ J84

After South's four spade bid, no lead is exciting. I suggest the ace of diamonds. Leading aces is not your first choice against a high level preempt, but when nothing else appeals, leading an ace is reasonable.

W	N	E	S
			5D
P	P	P	

WEST
♠ 2
♡ K10762
◇ 32
♣ AQ962

If you had a sequence like the KQ98 or possibly the QJ93, that would be a good start . But you don't. My guess here is the ace of clubs. I can switch to the stiff spade if that is right and a heart if necessary. The higher the preempt, the more likely leading an ace is correct. If, for instance, South opened two spades, I would lead the six of hearts or possibly the three of diamonds. I would not lead the ace of clubs. Against an opening five diamond bid, the ace of clubs becomes a good lead. Remember against a two spade contract, you need six tricks. Against a five diamond contract, you need just three.

In fact, I can accept almost any lead from this hand other than a trump. If you lead that, you deserve to find East with the ace of spades, in which case a spade lead and ruff and your ace of clubs would have set it.

The Auction Was Very Competitive.

When both sides are bidding a lot, your lead goals will change. Before looking at some hands, let me define what I mean by 'a lot'.

W	N	E	S
		1H	2S
3H	3S	P	P
P			

This is a competitive auction, but it does not qualify for a dramatic lead.

W	N	E	S
		1C	3D
3S	5D	DBL	P
P	P		

This almost qualifies. Your side was probably going to game, but North went to five diamonds before you could define your hands. Even though they are at the five level, you don't have to be overly worried about beating them. It is not necessary to be wild here either. You might have something like the following.

WEST
♠ AQ8763
♡ Q103
◊ 4
♣ Q98

They have a fit and may be planning to take some tricks on a cross-ruff. I would lead a club, partner's suit, or a trump. It is close. I would not lead the ace of spades. When you *know* the opponents are saving, you should make a normal lead.

Auctions like the following do qualify for 'a lot'.

NO ONE VULNERABLE

W	N	E	S
1S	2C	2H	3D
4H	5D	5H	6D
P	P	DBL	P
P	P		

WEST
♠ AQ10872
♡ QJ742
◊ Q
♣ J

If you would have bid six hearts rather than defend, that is not a terrible choice. If you do decide to defend, start with the ace of spades. If you look at the stiff club, make sure you don't do anything else with it, such as leading it. Leading a club is the best way in the world to let them make their bid. On hands such as this, setting the opponents is the important thing. Setting them two or three is secondary. Lead the ace of spades and go from there.

NORTH-SOUTH VULNERABLE

W	N	E	S
	1C	2H	3D
4H	5D	P	P
5H	P	P	6D
P	P	P	

WEST

♠ KQ10732

♡ K107

♢ 3

♣ AK3

Lead the king of spades. Leading a club may cost the contract. Here is the complete hand.

                NORTH
                ♠ A86
                ♡ 3
                ♢ KQ42
                ♣ QJ1098

WEST	EAST
♠ KQ10732	♠ 54
♡ K107	♡ QJ9654
♢ 3	♢ 10
♣ AK3	♣ 7652

                SOUTH
                ♠ J9
                ♡ A82
                ♢ AJ98765
                ♣ 4

West leads the king of spades, taken by dummy's ace. At trick two, declarer leads a club, won by West. West can take the queen of spades and that is it for the defense. If West leads a club, South has time to set up a club for a spade discard. If you think about it, leading the king of clubs can hardly gain. Only if you can take two clubs and a ruff will leading clubs be right. If you have two clubs tricks, you will always get them. It is when you have just one club trick that you don't dare lead one lest the hand be as shown here.

The Opponents Bid Carefully and Informatively and Stop At the Five Level

If you pay attention, you can make some remarkable leads. Great inspiration often occurs when the opponents get to the five level on their own initiative. Getting to the five level is just a short step removed from getting to a slam. Sometimes, the opponents did in fact look for a slam and have elected to stay out of it. When this happens, you should have a lot of information to help you with your lead. Also, since they stopped in five, it is likely that your side has some important assets which you can use to advantage.

W	N	E	S
			1S
P	2D	P	3D
P	3S	P	4D
P	4H	P	4NT
P	5D	P	5S
P	P	P	

WEST

♠ A76
♡ J10985
◇ 2
♣ J762

I spent a chapter discussing why you should not lead a singleton diamond after both opponents bid them. Here, you can expect your partner to have an ace so after leading the diamond, you have a plan. If East has the ace of diamonds, you get the first two tricks and your ace of spades. If East does not have the ace of diamonds, you intend to get in with the ace of spades, lead to whichever ace East has and get your diamond ruff that way. Why do you think East has an ace? You think so because they tried for slam via cue-bidding and Blackwood. It looks like they stopped in five spades because of two missing aces.

W	N	E	S
	1D	P	1H
P	2H	P	3C
P	3D	P	4D
P	4H	P	5H
P	P	P	

Without looking at your hand, you should lead a spade. They had a strong auction which ended with South's begging North to go to slam if he has spades stopped. North said no to the invitation. I can't imagine not leading a spade against this auction. Here is an extreme example of listen to the bidding and finding the killing lead. Here is the West hand on lead against the auction above. What card do you select?

WEST

♠ AJ4
♡ 863
◇ 762
♣ J873

Which spade did you lead? If you did not lead a spade, you did not pay attention to the auction. South asked North for a spade stopper and North denied one. If South had the king of spades, he would bid a slam himself and North just said he does not have it. The conclusion? Your partner has the king of spades.

Assuming you agree that your partner has the king of spades, you must decide that a spade is right and then to lead one. Which one do you lead?

You might think of leading the ace of spades and if you do, you will take the first two spade tricks. But that is all.

Refer to the next page to see how you did.

NORTH
♠ 872
♡ KQ7
♢ AQJ94
♣ 109

WEST
♠ AJ4
♡ 863
♢ 762
♣ J873

EAST
♠ K1065
♡ 94
♢ 1085
♣ 6542

The four of spades lead gets you three quick tricks for down one. The ace of spades lead gets you minus six hundred and fifty points. The jack of spades is too obscure to consider. Any other lead gets you no tricks at all.

SOUTH
♠ Q93
♡ AJ1052
♢ K3
♣ AKQ

Remember to listen to the bidding. On those occasions where the opponents tell you as much as they do here, you can use that information to advantage. Listen up and follow through!

AN OPENING LEAD QUIZ

The quiz section that follows is a little bit different than those you have seen in the past. Instead of giving you one hand and one auction, you are going to get one hand and multiple auctions.

Most of the time, the final contract will be the same. The auction, however, will be different. You should find your opening leads are not always the same.

Once in awhile, the final contract will not be the same. When this happens, it will be to show a theme and its variations.

Throughout the quiz, you are West. I hope you don't mind not always having good cards and easy choices.

Good luck.

#1	W	N	E	S
				1NT
	P	3NT	P	P
	P			

No One Vulnerable

#2	W	N	E	S
				1D
	P	1S	P	2NT
	P	3NT	P	P
	P			

WEST
♠ 87
♡ QJ7
◇ J9763
♣ A63

#3	W	N	E	S
		1H	P	2D
	P	2H	P	2NT
	P	3NT	P	P
	P			

1. Lead the six of diamonds. North didn't use Stayman so he will have seven or more minor suit cards. He may have four or five diamonds, in which case this lead will not work. A second choice exists in the queen of hearts. This lead can work well if partner has four or five hearts to an honor. The trouble with this lead is that it can blow your heart stopper. Since a diamond lead requires much less from partner to work, it is the best lead. Note that you have some potential entries. You can hope to get in to use the diamonds if they can be set up.

2. Lead the queen of hearts. South bid diamonds, which is discouraging. On some auctions, it is good to lead into the person who bid a suit, but not when they rate to have a strong suit. Given that diamonds won't work, you can fall back on the queen of hearts. A three card holding headed by a sequence is appealing as long as it is an unbid suit. If partner fits your lead, it will be effective. Recognizing that your first choice is bad, you should be pleased to have an alternative lead as good as this one. Don't lead the doubleton spade. It requires too much from partner to make the lead effective.

3. Lead the three of clubs. Both hearts and diamonds sound awful. Can a case be made for spades or clubs? You have eight points, which leaves room for partner to have eight himself. He might have bid one spade if he had a good five card suit. He didn't. While a club lead offers no guarantees, it does have chances. You might think that a spade is a safe lead in that it can't hurt. That isn't true. If partner has four spades to the queen, for example, you will give declarer four spade tricks while gaining nothing for yourself. Here is a second way to view the club lead versus the spade lead. If partner has four cards in each suit, a club lead may let you use partner's long card. A spade lead won't do much for partner's spades, even if they are quite good.

#1	W	N	E	S
				1S
	P	1NT	P	3H
	P	3S	P	4S
	P	P	P	

#2	W	N	E	S
				1C
	P	1H	P	1S
	P	2S	P	3S
	P	4S	P	P
	P			

WEST
♠ 1086
♡ AJ86
◊ K10942
♣ 5

#3	W	N	E	S	
			2H	3S*	*Strong
	4H	4S	P	P	
	P				

1. Lead the six of spades. DO NOT lead the ten. It might cost a trick. The bidding is so strong that you can't really hope for East to have enough strength to get in and give you club ruffs. What you can do for sure, though, is remove dummy's ruffing power. You can see two or three heart tricks in your hand if declarer is not allowed to ruff them in dummy. This sequence strongly dictates a trump lead. Your heart holding confirms this.

2. Lead the ten of diamonds. The lead to avoid is a singleton club. Never lead a singleton in a suit declarer has bid. You will play a high price even on hands when you get your ruff. You probably should not lead a trump either although it might turn out to be a safe lead on this hand. You don't have any reason to expect dummy to be ruffing clubs. Diamonds is the unbid suit and as such is always a serious contender for the opening lead. The auction suggests a diamond lead and your diamond holding does so too. Be happy you have the K109 of diamonds. It means you don't have to wish for much from partner. Be sure you lead the ten. If you lead the four, it can cost a trick (Chapter10).

3. Lead the ace of hearts. Leading aces is terrible in general so you need a strong reason for leading one. This happens here. East opened a weak two bid showing a good suit. You can lead an ace when partner does this. If East had opened with ONE heart, you wouldn't have enough assurance of a good suit to lead the ace. NOTE South's bidding. His three spade bid shows a good hand that needs only a little from partner to make a game. It is not a weak bid. South has something like this: AKQ754, 2, QJ5, AJ9. Incidentally, if the vulnerability was different, you should put pressure on North-South by jumping to five hearts at your first turn.

#1	W	N	E	S
		1C	1H	1S
	P	2S	P	4S
	P	P	P	

WEST
♠ 873
♡ 1063
◊ Q3
♣ K9732

#2	W	N	E	S
			1NT	2S
	P	P	P	

#3	W	N	E	S
		1H	P	1S
	P	2S	P	P
	P			

1. Lead the three of hearts. One thousand curses on you if you lead the ten of hearts and may your finesses never win if you lead the queen of diamonds. When your partner overcalls, you lead his suit unless you know what to lead. GUESSING that a diamond lead is good is nice for the company that sells ulcer medication but it is frustrating beyond anything for your partner. As to which heart to lead, you should never lead the ten or nine from three card or longer holdings unless it is part of a sequence (Chapter 17).

2. Lead the three of clubs or the queen of diamonds. The club lead is safer since you can count on partner to have something in clubs. The queen of diamonds is more dynamic and because partner rates to have values there, too, going for a ruff is semi-sensible. The problem with the queen of diamonds is that if it is wrong, the loss is great. Leading doubleton honors is risky in the best of times. Had partner opened with one diamond and South overcalled two spades, the queen of diamonds would stand out. Absolutely do not lead a trump. Lead trumps when you know they are right.

3. Lead the three of clubs. It is a reasonable lead in comparison with the alternatives. There is nothing exciting about any lead. In such circumstances, go ahead and lead something that has potential. Clubs is an unbid suit which suggests they are OK. There is a chance that a trump can work out. But I would not try it. My heart holding suggests declarer will be able to set them up for discards. You should not lead hearts for obvious reasons and diamonds are dangerous by definition. You want informed motivation to lead doubleton honors and on this hand you have only wishful thinking.

#1	W	N	E	S
	1D	DBL	4D	4H
	5D	5H	P	P
	P			

Problem Four
East-West Vulnerable

WEST
♠ A52
♡ 6
♦ AQJ76
♣ 5432

#2	W	N	E	S
			3S	4H
	4S	5H	P	P
	P			

1. Lead the ace of diamonds. When your partner bids or raises a suit strongly, it is acceptable to lead an ace. Your partner jumped to four diamonds, which qualifies nicely. Before leading the ace of diamonds, you should look for another lead, but on this hand, having looked elsewhere, you should feel comfortable that the ace of diamonds is right.

2. Lead the two of spades. Yes, I have stated at least ten times that you should not underlead an ace. It is good advice. The reason I suggest the two of spades is that you are desperate for partner to get in. You hope, in fact you rather expect, that declarer has the king of diamonds. If so, you want your partner to lead a diamond through declarer's king. The only way to get him in is with a spade. If you make the otherwise correct lead of the ace of spades, declarer will ruff the next spade and later, after drawing trumps, will discard a diamond on dummy's clubs. You will still get a diamond, but it will be only your second trick. This hand is in here for the reason that you must not be dominated by rules. Rules are good and normally will get you sound results. DO NOT use this hand as an excuse for underleading an ace just because you were moved to do so. In my estimation, you will correctly underlead an ace once every four or five thousand hands. By this reckoning, you will underlead an ace once every two years.

#1	W	N	E	S
				1H
	P	3H	P	4H
	P	P	DBL	P
	P	P		

Problem Five
East-West Vulnerable

#2	W	N	E	S
				1H
	P	1S	DBL	2H
	P	4H	P	P
	P			

WEST
- ♠ Q97653
- ♡ 107
- ◊ 932
- ♣ A3

#3	W	N	E	S
			1D	1H
	1S	2H	3D	3H
	P	4H	P	P
	P			

#4	W	N	E	S
	P	1C	P	1H
	P	3H	P	4H
	P	P	P	

1. Lead the three (!) of spades. This auction should sound odd to you. Your partner doesn't have a pile of trumps since you have two of them yourself. If partner had lots of high cards, he probably would have been heard from earlier. You should lead a spade and trust that your partner has made a lead directing double. This is a rare situation but when it comes up, you should know what it means. When partner doubles most unexpectedly, consider that he is looking for a special lead (Chapter 3, Part 8). Partner's hand is: ♠ — ♡ J83 ◊ K8754 ♣ KJ875. If you lead the ace of clubs, you can't beat four hearts any more. You need the ace of clubs as an entry to give partner a second ruff.

2. Lead the ace of clubs. Ace-leaders out there can rejoice. On this sequence, East made a takeout double showing diamonds and clubs. In essence, he bid both minor suits. Leading a doubleton ace is not that high on the list, but it does rate well when your partner has bid the suit for you. To a lesser extent it might be OK to lead a doubleton ace in an unbid suit.

224

3. Lead the two of diamonds. There is no reason to lead another suit, but there is a question about which diamond to lead. There are many available opinions about this. My suggestion (from Chapter 16) is that you lead low from three small cards except in certain circumstances. If you lead the nine, there is a danger that your partner will think you have two of them. These two similar hands show why.

NORTH
♠ AK62
♡ 8653
◇ J10
♣ 976

NORTH
♠ AK62
♡ 8653
◇ J10
♣ 976

WEST	EAST	WEST	EAST
♠ Q9873	♠ J4	♠ Q9873	♠ J4
♡ 102	♡ J	♡ 102	♡ J
◇ 93	◇ AKQ874	◇ 932	◇ AKQ874
♣ K843	♣ QJ52	♣ K83	♣ QJ52

SOUTH
♠ 105
♡ AKQ974
◇ 652
♣ A10

SOUTH
♠ 105
♡ AKQ974
◇ 65
♣ A104

East will win the first two rounds of diamonds. If he thinks you have two of them, a reasonable conclusion, he may decide to lead another diamond. If the diagram on the left is the one that exists, East's defense will work. West will ruff the third diamond with the ten of hearts and later the defense gets a club trick. If it turns out that life is as in the right hand diagram, the third diamond will be the only losing defense. Declarer will get rid of a club loser and will get his ten tricks. My guidelines won't be perfect, but they will make decisions a little easier.

4. Lead the six of spades. This is a boring lead problem that doesn't rate to teach anything dramatic. I can give you a good piece of advice though. If you never make a silly lead and if you don't allow yourself to over think yourself into making a genius lead, your leads will be better. It is not as if you will always make a good lead. It is that you will make more reasonable leads and fewer bad ones. Here there is no reason to lead the ace of clubs. Dummy bid them. A trump lead is actually dangerous. A doubleton ten spot can be important in trumps. Leading one can cost you a trick. Aside from this, there is no indication that a trump is wise. Choosing between the spade suit and the diamond suit is easy. Both are unbid suits which hints that they are leadable. Better to lead from a holding where you have something than from one where you don't.

#1	W	N	E	S
	P̄	1C	P	1H
	P	1NT	P	2H
	P	P	P	

WEST

♠ KQ5
♡ J542
◊ J
♣ QJ752

#2	W	N	E	S
				1H
	P	1S	P	2D
	P	2H	P	P
	P			

#3	W	N	E	S
				1H
	P	1S	P	2H
	P	P	P	

1. Lead the king of spades. Why lead a spade instead of the singleton diamond? Here is a sensational rule. If you have four trumps, getting ruffs should not be a priority. Put yourself in declarer's place. Do you not remember how hard it is to play in a 5-2 fit? You have to draw trump, which is a tough task when they divide 4-2. In the meantime, to make matters worse, they have established a suit and are leading it repetitively. To stop their suit, you must ruff in with one of your treasured trumps. Doesn't that sound familiar? 5-2 trump fits are not fun.

   West should keep this in mind. Rather than lead a stiff diamond and try for ruffs, West should lead the king of spades and hope that spades can be used to make declarer ruff. West's J542 of hearts are gold for the defense. They should not be used for ruffs when they rate to take a trick or two on their own. Leading a singleton when you have four trumps is so bad in general that you should lead the king of spades even if you have the 5432 of hearts.

2. Lead the queen of clubs. Once again the opponents are in what may be a 5-2 fit. Lead clubs and try to make declarer use his trumps to control the club suit. The difference between this hand and the prior is that spades were unbid on the first hand and clubs were unbid on this one.

3. Lead the queen of clubs, an unbid suit. South has promised six hearts on this auction. Still, trying for ruffs when you have four trump is a poor idea. If you led the jack of diamonds on any of these three auctions, you should reconsider. Had East bid diamonds, the diamond lead would be fine. Leading partner's suit is usually acceptable.

#1	W	N	E	S
				1NT
	P	3NT	P	P
	P			

Problem Seven
No One Vulnerable

WEST
♠ J974
♡ Q2
◇ A8
♣ Q8542

#2	W	N	E	S
		1D	P	1NT
	P	2NT	P	3NT
	P	P	P	

#3	W	N	E	S
				1H
	P	2D	P	2NT
	P	3NT	P	P
	P			

1. Choose between the four of spades and the four of clubs. The clubs are better but you should worry that North did not ask for a major suit. North has seven or more minor suit cards. If dummy has four clubs to, say, the J1063, it will be difficult to set them up. Clubs will be right some of the time. I am not saying they are not leadable. You could have the first five clubs. I merely doubt that they will be right a high percentage of the time. The reason for leading spades is that North's denial of a major suit hints that he may be weak in one or both majors. It is a close call actually which suit will work best. If you had just four clubs and four spades, the spade suit would be best by a lot.

2. Lead the four of spades. When South bid notrump, he denied a major suit. He may, however, have four or five clubs. Again, this is not a guaranteed fact, but the evidence suggests it is likely. This is frustrating hand in that if you lead a spade, the dummy might have 4-4-4-1 shape with a stiff club. In this case your spade lead will be futile and a club lead, in retrospect, outstanding. Some hands just do not come with assurances. Here is a possible hand for declarer to have.
♠ K3 ♡ J104 ◇ 1095 ♣ KJ976. It can happen.

3. Lead the four of clubs. This auction does not have the hidden inferences about clubs and spades. East is just as likely to have some clubs and spades. Lead your best suit with a clear conscience. Here is a possible hand for declarer to have.
♠ K105 ♡ AJ1083 ◇ J4 ♣ A97. South's spades and clubs are relatively equal, which they were not on the previous auction.

W	N	E	S
			1D
2S	3C	P	3D
P	3S	P	3NT
P	P	P	

Problem Eight
North-South Vulnerable

WEST
♠ KJ9753
♡ J108
♢ 96
♣ 72

#2

W	N	E	S
	1D	2C	2NT
P	3NT	P	P
P			

#3

W	N	E	S
			1NT
P	2C	P	2H
P	3NT	P	P
P			

#4

W	N	E	S
	1D	P	1NT
P	2NT	P	3NT
P	P	P	

1.   Lead the jack of hearts. Afraid that your partner might have the ace of spades and that you can take the first six tricks? This is impossible if you are playing with a thoughtful partner. If your partner has the ace or queen of spades, he should have doubled three spades to tell you that the lead was safe. Your partner might have two or three little spades, but he should not have an honor. The opponents did not look for hearts. There is a chance that he has four or five good ones and will appreciate a heart lead.

2.   Lead the seven of clubs. When your partner makes a two level overcall, he needs a good suit. Lead it. A spade lead could be best, but the number of times a spade lead is right is less than the number of times a club lead is best. An opening bid does not promise a good suit necessarily, but an overcalled suit does, especially a two level overcall. Be good to your partner.

3.   Before finding a lead, let's think about what their bidding shows. South opened a 15-17 point one notrump. North bid two clubs, asking for a major suit. South showed hearts. This caused North to bid three notrump. Why did North bid two clubs if he was not interested in hearts? The answer is that he must have been interested in spades. North has four of them for sure. As if you were looking over North's shoulder, you can see the four spades as clearly now as you will be able to see them when North puts the dummy on the table. This means your partner

has one spade or no spades. It will be an impossible task to get this suit established.

Assuming that a spade lead is hopeless, what should West lead? Let's look further at the clues. When North bid two clubs, East said pass. If East had good enough clubs for a club lead to work, East might have doubled two clubs. He didn't. I would reject the club suit too. This leaves you with two suits to choose from.

Lead the jack of hearts. This is definitely an expert conclusion (end of Chapter 11). You know declarer has four hearts (we hope not five). If you are reasonably lucky, your partner will have four hearts too. Your J108 of hearts will combine nicely with your partner's hearts if he happens to have a heart honor. Since you have only five points, your partner is entitled to have as many as ten. It is not asking too much to make the jack of hearts a killing lead.

4.   Believe it or not, if you gave this hand to a panel of experts, there would not be one standout answer. They would be equally torn between leading the fourth best spade and the jack of hearts. If East has a spade honor, a spade lead gets you off to a good start. If East has no spade honor, you will almost never set up the suit and even if you do, you won't be able to take your tricks, barring a miracle. The jack of hearts lead will work well most of the time, but it is not a powerful lead like the spade is. If you lead a heart, you run the risk that they will take the first ten tricks when you could have taken the first six yourself. The point of this problem is the same point I have made so often before. There are many hands which do have a clear lead. Even a hand as simple as this one can be a pain.

RULE - There is no set of rules

that will always get you off to the winning lead.

RULE - Your partner's hindsight is usually better

at opening leads than you are.

#1	W	N	E	S
				1C
	P	1H	P	1NT
	P	P	P	

Problem Nine
East-West Vulnerable

WEST
♠ 97
♡ KJ653
◇ K873
♣ Q4

#2	W	N	E	S
		1C	P	1NT
	P	P	P	

1. Lead the three of diamonds. A heart lead will go nowhere. Your partner has one or two hearts maximum. North rates to have four hearts to the ten at least and can have Q1082, which will put paid to your intentions of setting up the hearts. You might think about the nine of spades. If you think about the bidding, though, you will remember that East, who can have nine or ten points, did not bid one spade. He does not rate to have five fair spades. If he has four of them, it means a spade lead will be right into the opponents' seven card fit. This is an unpleasant hand to lead from when you know that your best suit is not a good choice. Basically, you are hoping that by not leading a heart, you will have avoided a bad lead. You are not hoping that you are finding a great lead.

2. Sometimes during a lecture I present some quiz questions. Once in awhile, I wonder if some players don't work too hard with their opening leads. On this hand, I and 99% of the players in the world would lead the five of hearts. Neither opponent has suggested they have hearts. Hearts is your longest suit and you have good honors. Leading a heart seems automatic. Yet some players find a reason for either a spade lead or a diamond lead. They inform me that they don't want to give away a free heart trick or some such reason. My advice is that after you finish this book, you do the following when on opening lead. Take the card that looks best to you and mentally hold it in readiness. Your instincts rate to be pretty good. Then, before releasing the card on the table, ask yourself if there are any guidelines that suggest another lead. Fretting should be your least important concern rather than your driving concern.

#1	W	N	E	S
				1S
	P	2S	DBL	3S*
	P	P	P	

*Competitive

WEST
♠ 872
♡ K2
♢ J8763
♣ Q106

#2	W	N	E	S
		1D	P	1S
	P	3S	P	P
	P			

#3	W	N	E	S
				1NT
	P	2H*	P	2S
	P	2NT	P	3S
	P	P	P	

*Transfer

1. Lead the king of hearts. East's takeout double suggested heart strength. Leading a doubleton honor is not a good idea unless you have input about that suit from partner. Had East not doubled two spades, leading the king of hearts would be very scary. Incidentally, did you think about bidding four diamonds over three spades? It was worth a thought.

2. Lead the two of spades. Declarer has a wretched hand opposite a seventeen count. Since you have diamonds stopped, you aren't worried that declarer will draw trumps and run diamonds forever. Start a spade and let declarer guess his way through the hand. Do not lead the king of hearts on this one.

3. Lead the two of spades. Partner didn't double two hearts so there is no excuse for leading them. Leading against a strong notrump opener can be difficult if you don't have a safe sequence lead. Declarer is known to have high cards so leading from broken holdings like the Q106 of clubs is nervous stuff. The diamonds are not promising either. They would be fine to lead against a notrump contract, but not when a one or two notrump opening bidder is playing in a suit.

#1	W	N	E	S
				4S
	P	P	P	

Problem Eleven

No One Vulnerable

#2	W	N	E	S
				1S
	P	3S	P	4S
	P	P	P	

WEST
♠ 74
♡ 98
◊ AQ63
♣ K8763

#3	W	N	E	S
				1S
	P	2NT	P	3H
	P	3S	P	4S
	P	P	P	

1. Lead the ace of diamonds. Leads against high level preempts are never easy because you know so little about the hand. Usually when the opponents play at the four level, there has been some bidding. Not this time. NOTE that leading the ace of diamonds is not a routine lead. If you had the KQ of clubs, you would lead them instead. Against high level preempts, leading an ace becomes a moderately acceptable lead as opposed to a taboo lead, but it is still not a priority lead. My second choice is between a club and a heart with the club getting the nod. Either can work. One lead I will not make with this hand is a spade. Never lead a trump against an auction like this one. Declarer got himself to four spades without a whisper of support from partner. For all you know, dummy is void in spades. Your partner, holding the Jxxx or the Qxx, will not be amused with your choice. All in all, it is scary to be on lead against such a sequence when you don't have an easy choice.

2. Oh, my. Don't lead diamonds. Otherwise, make your best guess. There will be days like this. The opponents have had an uninformative sequence and you are going to pay a price for it. The less you know about the opponents' hands, the less likely you will find the correct lead. Keep this kind of bidding in mind when you are bidding. If you go in for slow, super-scientific auctions, you may get to good contracts, but you will also get informed opening leads. NOTE the difference between this situation and the next one where the opponents' bidding was more descriptive.

3. Lead the six of clubs. Neither major is worth leading. It has to be one of the minor suits. Since leading the ace of diamonds is pretty terrible, the club is your choice. Yes, leading a club can be ineffective. At least it has a chance. It is likely that dummy has the king of diamonds and leading the ace will establish a trick for declarer.

NORTH		NORTH	
♠ J85		♠ J85	
♡ K104		♡ K104	
◊ KJ82		◊ KJ82	
♣ A52		♣ AJ2	

WEST	EAST	WEST	EAST
♠ 74	♠ K63	♠ 74	♠ K63
♡ 98	♡ J53	♡ 98	♡ J53
◊ AQ63	◊ 9754	◊ AQ63	◊ 9754
♣ K8763	♣ J94	♣ K8763	♣ Q104

SOUTH		SOUTH	
♠ AQ1092		♠ AQ1092	
♡ AQ762		♡ AQ762	
◊ 10		◊ 10	
♣ Q10		♣ 95	

In the left hand diagram, West leads the six of clubs and feels a sinking sensation when declarer calls for the two. South wins East's jack with the queen, leaving West wondering about his choice. Sooner or later, West gets his ace of diamonds and declarer takes twelve tricks via the spade finesse. You can bet that West and East are both scrutinizing the North-South hands now. It turns out that West's lead did not cost a trick. It created a heart-stopping moment for West at trick one, but since South could lead toward the king of diamonds and set up a trick for a club discard, nothing mattered.

In the right hand diagram, the club lead is necessary. It sets up a club trick before South can set up and use the king of diamonds. All this adds up to a simple overtrick, but it could also be the setting trick that is stake.

#1	W	N	E	S
		1C	1H	1S
	4H	4S	P	P
	P			

Problem Twelve

North-South Vulnerable

WEST
♠ 32
♡ K9762
◊ J865
♣ 104

#2	W	N	E	S
				1S
	P	2C	P	2S
	P	4S	P	P
	P			

#3	W	N	E	S
				2NT
	P	3C	P	3S
	P	4S	P	P
	P			

1. Lead the king of hearts. Your side has at most one heart trick coming. If you lead low, your partner will win the trick but he may not be able to do anything constructive from his side of the table. If you lead the king, you rate to win the trick. This will allow you to make whatever shift is indicated. Perhaps it will be right to switch to diamonds. Perhaps a club is best. This lead is more common than you might think. Holding four or five cards headed by the king in partner's suit, leading the king can be effective since it allows you to remain on lead for a switch if that is best and to continue hearts if that looks right.

2. Lead the six of hearts. Attack. They have strength AND they have a source of tricks in clubs. Leading from a king in an unbid suit is often a good idea. Against auctions like this one, it is even more likely to succeed. The other unbid suit, diamonds, is unattractive since it has only a jack to contribute. When the opponents have a fit, game points, and a known side suit to use for tricks, you can't afford to be passive. It is not the worst thing to lead from a jack, but it is not a good thing either. The heart suit rates as the only real choice here.

3. Lead the two of spades. It is very dangerous to lead from these red suit holdings after an opening two notrump bid. In a similar vein, it is wrong to lead a club. You frequently lead passively when your RHO opens two notrump and later plays in a suit contract. Had East doubled three clubs, you would have led them.

#1	W	N	E	S
				1S
	P	2NT	P	3H
	P	4D	P	4NT
	P	5D	P	6H
	P	P	P	

Problem Thirteen

No One Vulnerable

WEST
♠ A8632
♡ 8
◇ 10987
♣ Q53

#2	W	N	E	S
		1D	P	1H
	P	1S	P	2C*
	P	2H	P	3D
	P	4H	P	4NT
	P	5H	P	6H
	P	P	P	

*Fourth suit forcing

#3	W	N	E	S
				1NT
	P	2D*	P	2H
	P	4C**	P	4S
	P	6H	P	P
	P			

*Transfer to hearts
*Asking for aces

1. Lead the ace of spades. Finding this lead is a simple function of listening to the bidding. South opened one spade and North bid two notrump showing a balanced game forcing hand. South eventually ended up in six hearts. Simple arithmetic shows that South has five spades or more and North has two spades or more, which means East has one spade or fewer. Lead the ace of spades and give East a ruff. Just because you have a bad hand does not mean you can quit thinking.

2. Lead the three of clubs. Here is the idea. South's two club bid is what they call the 'Fourth suit forcing'. He is not bidding clubs so much as he is starting a forcing auction. Standard bidding has its difficult moments when you have a good hand and no comfortable way to tell partner. The 'Fourth suit forcing' was invented to cater to these hands. By the time the bidding was over, South had shown a heart suit that didn't need much support, diamond support for North, and possibly a singleton spade. South might have all the club honors, but he might just have the ace. If so, leading a club gives you a chance to set up a trick to cash when you get in with the ace of spades. If you lead the spade ace, you rate to set up a trick or two for declarer's immediate use.

3. Lead the ten of diamonds. Some useful things happened in this bidding. Your partner did not double four clubs. He might have done so if he wanted a club lead. NOTE, by the way, that you did not double four spades. Why tell the opponents where the ace of spades is when you are going to be on lead yourself? One more point. Keep your fingers off the ace of spades. The notrump bidder is on your right so you rate to be giving up a free trick to declarer's king. Leading the stiff heart is too awful to think about. The ten of diamonds is an easy choice to fall back on. It is safe and there are no arguments against it.

#1	W	N	E	S
	P	P	1S	2H
	4S	5H	5S	P
	P	6H	DBL	P
	P	P		

Problem Fourteen
East-West Vulnerable

WEST
♠ QJ109
♡ 8
◊ 1097432
♣ K2

#2	W	N	E	S
				1H
	P	2D	P	3C
	P	4H	P	4NT
	P	5H	P	6H
	P	P	DBL	P
	P	P		

#3	W	N	E	S
				1H
	P	2NT	P	3D
	P	3H	P	4C
	P	4NT	P	5S
	P	6H	DBL	P
	P	P		

#4	W	N	E	S
			3S	4H
	4S	4NT	P	5D
	P	6H	DBL	P
	P	P		

1.   Lead the queen of spades. When your side is bidding strongly and the opponents compete, it is likely that they are sacrificing in the hopes of going down less than the value of your game. If you can make five spades, you get 650 points. If they can go down 300 or 500 in six hearts, they will show a profit. On this auction, East went on to five spades when North bid five hearts but doubled North's six heart call. In essence, East is saying to North, "enough is enough." East's double is not lead directing. It is saying that your side is high enough and will have to be content with whatever penalty is available against six hearts. There is nothing in East's double to suggest a special lead. The queen of spades is your normal lead and there is nothing in your hand to suggest another lead. Leading the king of clubs is unacceptable. NOTE, incidentally, West's good four spade bid. West can see that bidding two spades will be ineffective. Better to bid four and put pressure on the opponents. The bid is defined as showing good trumps and shape and not many high cards, which is just what you have.

2.   Lead the four of diamonds. This is the classic lead-directing double. North probably has a diamond void and hopes to get a ruff plus some other trick. A lead-directing double of a slam indicates your partner wants you to lead dummy's first bid suit. On this hand, your six diamonds make a diamond ruff for partner a likely message, so that is your choice. NOTE that partner will look at your opening lead and will try to draw a suit preference inference from it. By leading the four, you hope partner will realize you are indifferent about what he returns at trick two.

236

3.   Lead the four of diamonds. There will be auctions where a lead-directing double can't mean to lead dummy's first bid suit since he may not have bid a suit. That happens here. North bid a natural two notrump and then showed heart support. South cue-bid four clubs (not Gerber for aces) and North decided he had the missing cards that South needed for slam. After Blackwood, North went to six hearts. East's double is either lead directing or perhaps he has the QJ109 of hearts and is doubling because they have gotten to an unmakeable slam. West can't tell what East's intentions are so treats it as if it was a lead-directing double. What do you think the double asks for? Since dummy didn't bid a suit, the double asks for the lead of one of opener's suits. With this hand, West can see that East is ruffing diamonds so leads one.

NORTH
♠ A85
♡ KJ5
◊ K85
♣ QJ97

WEST   EAST   The diamond lead is necessary to defeat six hearts. Of
♠ QJ109   ♠ K7643   note is that if someone runs to six notrump, that will
♡ 8   ♡ 9432   be cold without a spade lead and will require a finesse
◊ 1097432   ◊ —   if a spade is led. In this case, the club finesse loses so
♣ K2   ♣ 8543   six notrump will go down. All very exciting. If you
                                    were East, would you know to lead a spade if your
          SOUTH   opponents ran to six notrump?
          ♠ 2
          ♡ AQ1076
          ◊ AQJ6
          ♣ A106

4.   Lead a diamond. Once again, East's double is lead-directing. The opponents haven't bid any suits at all other than the trump suit so the double has yet a third meaning. East's double says that six hearts will go down if West guesses the right lead. Spades is out of the question because that is the suit that West would lead without East's double. A lead-directing double is very specific about that. It says, among other things, that the opening leader must lead something besides the East-West suit. Once West puts his mind to it, it is easy to see that East is looking for a diamond ruff . For his double East can have either of these two hands: ♠ AK87542 ♡ 1072 ◊ — ♣ J64 or ♠ K876542 ♡ 762 ◊ — ♣ QJ8. On the first hand, East reasonably hopes he can get a diamond ruff and a spade trick. No guarantees, but fair hopes. On the second hand, East wants a diamond ruff and has only a prayer for a second trick. East's double is still reasonable since it is possible that East-West have an ace somewhere in addition to the diamond ruff. Another way of looking at East's problem is to say that defeating the slam without a diamond ruff is unlikely. Doubling gives East the best chance to go plus on the hand.

#1	W	N	E	S
				3NT*
	P	P	P	

Problem Fifteen

No One Vulnerable

*Long solid minor

#2	W	N	E	S
		1S	P	1NT
	P	2NT	P	3NT
	P	P	P	

WEST
- ♠ 73
- ♡ QJ95
- ◊ AQ105
- ♣ 852

#3	W	N	E	S
		1H	P	1S
	P	2H	P	2NT
	P	3NT	P	P
	P			

1.   Lead the ace of diamonds. This is an unusual lead for sure. The reason for this lead is that you know they will have or probably will have enough tricks when they get in. The idea behind the ace of diamonds lead is that you want to see dummy in order to judge whether to lead more diamonds, switch to hearts, or switch to spades. This is just about the only sequence to three notrump where leading the ace of diamonds is correct.

2.   Lead the queen of hearts. If you had the QJ62 of hearts, your correct lead would be the two of hearts. It is because you have the nine, giving you a more substantial sequence, that you lead the queen.

3.   Lead the eight of clubs. This is one of those cases where you lead high from three small against notrump. You want partner to lead diamonds if he gets in. If he wastes his entries leading clubs, thinking he is setting up your suit, the defense will go nowhere. The other leads are poor. Declarer bid spades. Leading from two or three or four little cards into the person who bid the suit is just lunacy. Leading a heart is also futile given that North bid them twice. A diamond lead is uncertain since you don't want to give up a free trick. Leading from a five card suit headed by the AQ against notrump is OK since you hope to lose one trick and get back four. With the AQ105 of diamonds, you can hope for all four tricks without losing one first. Perhaps your partner has the jack of diamonds and an entry or two. The club lead can obviously work poorly if declarer is loaded there, but the reasons for leading clubs are valid in principle. Have I mentioned yet that it is not easy to make good leads all of the time?

#1	W	N	E	S
				1C
	P	1H	P	1NT
	P	P	P	

Problem Sixteen

No One Vulnerable

WEST
♠ 63
♡ QJ1075
◇ A42
♣ J104

#2	W	N	E	S
		1C	P	1NT
	P	P	P	

#3	W	N	E	S
			P	1D
	P	1H	DBL	1NT
	P	P	P	

1.   The best lead is not clear. Before looking for the correct lead, consider the obvious, but incorrect, queen of hearts lead. For hearts to work for you, you need to find your partner with the ace, king, or nine. If you lead the queen and partner has one of these cards, it won't help you much if they play it at trick one in an effort to unblock for you (Chapter Ten). The right lead is either the seven of hearts or the jack of clubs. Leading the little heart caters to the possibility that partner has a heart honor. If so, he will play it at trick one and the rest of your heart suit will benefit. The second choice of the jack of clubs is sane, but I prefer the heart since a little bit of luck will produce four tricks. Given that partner is marked with about eleven points, he can have a heart honor.

2.   Lead the queen of hearts. Reiterating an earlier statement. Consider your normal lead and decide if there is a reason to lead otherwise. Here, no one bid hearts so the queen of hearts is the logical and also correct choice.

3.   Lead the jack of clubs. East made a passed hand takeout double showing spades and clubs. Here, in contrast with the previous hand, you know partner has length and strength in clubs. The J104 are excellent filler cards for partner's clubs. He could have four clubs to the king-queen or ace-queen. He could have five of them. Even if he has only four to the ace, king, or queen, your lead will be constructive for you. Your other choice, the seven of hearts, can work, and it is still a thinking lead. But, with partner announcing clubs during the auction, it is better to lead a suit you know your side has for sure.

#1	W	N	E	S
				1D
	P	1S	P	1NT
	P	P	DBL	P
	P	P		

Problem Seventeen

No One Vulnerable

WEST
♠ 63
♡ J10765
◇ AJ6
♣ Q82

#2	W	N	E	S
				1NT
	P	P	DBL	P
	P	P		

1. Lead the six of spades. Are you wondering why you didn't bid two hearts? Partner's double of one notrump is one of the mysteries of life. Is it for takeout or is it for penalty? Some players think that double is a reopening double. The idea is that if the opponents stop in one notrump, perhaps your side can make something. Personally, I hate that treatment. The treatment I like and suggest is that you play East's double as penalty. It says that East has around fifteen points with excellent spades, the suit bid on his right. He is hoping that what few points I have will be sitting over declarer and will be sufficient to stop him from running his suit or suits.

   If that is what East's double means, there is no reason to bid two hearts. Partner is not asking for hearts and could have two of them or even one. Partner's double specifies good spades and I will lead one for him.

2. Lead the six of hearts, a normal fourth best. If the suit was a little better, say, the J10865, the jack would be correct. Again, just like in the previous discussion, partner's double is not for takeout. In this case he is showing the equivalent of a strong opening notrump or better. He should not double with a weaker hand. A common error is for someone holding twelve points to double a strong notrump in the pass-out seat feeling that this is good bridge. It is not. If the dummy comes down with as few as five points, you will end up on defense with fewer points than they have. And, since defending against one notrump is tougher than most any other contract, doing so with less than half of the high card points is a loser. Keep your double of one notrump at fifteen points regardless of whether you are over the notrump bidder or are reopening.

#1	W	N	E	S
			1H	1S
	2H	2S	3H	3S
	P	P	P	

Problem Eighteen
No One Vulnerable

WEST
♠ K63
♡ 9652
♢ A2
♣ 10983

#2	W	N	E	S
				1D
	P	1H	P	1S
	P	3S	P	P
	P			

#3	W	N	E	S
			1D	1NT
	P	2C	P	2S
	P	3S	P	P
	P			

1. Lead the ace of diamonds. You rate to get in with a spade and you have hopes to get partner in for a diamond ruff. Part of your reasoning for this lead is that you have four hearts. This diminishes the number of heart tricks you will take.

2. Lead the ten of clubs. Leading the diamond ace on the first auction was acceptable since you knew East had points and could get in. On this auction, there are two reasons why leading diamonds is bad. For starters, South opened one diamond. That, by itself, should be enough reason to lead something else. The second reason is that on this auction, you can't be sure that you can get partner in to give you a diamond ruff.

3. Lead the ten of clubs. The ace of diamonds is not bad, but South's notrump overcall tells you he has good diamonds. Leading a diamond may get you a ruff, but it may cost you a trick or two in the process. This kind of layout is common.

NORTH
♢ 964

WEST
♢ A2

EAST
♢ J1075

SOUTH
♢ KQ83

South can hold his diamond losers to one by finessing the eight, but in reality, he will lead to the king. West gets something good with his ace and later, East gets a second trick. This is a likely scenario given that South overcalled one notrump.

#1	W	N	E	S
		3C	P	3NT
	P	P	P	

Problem Nineteen

North South Vulnerble

#2	W	N	E	S
				1C
	P	1H	P	2D
	P	3C	P	3NT
	P	P	P	

WEST

♠ 653

♡ KQ7

♢ Q7652

♣ Q8

1. Lead the king of hearts. They are likely to have enough fast tricks if you lead a diamond. The heart lead wins if your partner has long hearts with the ace or if he has long hearts with the jack along with another timely entry. A diamond lead wins only when partner has both diamond honors or one diamond honor and another quick entry. In terms of the high cards you need to make either lead successful, the heart lead requires less. NOTE that if the bidding had been a routine 1NT - 3NT auction, you would lead the five of diamonds. North's three club opening gives you something extra to worry about. The fact that you have the doubleton queen of clubs gives you all the more to worry about since it appears that the club suit will work for declarer.

2. Well? South's two diamond bid certainly discourages a diamond lead. A club is impossible, of course, so your choice has to be between hearts and spades. I think the right lead is the king of hearts. A miracle has to happen for a spade lead to work. South has strength and he thinks he has spades stopped. He is right. Whatever he has in spades will turn out well for him. If they have a weak spot, it is likely to be hearts. North responded one heart, but since his suit can be as weak as four little ones, there is potential here for the defense. There is another clue that says hearts is a good lead. Declarer bid clubs, diamonds, and then bid notrump, showing something in spades. South could have a singleton heart. In fact, it is probable. If South had a doubleton heart along with all the other values he has shown, he might have jumped to two notrump on the second round instead of bidding two diamonds. Be alert to this kind of auction. The layout on the next page is typical of the auction.

#2	W	N	E	S	Auction repeated for reference
				1C	
	P	1H	P	2D	
	P	3C	P	3NT	
	P	P	P		

NORTH
- ♠ K942
- ♡ 10863
- ◇ J3
- ♣ AJ2

WEST	EAST
♡ 653	♠ Q107
♡ KQ7	♡ J9542
◇ Q7652	◇ 108
♣ Q8	♣ 653

SOUTH
- ♠ AJ8
- ♡ A
- ◇ AK94
- ♣ K10974

If West leads a spade against three notrump, South will make eleven or twelve tricks. If West ignores the bidding and leads a diamond, South can make up to thirteen tricks. If West leads the king of hearts, South can still make a ton of tricks, but if he misguesses clubs, he will take just eight. Down one with a heart lead will happen.

Here are two more auctions which hint that leading dummy's suit is worthwhile.

W	N	E	S
			1D
P	1S	P	3C
P	3D	P	3NT
P	P	P	

South has bid two suits and showed some length in a third. He rates to be very short in responder's suit.

W	N	E	S
			1D
P	1H	P	2C
P	2D	P	2NT
P	P	P	

The same principle applies here, but in even stronger fashion. South's bidding shows about eighteen points, but since he didn't jump in notrump, but instead bid suits, he rates to have a 3-1-6-4 shape. North has a minimum hand since he passed two notrump. A heart lead rates to be the killer.

#1	W	N	E	S
				1NT
	P	2NT	P	P
	P			

WEST
♠ 1092
♡ 82
◊ Q73
♣ KQ1096

#2	W	N	E	S
	P	P	2H	2NT
	P	P	P	

#3	W	N	E	S
		1C	2C*	2NT
	P	P	P	

*5-5 in the major suits. 8 + points

1. Lead the queen of clubs. This is a conventional lead. If you lead the king of clubs, your partner, if he has the jack, won't know it is an important card for you and will not tell you if he has it. If you lead the queen, your partner, if he has the jack, will think that something odd is happening. Given that you have agreed to lead the queen from the KQ109 of a suit, he will realize that you must have done so here. He will play the jack and you will know to continue the suit without fear.

2. Leading the queen of clubs here is probably OK. East opened two hearts in third seat and is likely to have a poorish suit. In third seat, you can take liberties with your weak two bids. There are no guarantees that a club lead is better than a heart, but it is a distinct possibility. If East had opened two hearts in first position, I would lead his suit. You need a pretty good reason not to lead partner's suit. This hand offers two reasons. You have a very good suit plus you have reason to be suspicious of partner's suit.

3. Lead the ten of spades. North opened one club so there is not too good a chance that you can set up the club suit. You know your partner has five spades, which makes your 1092 of spades a good holding to lead from. You hope to get in with a club to continue spades.

#1	W	N	E	S
				1S
	P	2H	P	2S
	P	3S	P	4S
	P	P	P	

#2	W	N	E	S
				1S
	P	2D	P	2S
	P	3S	P	4S
	P	P	P	

WEST
♠ 763
♡ J1063
◇ 43
♣ AJ83

#3	W	N	E	S
				1S
	P	2S	P	3S
	P	4S	P	P
	P			

1. Lead the four of diamonds. Do not lead trump. They have game points and they have a known suit to work on for tricks. Your J1063 of hearts will not stop the suit for long. There are some good reasons for the diamond lead. It is an unbid suit which is a small recommendation. The bigger reason is that you are almost broke. This increases the chances that your partner will have some points. If they are in diamonds, you are off to a good start. A club, as always, is barred since they are headed by the ace. Do not lead ace-high suits against a suit contract.

2. Lead the jack of hearts. North bid diamonds this time so there is no future in them. The jack of hearts is a good solid choice. It is an unbid suit for starters and because it is a sequence, it requires less from partner than some other holdings you might have.

3. Lead the jack of hearts. This time, your lead is uncertain. Hearts is an unbid suit, but you also know less about the hand than you did on the previous auction. All in all, this is not an easy hand to lead from. Be grateful you have the J1063 of hearts and not the J863 of hearts, which would be much less palatable. The difference between informative auctions and uninformative auctions is brutal. Be sure to listen to the bidding and use all the information that is there.

#1	W	N	E	S
				2NT
	P	4NT	P	6NT
	P	P	P	

Problem Twenty-Two
No One Vulnerable

WEST
♠ 87
♡ 862
◊ K8653
♣ Q85

#2	W	N	E	S
				1C
	P	1S	P	3C
	P	3H	P	3NT
	P	6NT	P	P
	P			

#3	W	N	E	S
		1S	P	2NT
	P	3S	P	3NT
	P	6NT	P	P
	P			

1. Lead the two of hearts. This sequence shows point count. They have thirty-three or so points. Your partner has one or two. You suspect from the bidding that they do not have a long suit for a source of tricks. For them to get twelve tricks, they may have them on top but equally likely, they will require a finesse or two. Your best shot is the two of hearts, hoping to find a lead that does not cost you a trick. Declarer will have to work for his tricks.

2. Lead the five of diamonds. Here, they have suits all over to get tricks from. Declarer has six clubs so that will be one of the places he looks. You rate to get in with the queen of clubs, which will be a start, but the second trick is less certain. I think leading the diamond is a fair shot. If it gives a free trick to declarer, it is unlikely to be a crucial trick. There is nothing about the bidding to suggest they have the top diamonds. A good partner will have the queen or he will be understanding if he doesn't.

    The diagram on the next page shows the kind of setup you are rooting for. It is not farfetched at all. North showed good spades and hearts and South showed good clubs and a diamond stopper. Nothing about the bidding confirmed that they had all the missing diamond honors.

#2	W	N	E	S
				1C
	P	1S	P	3C
	P	3H	P	3NT
	P	6NT	P	P
	P			

Auction repeated for reference

NORTH
♠ AKQ94
♡ AQJ7
◇ Q4
♣ 106

WEST
♠ 87
♡ 862
◇ K8653
♣ Q85

EAST
♠ J10632
♡ 1054
◇ J72
♣ 73

SOUTH
♠ 5
♡ K93
◇ A109
♣ AKJ942

Look what happens with a 'safe' heart or spade lead. Declarer wins, takes a club finesse, and claims twelve tricks. Now play it with a diamond lead. If I were declaring this hand, I might think West more likely to lead from the jack of diamonds than from the king. After all, who leads from a king against six notrump? If dummy plays the four, East's jack forces out the ace and in the fullness of time, South finesses in clubs and goes down one, losing to the queen of clubs and the king of diamonds.

But what if declarer plays the queen of diamonds, you ask? The answer is that declarer takes the club finesse and makes twelve tricks. Your diamond lead didn't cost a thing. Actually, that is not true. It gave declarer a terrifying moment at trick one, and that is worth a small amount of solace. NOTE that North's bidding was greedy. Six clubs was almost cold.

3.   I don't know what to lead. On the previous hand, you expected that declarer had enough tricks when he got in. Attacking with a diamond lead was OK. On the auction here, you know that opener has six or more spades and about nineteen high card points. He probably has a balanced hand else he might have insisted on playing in spades. What you can't tell for sure is whether declarer has enough tricks. North and South have points but they may not have a suit to set up other than spades. In this case, there is a good case for making a passive lead such as the eight of spades. But there is no assurance of this. Possibly a club or a diamond is best. You can't really tell, though. NOTE that a spade lead is probably safer than a heart lead. A heart lead might help declarer play that suit. A spade lead won't give away a trick unless you are very unlucky.

#1	W	N	E	S
				1H
	DBL	P	P	P

#2	W	N	E	S
				2H
	DBL	P	P	P

#3	W	N	E	S
				3H
	DBL	4H	4S	P
	P	5H	DBL	P
	P	P		

Problem Twenty-Three
Both Sides Vulnerable

WEST
♠ KQ8
♡ 2
♢ AJ875
♣ QJ104

1. Lead the two of hearts. This lead is automatic. You made a takeout double and partner passed for penalty. He is, in effect, saying that your side can make one heart. In such a situation, you should play as if you were the declarer. Draw trump and then take your winners. If you lead winners before trumps are gone, they will be ruffed. Lead trumps and stop declarer from getting ruffs he doesn't deserve (See Chapter Seven).

2. Lead the queen of clubs or possibly the king of spades. Declarer's trumps are too good for you to be able to draw them as you hoped to do in the previous situation. When they are at the two level or higher, your best bet is to take your high card tricks and whatever trump tricks you are entitled to. Of course, if it turns out that there is a ruffing value in dummy, you will change course and lead trumps so as to stop declarer from getting a ruff.

3. Lead a trump. When you bid a game or a slam and your opponents take a save, leading a trump is often a good idea. Your hand tells you that dummy won't have a good suit to run. The real danger is that dummy will have distribution and will ruff some of your winners. By leading a trump, you can stop some of that nonsense. If you can get partner in early in the play, he can lead a second trump.

#3

	W	N	E	S	Auction repeated for reference
				3H	
	DBL	4H	4S	P	
	P	5H	DBL	P	
	P	P			

That may ruin declarer's plan. Here is a likely scenario based on the auction here.

NORTH
♠ A643
♡ QJ3
◊ 2
♣ 98753

WEST
♠ KQ8
♡ 2
◊ AJ875
♣ QJ104

EAST
♠ J9752
♡ 108
◊ KQ63
♣ AK

SOUTH
♠ 10
♡ AK97654
◊ 1094
♣ 62

With a spade lead or the ace of diamonds lead, declarer will be able to get two diamond ruffs in dummy. He will still go down a trick, but you can set five hearts two with a trump lead, which is better. A club lead doesn't set them two tricks because it gives declarer time to set up a club trick. Your stiff trump is the winner. Yes, it goes against most guidelines, but the situation suggests it is right on this occasion.

#1	W	N	E	S
				1H
	P	2C	P	2H
	P	4H	P	P
	P			

Problem Twenty-Four
East West Vulnerable

WEST
♠ 87643
♡ 752
◊ K982
♣ A

#2	W	N	E	S
	P	P	1C	1H
	1S	4H	P	P
	P			

#3	W	N	E	S		#4	W	N	E	S
	P	P	P	1H						1H
	P	2H	P	2S			P	1S	P	2C
	P	4H	P	P			P	3H	P	4H
	P						P	P	P	

1. Lead the two of diamonds. North bid two clubs over one heart so leading the ace of clubs, even if it gets you a ruff, is really an exercise in surrendering the timing to the opponents. This is what you are risking.

NORTH
♠ Q2
♡ K96
◊ A53
♣ QJ1086

WEST
♠ 87643
♡ 752
◊ K982
♣ A

EAST
♠ A105
♡ 83
◊ Q107
♣ 97543

SOUTH
♠ KJ9
♡ AQJ104
◊ J64
♣ K2

On the lead of the ace of clubs, West will continue, if he judges correctly, by switching to a spade. East wins and gives West a club ruff and declarer leans forward and claims. Making four.

If West keeps the club ace and instead leads the two of diamonds, the defense will get two diamonds, one spade, and the ace of clubs for down one. The defense doesn't get a club ruff, but it gets two diamond tricks in return. A fair trade for the defense. Leading a stiff ace in one of the opponents' suits is often ineffective for the reasons shown here.

2.   Lead the ace of clubs. It is OK to lead it since you are leading partner's suit. East may have the king and queen of clubs and if you don't cash your ace, it will be hard to get all the club tricks you have coming. Leading partner's suit is usually right and is definitely politically correct.

3.   Lead the ace of clubs. Clubs is an unbid suit, which means there is not as acute a danger as there was in the first auction. If your diamonds were headed by the KQ108 instead of the K982, they would get the nod. Leading from strong sequences is generally better than leading shortness except in the case where partner bid your short suit.

4.   Lead the two of diamonds. The unbid suit is usually worth looking at so it deserves consideration. Leading the ace of clubs is a bad idea here. Just like on question one, an opponent has bid this suit. While leading the ace of clubs does not have to cost you, and admitting that it can gain some of the time, leading it will cost you a club trick on many occasions. Here is one such.

#4	W	N	E	S
				1H
	P	1S	P	2C
	P	3H	P	4H
	P	P	P	

Auction repeated for reference

NORTH
♠ AQ105
♡ KJ6
◊ J104
♣ 953

WEST   EAST
♠ 87643   ♠ KJ2
♡ 752   ♡ 93
◊ K982   ◊ Q653
♣ A   ♣ Q1082

SOUTH
♠ 9
♡ AQ1084
◊ A7
♣ KJ764

If I could make up a few perfect rules about what to lead, I would do so. Unfortunately, I can not. I can, however, give you a couple of rules about what not to lead. Leading the ace of clubs, a suit declarer has bid, is a guaranteed overall loser. This hand is a typical example. With a diamond lead, declarer will go down. At some point, he will finesse the jack of clubs, which works well, but the four-one club break will be a killer. If, however, West leads the ace of clubs, South has no difficulty taking ten tricks. Keep those aces in your hand until their time!

251

#1	W	N	E	S
		1H	P	1S
	P	3S	P	4S
	P	P	P	

WEST
♠ 76
♡ AK102
◇ 1096
♣ J852

#2	W	N	E	S
		1D	P	1S
	P	2C	P	2H
	P	2S	P	3S
	P	P	P	

1.   Lead the ten of diamonds. Whatever heart tricks you have rate to keep. Lead the king of hearts if you must, but be aware that you are giving declarer a head start if he needs to set up the hearts. The main reason for leading hearts is on the off chance that your partner has a stiff heart and can ruff the third round. This is unlikely. Better to start with the ten of diamonds and try to set up your tricks instead of helping declarer set up his.

2.   Lead a spade. North took a preference to spades and rates to have short hearts. Perhaps North has just one heart and two spades. If so, you will be able to lead trumps now and then again as soon as you get in with a heart. Leading hearts instead of spades can hurt for many reasons. Say this is the heart suit.

♡ 64

♡ AK102   ♡ 873

    ♡ QJ95

If you lead hearts, declarer will need only one ruff in dummy to hold his losers to two. A heart lead gives declarer a heart trick as well as making it easier for him to get ruffs in dummy. The difference from declarer's point of view is a large one since the lead makes his work much easier.

#1	W	N	E	S
		2S*	P	3H
	P	4H	P	4NT
	P	5C	P	6H
	P	P	DBL	P
	P	P		

*Weak two bid

WEST
♠ A86542
♡ 32
♢ 843
♣ K6

#2	W	N	E	S
		1C	3S	4H
	5S	6H	P	P
	P			

1. Lead the two of spades (any spade other than the ace). If you listen to the bidding, the right lead will jump out at you in a second. It just requires that you see the logic. Here, North opened with a weak two spade bid. This is surprising, but when you have played bridge for a year or two, these things do happen. East, who has been quiet, doubles the final six heart bid. His double is a lead directing double. From your hand, it is clear that East has a void in spades. You should lead spades, but the issue here goes beyond that. Let's say you lead the ace of spades. Dummy is going to have something like the KQJ1073 of spades. Your ace will live, but declarer will be able to overruff the second round of spades so you won't get a second trick there. Worse, declarer will now have a bunch of spade winners to use after drawing trump. It is unlikely that you will get another trick. What you have to do is lead a LOW spade for partner to ruff. This way, you will keep the ace of spades to stop the spade suit from running. If declarer has a side loser, it will still be there for the defenders to take.

2. I guess to lead a trump. Leading a spade will give the opponents a sluff and a ruff. This is a rare occurrence, but since it is predictable here, you should avoid it. The king of clubs is just too risky to contemplate and a diamond doesn't rate to find partner with enough to make it worthwhile. Lead a trump and sit back for any tricks you have coming.

#1	W	N	E	S
	1H	2H*	3H	3S
	4H	4S	P	P
	P			

*Spades and a minor

WEST
♠ 7
♡ AQ10875
◇ KQ98
♣ J2

#2	W	N	E	S
				1S
	2H	3S*	P	4NT
	P	5D	P	6S
	P	P	P	

*Limit raise

1. Lead the king of diamonds. North has used one of the modern bidding devices called the Michaels Cue Bid. Two hearts shows five spades and five cards in one of the minor suits. The idea behind this bidding is that it is more useful to use a cue bid to show certain distributional hands than to show a strong hand. The bid is a little like the popular Unusual Notrump overcall that is used to show the minor suits. The reason for leading the king of diamonds is that if you lead the ace of hearts, you may set up declarer's king. Something like this hand is possible.

NORTH
♠ A10984
♡ 3
◇ A2
♣ KQ1096

WEST	EAST
♠ 7	♠ QJ5
♡ AQ10875	♡ J942
◇ KQ98	◇ J1053
♣ J2	♣ A8

SOUTH
♠ K632
♡ K6
◇ 764
♣ 7543

If West leads the ace of hearts, declarer makes four spades. Dummy's two of diamonds goes away on declarer's king of hearts. The defense makes a spade, a heart, and a club. With the king of diamonds lead, declarer is quietly down one. If you are willing to take the chance that East always has the king of hearts for his raise, go ahead and lead the ace. But if East should disappoint you, as he does here, you are out a trick and the opponents have a game that should have been set.

The question of leading aces is an ongoing one. I have stated that leading them against low level contracts is generally awful. On this hand, the opponents are at the four level, but it is still not correct to lead the ace. With a solid alternative lead in the king of diamonds, the heart ace should be avoided. Have I stated anywhere in this book that opening leads is an art and not a science?

2. Lead the king of diamonds. There is too much risk in leading the ace of hearts. You may set up dummy's king of hearts or you may set up declarer's king of hearts. Either may be a disaster. The king of diamonds is a solid start toward setting up a defensive winner. Hopefully, you will get a heart and a diamond after this lead. If you lead the heart first, your diamond may go away. This is not as certain a choice as the king of diamonds was on the previous hand. Still, it is a good selection for solid reasons.

What kind of auction *would* call for leading the ace of hearts with this hand? Try this one.

W	N	E	S
	1D	P	1S
2H	2S	4H	4S
5H	5S	P	P
P			

Leading the ace of hearts is reasonable now. East raised hearts strongly. Also, your other choice of leads, the diamond king, is not as appealing with North's having bid them. Combined with the opponents being at the five level, the heart ace has lots to recommend it.

#1	W	N	E	S
			1S	P
	2S	2NT	4S	5C
	P	P	DBL	P
	P	P		

WEST
♠ 87542
♡ KJ108
◊ Q2
♣ 75

#2	W	N	E	S
				1D
	P	1S	P	2C
	P	3D	P	P
	P			

#3	W	N	E	S
				1D
	P	1H	P	2C
	P	P	P	

1. Lead the eight of spades. This is analogous to leading the top of three small. The idea is to make sure partner doesn't think you have anything in spades. What if these are the spades around the table?

♠ K3

♠ 87542   ♠ AJ1096

♠ Q

If you lead your fourth best, East might finesse the nine, not realizing that South has the stiff queen. This is a good way to ruin what should have been a good result. By leading the eight, East will see that it is not a fourth best lead and can only be some sort of top-of-nothing lead. However the defense proceeds after your opening lead, your partner should be sensibly informed about how to continue.

2. Lead the jack of hearts. This auction screams for a heart lead and your heart holding further suggests leading them. If you are feeling any qualms at all about this lead, go back and reread Chapter Two. In my opinion, the jack of hearts is the only acceptable lead. Leading a spade on the theory that you hate to lead from a king is ostrich-thinking of the worst kind. Yes, once in awhile, you will lead into the AQ and lose a trick. But more often, a spade lead will give declarer a head start setting up tricks for discards. On this hand, you should actually feel happy about leading a heart. Your holding is very strong so you need only the queen from partner's hand to get the defense off to a good start.

3. Lead the seven of clubs. Hearts were bid by dummy so your holding is not as appealing as it was in the last question. Your spades are miserable to lead since you have so little in the suit. For a spade lead to work, you have to find a lot of spade honors in partner's hand. Above all else, however, this is an auction that demands you lead a trump. It will be right to lead a trump over 75% of the time. This hand offers no reason to do something else.

Here is an imaginary hand seen from declarer's point of view.

SOUTH
♠ 63
♡ Q6
◇ K9875
♣ AKJ4

Let's say you opened this hand with one diamond. Your partner bid one heart, and you rebid two clubs. Everyone passes and LHO gets his lead ready. Before you see the opening lead, you can reflect that your partner is going to have three or four clubs and two or fewer diamonds. Does it not seem obvious to you that you are going to need to ruff your diamonds in dummy in order to set them up? Does it not also seem obvious that a trump lead won't be good for you?

Problem Twenty-Nine
No One Vulnerable

#1	W	N	E	S
		2C	P	2H
	P	2S	P	2NT
	P	3H	P	4H
	P	4NT	P	5D
	P	6H	P	P
	P			

WEST

♠ K2
♡ QJ6
◇ 1087
♣ 87432

#2	W	N	E	S
		1D	P	1H
	P	3D	P	3H
	P	4H	P	4NT
	P	5C*	P	6H
	P	P	P	

*Three key cards

1. Lead the two of spades. You are hoping to fool declarer into believing you have a stiff spade. South does not know you have a trump trick. He may think that by going up with the ace of spades in dummy and drawing trump, he will be safe. With luck, you will get a heart and a spade out of this.

2. Before deciding what to lead, ask yourself how the bidding went. Do you remember for sure? The answer is that you should lead the two of spades. A diamond lead is foolish, but a club lead is possible. Or is it? If you followed the bidding, you will see that your partner passed over five clubs. If East wanted a club lead, he would double five clubs. He didn't double. East doesn't rate to have the king of clubs. The spade lead is correct since you are entitled to hope for East to have the queen. If he does, six hearts may go down. Every now and then, East shows up with the ace of spades! Even if East has nothing in spades, the lead should not cost you. Declarer rates to have enough tricks if you leave him time to get them.

#1	W	N	E	S
		1D	P	1H
	1S	P	P	3D
	P	3S	P	3NT
	P	P	P	

Problem Thirty
No One Vulnerable

WEST
♠ K107653
♡ 92
◇ A2
♣ J102

#2	W	N	E	S
	2S	DBL	P	3D
	P	3S	DBL	3NT
	P	P	P	

#3	W	N	E	S
	2S	3C	P	3NT
	P	P	P	

1.   Lead the jack of clubs. East had a chance to raise spades and did not. This in
      itself is only mildly significant. East could have the queen or even the ace of
      spades and not have a raise. On the next round, East had a chance to double three
      spades. Again, he did not. It is fair to assume that he would double if he had the
      right hand. And what does it take to double three spades? The answer is that East
      should double when he has one of the top three spade honors. East should not
      double three spades just to make a noise. He should double when he has
      something useful to tell partner. Look at it from West's perspective. If you were
      West, wouldn't you like to know for sure if your partner had a spade honor?
      Given that West chooses not to lead a spade, the club lead is a fine alternative.
      West has only eight points. East could have six or seven points and a good five
      card club suit. The club lead is a learned choice which will work some of the
      time.

2.   Lead the six of spades. This time your partner showed something in spades so
      leading one is obvious. Compare the difference in your mood between having a
      helpful double from East and having no double from East as in the previous
      auction.

3.   Lead the six of spades. On this auction, East did not raise spades so that is a hint
      that he doesn't like spades. You can't be sure, though, since East did not have
      the opportunity to double a cue bid. The evidence here is not sufficient to stop
      you from leading a spade. Actually, if you did lead the jack of clubs, I don't
      think that is a terrible choice. The main point of this hand is how partner's
      contribution OR LACK of contribution to the auction affects your choice of
      leads.

#1	W	N	E	S
				1D
	P	1H	P	3C
	P	3D	P	3NT
	P	P	P	

Problem Thirty-One
No One Vulnerable

#2	W	N	E	S
				3NT*
	P	P	P	

*Gambling

#3	W	N	E	S
		1C	P	1D
	P	1S	P	2NT
	P	3NT	P	P
	P			

WEST
♠ 64
♡ QJ4
◇ J762
♣ 10763

1. Lead the queen of hearts. South has diamonds and clubs and has a spade stopper too. He doesn't have room for many hearts. He might have a small singleton. North did not rebid his hearts. One of the first things you should do when partner jump shifts or reverses is show a five card suit. The fact that North did not rebid hearts suggests he has just four of them. A modest point in addition is that your partner did not bid one spade. With five spades and ten points, he might have done so. Here is what you would like to find.

NORTH
♠ Q853
♡ 10873
◇ K95
♣ J5

WEST
♠ 64
♡ QJ4
◇ J762
♣ 10763

EAST
♠ K1072
♡ A9652
◇ 8
♣ Q94

SOUTH
♠ AJ9
♡ K
◇ AQ1043
♣ AK82

NORTH
♠ J853
♡ K732
◇ K95
♣ Q5

WEST
♠ 64
♡ QJ4
◇ J762
♣ 10763

EAST
♠ K972
♡ A9865
◇ 8
♣ J94

SOUTH
♠ AQ10
♡ 10
◇ AQ1043
♣ AK82

Look at the first diagram. If you lead the queen of hearts, your partner will have to allow South's king to win. But, when the defenders get in, they can run off the next four hearts. If West leads the six of spades, the unbid suit, South will make nine or ten tricks according to how well the defenders continue.

If you are really lucky, the hand will be as in the right hand diagram. In this diagram, the queen of hearts gets you the first five tricks. If you lead the six of spades, they will take nine tricks for sure. Reflect how often you have bid a weak suit and later played in three notrump. Haven't you found that your weak spot is often this suit?

2.   Lead the queen of hearts. You have a generally crummy hand. Your best chance is to find partner with a decent suit and the only suit you have help for is hearts. A three card sequence in an unbid suit is often a good selection.

3.   Lead the queen of hearts. On all three hands in this set the correct lead is the queen of hearts. The reasons for it are always different, though. In this case, you are leading the queen of hearts because it is an unbid suit. This is not the only reason, of course. If you had a singleton heart, you would not lead it. Leading stiffs against notrump is done ONLY when partner has indicated the lead during the auction. On this auction, no one bid hearts so it is logical that you look at them first. Finding the QJ4 to lead from is a big plus. If the hearts were 853 instead of the QJ4, I would still lead them, but would be far less happy to do so.

No One Vulnerable

#1	W	N	E	S
				1NT
	P	2C	P	2H
	P	3NT	P	P
	P			

WEST
♠ AQJ93
♡ A62
◊ 87
♣ 1064

#2	W	N	E	S
				1S
	P	2C	P	2NT
	P	3NT	P	P
	P			

1.   Lead the ace of spades. Finding this lead requires a review of the bidding. North bid two clubs, looking for a major fit. South showed hearts and North went to three notrump. North must have four spades else why bid this way? The reason you lead the ace is to learn how to continue the suit.

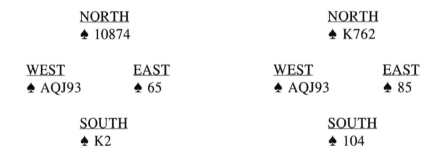

NORTH
♠ 10874

WEST   EAST
♠ AQJ93   ♠ 65

SOUTH
♠ K2

NORTH
♠ K762

WEST   EAST
♠ AQJ93   ♠ 85

SOUTH
♠ 104

In the diagram on the left, making the "book" lead of the queen does not work. South wins with the king and dummy remains with the 1087 leering at you for the rest of the hand. Had you led a small spade, the spade suit would come home for you since the ace would drop the king on the next round.

The trouble is that if you happen to hit on a small spade for your lead, you might find the spades as in the second diagram. Leading a small spade will get you a different kind of disaster. South will win with the ten and now the king in dummy will remain to stop you from running the suit.

One might think that you should not lead the suit at all. Not true. If you lead the ace, you will see the dummy and will know how to continue. If dummy has four to the ten, you can continue with a little spade, hopefully forcing opener to take his king. In the second diagram, you will see that continuing the queen of spades will set up the suit and you will do so. If dummy has the K1072 of spades, for instance, you won't get all the spade tricks you wanted but then you were not destined to get them on this hand. Likewise, if you lead the ace and a little one as in the first diagram and South has three of them, you won't be able to run the suit. But you weren't going to do that in any case. Leading the ace will get you the most tricks possible.

2.   What you should lead is not certain. What you should not lead is. Do not lead a spade and do not lead a club. When an auction begins with a two over one bid by your LHO, you virtually never lead one of their suits. A speculative two of hearts lead is OK, hoping to find your partner's suit, but so is the eight of diamonds. Your goal is to avoid giving declarer a free trick. He may decide to play the spades himself. That would be nice for you. If you lead one, declarer won't lead them himself since he will know there is a danger there.

#1	W	N	E	S	Problem Thirty-Three
	1C	P	1H	1S	No One Vulnerable
	2H	2S	DBL	P	
	P	P			

#2	W	N	E	S
		1C	P	1S
	P	2S	P	P
	DBL	P	P	P

WEST
♠ 7
♡ QJ7
◇ A653
♣ AQ874

1. Lead the seven of spades. Your side found a fit and then your partner doubled them in their fit. This is unusual. When both sides have a fit, the bidding usually goes on to the three level before the doubling starts. When East hits two spades, he is announcing a strong spade holding. He suspects you have a singleton spade since he is looking at four of them himself. If he had three only spades, he would not double. Here is the complete hand.

NORTH
♠ K62
♡ 92
◇ 10984
♣ K953

WEST
♠ 7
♡ QJ7
◇ A653
♣ AQ874

EAST
♠ QJ109
♡ AK108
◇ J72
♣ 102

The queen of hearts gives declarer time to get at least one heart ruff in dummy. He might get two if the defense misfires. A trump lead, however, stops all heart ruffs in dummy. Declarer will lose two spades, four hearts, and two aces for down three. south will be punished for a marginal overcall. here is a notable aside. Look at the West hand again. It raised to two hearts with just three card support. this is a bid that many players refuse to make, feeling that they need four trumps to raise a one level response.

SOUTH
♠ A8543
♡ 6543
◇ KQ
♣ J6

2. Lead your spade. Partner passed you in a takeout double. This is a little like the situation where you double a one bid and partner passes it out. This is NOT like the situation where you double a weak two bid and partner passes it out. After a weak two bid, you know that declarer has a good six card suit. On the auction here, it sounds like declarer has a so-so four card suit and your partner has five good ones. Get the trump on the table. PS. That was a good reopening double. Would you have found it?

#1	W	N	E	S
		1NT	P	2D*
	P	2H	P	3C
	P	3H	P	4C
	P	4D	P	4S
	P	5S	P	6C
	P	P	P	

*Transfer

Problem Thirty-Four

North South Vulnerable

WEST
♠ A9743
♡ A83
◇ 3
♣ 10987

1. This is one of my all time favorite hands. The winning lead turns out to be a bit odd. I will show it to you in a moment.

    You will agree that having two aces against a slam is not an everyday event. It occurred in the Portland Regional Swiss Teams in February of 1994. Due to the fact that this was the last event of the tournament, it was scheduled much too early in the morning. I had rolled out of bed moments before and had arrived at the table with coffee in one hand, the convention card in another, and an apple stuffed into a shirt pocket. My partner, Grant Baze, was already at the table and he, drat him, looked like he had been up for an hour. Smiles and elegance he was. I managed to finish half of the cup of coffee but had to stop to help shuffle the boards. This was the first hand of the day.

    The auction was revealing, albeit a bit disjointed. North showed a strong notrump and South transferred to hearts and then bid clubs. In turn, South showed 5-5 in his suits and North showed he liked hearts. Finally, they started cue-bidding. North's four diamonds showed the ace of diamonds and South's four spades showed the ace or a void or a singleton. My hand suggested it was not the ace. North, I think, was not sure what was happening at this point and solved his insecurities by cue-bidding the king of spades. South's six club bid was an offer to North to choose between hearts and clubs. After more than a little huddle, North passed making the final contract six clubs. At Swiss Teams, the important thing is to get to your good slams. It is not as important to be in six of a major instead of six of a minor in case both slams are making.

    So, what is the right lead? The ace of spades is a possibility and so is the ace of hearts. Perhaps East is ruffing the second round of hearts. A singleton diamond? Or perhaps the ten of clubs. That will be a safe lead.

In order, most of these leads can be rejected. The ace of spades might work, but I think that the four spade bid showed a void. Why? South was a good bidder. If he had a singleton spade, he would have used Blackwood as the easiest tool. If he had a spade void, Blackwood wouldn't help him. A cue bid would be the best approach. I did not expect the ace of spades would cash. The ace of hearts did not seem right either. For it to work, my partner needs a stiff heart and that is unlikely. If North-South had nine hearts, they would be in six hearts. The six of diamonds is just awful. You have two aces. Your partner isn't going to get in to give you a ruff. Also, just for the record, East did not double four diamonds. Doubling cue bids for the lead is a popular bidding tool. Grant Baze would not overlook a lead directing double if he really liked a diamond lead. The ten of clubs is, as noted, a safe lead, but it is depressingly boring. Nonetheless, the four card sequence can't hurt. Something about the above thoughts coalesced into a new thought. It was a combination of these two. One, if I lead the ace of spades, it will get ruffed. Two, I have four trumps. Thirty-five years ago, I worked for the US Forest Service. During a lunch break, I read a hand from *Cut For Partners,* by S.J. Simon, wherein the Unlucky Expert was on lead against a slam with two aces. Could the Unlucky Expert's hand have found its way to my table thirty-five years later? In essence, the Unlucky Expert underled an ace in order to make declarer ruff. Then on getting in with his second ace, he was able to make declarer ruff a second time. I have been waiting for this situation for a lifetime of bridge. No way would I wait longer for it to come back. I led the four of spades. Dummy was known to have the king of spades. If it did not also have the queen, declarer might not play the king at trick one. If South has to ruff the first spade and can be forced to ruff a later spade, it might be possible to get a trump trick out of this. Here is the entire hand.

NORTH
♠ KJ82
♡ Q104
◊ AQ6
♣ KJ5

WEST
♠ A9743
♡ A83
◊ 3
♣ 10987

EAST
♠ Q1065
♡ 65
◊ 1098752
♣ 3

SOUTH
♠ —
♡ KJ972
◊ KJ4
♣ AQ642

Declarer played the jack of spades (who underleads an ace against a slam?) and East produced the queen. South ruffed, but was not able to draw trump and use the clubs. Declarer did draw two trumps and then led hearts. West won and led the ace of spades. This left West with more trumps than South and the slam went down one.

#1	W	N	E	S
				1S
	P	2S	P	P
	P			

Problem Thirty-Five

No One Vulnerable

#2	W	N	E	S
				1S
	P	P	DBL	2C
	P	2S	P	P
	P			

WEST
♠ J72
♡ 1096
◇ KJ83
♣ J94

#3	W	N	E	S
				P
	P	1D	P	1S
	P	P	2C	2S
	P	P	P	

1. Lead the ten of hearts. When your opponents bid one suit, you know as little about the hand as possible. You do know that they don't have a lot of points and you are not specifically warned that there is a suit in dummy that will be good for discards. In this situation, the need to attack is not as acute as in some other stronger and more descriptive auctions. Either minor could work out, but with a sequence in hearts, that is the chosen lead.

2. Lead the two of spades. North has a weak hand but does have a preference for spades over clubs. You have the J94 of clubs which by itself does not suggest declarer has a lot of club losers. But, your partner's takeout double suggests he has some clubs. Between your J94 of clubs and whatever partner has, you may have a couple of club tricks if declarer doesn't have time to ruff them in dummy. Get the trump out there.

3. Lead the four of clubs. As a rule, you don't lead trumps unless you have a reason to do so. As a rule, you lead partner's suit unless you have something better to do. Everything points to a club lead so that should be it. Do not lead the jack. Leading the top card from a broken three card holding is a losing lead. Keep away from such thoughts.

#1	W	N	E	S
				1NT
	P	3NT	P	P
	P			

Problem Thirty-Six

No One Vulnerable

WEST
♠ AK53
♡ 763
◊ 1098
♣ Q53

#2	W	N	E	S
				1C
	P	1S	P	1NT
	P	2NT	P	3NT
	P	P	P	

1. Lead the king of spades. When you have a four card suit to the ace-king, you lead the king against notrump so that you will be in at trick two. If you are off to a good start you can continue, and if you are wrong, you can switch. If your spades were AK532, you would lead the three. The reason is that you may block the suit by leading the king. Here are some spade holdings which would be ruined defensively if you started with a high one.

#1		#2		#3	
NORTH		**NORTH**		**NORTH**	
♠ QJ4		♠ Q96		♠ 1084	
WEST	**EAST**	**WEST**	**EAST**	**WEST**	**EAST**
♠ AK532	♠ 106	♠ AK532	♠ J74	♠ AK532	♠ Q6
SOUTH		**SOUTH**		**SOUTH**	
♠ 987		♠ 108		♠ J97	

In the first case, leading the king means you can't use the suit unless you have an outside entry. If you lead the three and if your partner can get in, he will return the suit and you will cash the next four tricks. In the second case, you can get four tricks by leading the king and then little, but if you lead the three, you have a chance to take all five tricks if declarer misguesses the spades. And, in the third case, leading the king does the worst damage of all. You were in a position to run off five spades. Leading the king costs you three tricks unless you can manage to get in somehow in another suit.

2. Lead the ten of diamonds. Four to the ace-king is an OK suit to lead against notrump, but not when it has been bid by the opponents. You know that dummy has four or more spades so leading them will not gain you a trick. If your partner has the queen of spades, you can take your three spade tricks later (hopefully).

#1	W	N	E	S
				1H
	P	1S	P	2D
	P	3C	P	3NT
	P	P	P	

Problem Thirty-Seven

No One Vulnerable

#2	W	N	E	S
				1H
	P	1S	P	2D
	P	3C	DBL	3NT
	P	P	P	

WEST
♠ K43
♡ AJ43
♢ 10975
♣ 43

#3	W	N	E	S
				1NT
	P	2NT	P	3NT
	P	P	P	

1. Lead the ten of diamonds. This might surprise you. If partner has nothing in diamonds, you have lost nothing. If partner has an honor, you may be off to a good start. You would like to find the diamonds looking like this, or something similar.

NORTH
♢ Q2

WEST   EAST
♢ 10975   ♢ K64

SOUTH
♢ AJ83

In an ideal world, you will get two tricks out of this. You may actually gain more than this by virtue of not finding a poor lead which loses a trick. The other suits are not appealing. Hearts are poor given South's opening heart bid. Spades have some potential, but when it doesn't work, it will be bad with a vengeance. A club is possible, but that too has a downside. If clubs are a good lead, East must have a good holding. If he has that, he might have doubled three clubs. Here is a rule you can live with. When an opponent bids "the fourth suit" he often does so without a real holding in the suit. If you want partner to lead this suit should he be on lead, you can double to get it. Partner didn't double three clubs so you can't be optimistic about leading that suit.

Let me digress a moment. Here is a possible hand for North.

NORTH
♠ AQJ86
♡ Q5
◇ KJ2
♣ J75

When South opens one heart, North responds one spade. Over South's two diamond rebid, North is stuck for a bid. A common solution with hands like this one is to bid the fourth suit, in this case, three clubs. The idea is that you are making a forcing bid which will get some further noise from partner. This bidding tactic is common today and is, in fact, a very good adjunct to add to your system. In any event, if an opponent bids one of these "fourth suit" bids you should look for the opportunity to make a lead directing double when you have a good five card suit or even a really good four card suit. You should double three clubs with holdings like these: QJ1085, KQ875, or KQJ8. The opponents often end up in three notrump and if so, you want partner to lead this suit.

Going back to the original question, West has the 43 of clubs. Had East doubled, the right lead would be the four of clubs. East's silence suggests looking elsewhere. NOTE that you should lead clubs if you have good clubs. With Q10763, leading a club is fine. Partner's silence over three clubs says he isn't anxious for you to lead them. He may, however, have enough strength in clubs that your suit can be set up in a lead or two.

2.   Lead the four of clubs. It is nice to have a thoughtful partner who indicated a club lead for you. Without the double, you would not lead a club. Comfort at the bridge table is not having to guess what to do. Thank you, partner.

3.   Lead the three of hearts. When responder bid two notrump, he denied the major suits and perforce suggested the minors. This is not an ideal holding for a heart lead since it can give away a trick, but it does have potential. Your partner is marked with seven points and they may include something in hearts. A nice bonus is that partner can sometimes have length in hearts. If he has five to the king, you will have three notrump set before declarer takes a single trick.

#1	W	N	E	S
	P	P	P	1NT
	P	P	P	

Problem Thirty-Eight
No One Vulnerable

#2	W	N	E	S
			1D	1NT
	P	P	P	

WEST
- ♠ J942
- ♡ Q62
- ◇ 84
- ♣ Q1094

#3	W	N	E	S
	P	P	1D	P
	1S	P	P	1NT
	P	P	P	

#4	W	N	E	S
			P	1C
	P	P	1D	1NT
	P	P	P	

None of the four leads in this set of answers is clear-cut. You like more bidding than you get here to judge the best lead and you don't have anything that stands out on these four sequences.

1. Lead the ten of clubs. East has eleven points. With more, he would have opened in third seat. With less, the opponents would have enough to bid or at least try for game. Given East has a fair hand, you can expect he would have bid if he had a major or if he had both majors. It is likely he has a balanced hand with a smattering in all suits. Your good club spots make this suit your best choice. In the long run, this will be your best lead. It will, however, be poor on quite a few hands. It is the nature of boring hands that you can't find scintillating leads.

2. This sequence is a pain. South has a good hand but did not look for a major suit. He may be well heeled in clubs and diamonds. East may have opened one diamond with four-four in the majors and a three card diamond suit. This suggests a spade lead might be best. Still, not leading partner's suit is dangerous since when you don't lead it and it was right, you tend to hear about it. I think it is close with the nod going very slightly to the two of spades.

3.   Lead the two of spades. East's pass to one spade says he has a light opener, but he also has three spades. It is bad bridge to open light in third seat and then pass partner's one level bid without a tolerance for partner's suit. You have to have enough support that your partner won't struggle in a terrible contract. East, therefore, rates to have three spades and likely has an honor or two. East can also have diamonds, but South rates to have them too.

4.   Lead the eight of diamonds. Here, East will have a real diamond suit. He will not balance with a crummy four card suit. Since East did not look for a major and since his diamonds should be good, leading his suit is right. Clubs, being bid by South, are out of the question. It is important to see that East's one diamond bid in this auction shows a good suit whereas the one diamond opening bid in auctions two and three gives no assurances of good diamonds.

#1	W	N	E	S
		1D	P	1S
	P	3S	P	4C
	P	4D	P	5S
	P	6S	P	P
	P			

No One Vulnerable

#2	W	N	E	S
			2H	4S
	P	4NT	P	5D
	P	6S	P	P
	P			

WEST
♠ 865
♡ A73
◇ 743
♣ 10986

#3	W	N	E	S		#4	W	N	E	S
		1H	P	1S				1C	P	1S
	P	2NT	P	3S			P	3S	P	4NT
	P	4S	P	4NT			P	5S	P	6S
	P	5H	P	6S			P	P	P	
	P	P	P							

1.   For all the marbles, you can underlead the ace of hearts. The auction has given you a world of information. The opponents first found their spade fit and then cue-bid clubs and diamonds. The two bids that give the show away for you are South's five spades and North's six spades. Five spades asks North if he has heart control. Six spades says he does. If North didn't have a heart control, he would pass five spades. What you hope for is that North has the king of hearts and that declarer misguesses the suit when you lead low. Here is the heart suit you are hoping for.

NORTH
♡ K85

WEST
♡ A73

EAST
♡ Q10942

SOUTH
♡ J6

The ace of hearts will get you one trick and no more. The three of hearts puts you in the running for two tricks. Of course, if East doesn't have the queen of hearts, you might not get your ace. It is, at least, a reasonable effort. Be sure of your facts before you try this one.

This hand brings up a true story.

274

I will allow my partner to be anonymous. On the exact auction above, my partner underled the ace of hearts. Declarer won the first trick with the king(!), discarded the jack of hearts, and later conceded a trick to the ace of trumps! Bad result? It was a tie. The auction and the lead were the same when the hand was played at the other table. This story occurred in the Vanderbilt KO's involving eight players who had a total of 31 national event wins among them as well as a few world championships. Amazing stuff.

2. Lead the ace of hearts. Easy. Partner bid them strongly and the opponents are in a very high contract.

3. Lead the ten of clubs. The ace of hearts is awful. North bid the suit so you run the risk of setting up their side suit. The club is right by a mile. You hope to set up a trick before declarer gets the heart suit going. It is true that a diamond lead might be the winner. The club suit is solid, though, so is safer in the event it turns out not to be effective. Incidentally, a trump is at least as awful as the ace of hearts. You must try to set up a trick and this is your last chance to do it in time to be useful.

4. I do not know what to tell you. If South has bid foolishly, your side may have two heart tricks, in which case you should lead the ace of hearts. It is also possible that South has the king of hearts and will welcome the lead of the ace. I can tell you that I would never underlead the ace here. I judge that it is about fifty-fifty whether you lead the ace of hearts or something else. Actually, if you decide to lead something else, that is a problem in itself. A trump lead is probably safe, but not a certainty. A club lead also looks safe, but perhaps not. And a diamond lead might be right into declare's second suit. South bid uninformatively and that is always annoying. My best advice is not to have hands like this one very often.

#1	W	N	E	S
				1NT
	P	2NT	P	3NT
	P	P	P	

#2	W	N	E	S
		1S	P	1NT
	P	3NT	P	P
	P			

WEST
♠ J103
♡ 874
◇ 873
♣ Q987

#3	W	N	E	S
		1H	P	1S
	P	2C	P	2NT
	P	3NT	P	P
	P			

#4	W	N	E	S
		1H	P	1S
	P	2D	P	3NT
	P	P	P	

1. Lead the jack of spades. With a bad hand and with the dummy expected to have lots of minor suit cards (dummy did not look for a major suit), you should lead the jack of spades and hope you are striking partner's suit. The J10 combination is a solid start since it means you need less help in the suit from partner than if you chose to lead from the three worthless hearts.

2. Lead the seven of clubs. Not so clear this time. North has five spades so he will have a doubleton somewhere. It could be clubs. South responded one notrump, which says little about his shape. There is hope that your partner has clubs so you should go ahead with the suit. This is not a great lead. It is merely better than the alternatives.

3. Lead the eight of diamonds, or if you prefer, lead the three. Not a big deal here. The point is that they have bid the other three suits. The unbid suit is a good place to start and unless there is a good reason to do otherwise, leading the unbid suit is often right.

4. Lead the seven of clubs. The same thinking applies as on the previous auction. On the first auction, where the opponents bid 1NT - 2NT - 3NT, it was wrong to lead a club for a multitude of reasons. Here, the other three suits have been bid. Given the bidding, this club holding is attractive to lead from. It all depends on how the bidding has gone.

#1	W	N	E	S
				1H
	DBL	2H	2S	3H
	P	P	P	

Problem Forty-One

Both Sides Vulnerable

#2	W	N	E	S
				2H
	DBL	P	2S	P
	P	3H	P	P
	P			

WEST
♠ K103
♡ 76
◊ AQ2
♣ KQ983

1.   Lead the king of clubs. It is possible that a spade is better, but the king of clubs is a decent lead. The main point on this hand is that East's two spade bid can be made with four spades to the nine spot or equivalent. You asked him to bid and he is entitled to do so with something like this example hand.

EAST
♠ 9842
♡ 1063
◊ K43
♣ A72

This hand is not enormous nor are the spades very good. It is still worth a two spade bid because the cost of passing is so great. East has almost nine support points and he has four spades. You said you had spade support with your double so East's bidding them over two hearts is quite correct. After all, you will have four spades for your double as often as not. The price for not bidding two spades? It is huge. You let the opponents play in a partscore and you give up on what might be a partscore or game for your side.

2.   This time, it is clear to lead the king of clubs. You asked partner to bid and his two spade bid was an answer, not an opinion. On the previous auction, East did not have to bid. He could have passed over two hearts. On this auction, you doubled two hearts and East was OBLIGED to bid. The chances are good that East has nothing in spades.

#1	W	N	E	S
				1C
	1S	DBL*	2S	3C
	3S	5C	P	P
	P			
			*Negative	

#2	W	N	E	S
				3C
	P	5C	P	P
	P			

#3	W	N	E	S
		1D	P	2C
	P	2NT	P	3D
	P	3NT	P	4C
	P	5C	P	P
	P			

Problem Forty-Two

Both Sides Vulnerable

WEST
♠ AJ8763
♡ K643
◇ 3
♣ 107

1. Lead the ace of spades. Against a five level contract, leading an ace can be reasonable. Here, East raised spades, which suggests a spade lead. Assuming it wins, you can switch to the stiff diamond or a heart according to what looks best. Had North bid four clubs instead of five, leading the stiff diamond would be better. One reason for this is that if partner wins the diamond and gives you a ruff, you may be able to get to his hand with the king of spades for a second ruff. Your goal against five clubs is three tricks so getting two ruffs is not as significant.

2. Lead the ace of spades again. Any lead can be right and leading the ace will give you a shot at finding the right continuation.

3. Tough. I suggest the three of hearts. There are two big dangers in leading the ace of spades. One is that declarer may ruff it. He does seem to hate notrump so a spade void is a possibility. Also, dummy has spade strength. Leading the ace may set up a trick or two for declarer. On the first two sequences, there was no specific worry that dummy would have the king or the king-queen of spades. A heart lead may set up a trick or it may help you cash two hearts immediately. Do not lead your stiff diamond. Both opponents have bid them. The hand on the facing page shows a likely setup.

NORTH
- ♠ KQ2
- ♡ Q872
- ◇ K1052
- ♣ K8

WEST
- ♠ AJ8763
- ♡ K643
- ◇ 3
- ♣ 107

EAST
- ♠ 10954
- ♡ A5
- ◇ J976
- ♣ 432

SOUTH
- ♠ —
- ♡ J109
- ◇ AQ84
- ♣ AQJ965

Against this layout, they will make five or six if you lead the ace of spades, five if you lead your stiff diamond, and will go down one if you lead the three of hearts. It does not have to be this way, but I think the result on this hand reflects the merits of each of the three leads. For whatever it is worth, a trump lead lets them out with eleven tricks. It is noted only for a confirmed trump leader who hasn't yet given up this habit. It looks like the diamond lead sacrifices East's diamond trick, but that is only a temporary thought. South will set up the hearts and discard his losing diamond. Still, the diamond lead might have cost the defense if the cards were different.

#1	W	N	E	S
				1S
	P	2S	P	P
	P			

Problem Forty-Three
No One Vulnerable

WEST
♠ K104
♡ 873
◊ Q64
♣ QJ84

#2	W	N	E	S
			1H	1S
	2H	2S	P	P
	P			

#3	W	N	E	S
		1C	P	1S
	P	2S	P	P
	P			

1.   Lead the queen of clubs. Fretters will claim that the dummy always has the K102 of clubs and declarer always has the ace and the lead gives away a trick. When I ask them what they should lead, they look at me and shrug their shoulders as if I am an idiot. OK. Let's look at the alternatives. A trump lead will lose a trick almost any time your partner has an honor and it can lose a trick when he doesn't. On balance, a trump lead from the K104 will cost about half a trick. I can do without that. A heart lead looks safe, but unless partner has a lot of stuff in hearts, leading one will often help declarer more than you. A diamond? Why should a diamond lead be a good lead and a club lead not? For a diamond to work, you need partner to have the ace or king and even then, your lead may cost you. Is it not better to hope that partner has something in the suit you lead? Not leading a club for the sake of worrying is the worst kind of logic. If partner has the ace, king, or ten of clubs, your lead will be a good start. At the very least, this may be the club suit. The queen of clubs lead takes awhile to work here but it does work eventually.

NORTH
♣ K76

WEST	EAST
♣ QJ84	♣ 932

SOUTH
♣ A105

You lead the queen. Perhaps South takes it with the ace. When East gets in, he returns a club and your side is able to establish a club trick. All you needed in this setup was for partner to have the nine. I have no idea why people worry about leads like this and are willing to make horrible leads instead.

2. Lead the eight of hearts. East heard your raise and will know you are not leading a doubleton heart. He will read your lead as top of nothing and will do whatever looks best based on this information. If your clubs were headed by the QJ104, you would lead them in preference to the heart. But they are headed by the QJ84. This is a good holding when you don't know of a better lead, but here your partner gave you some important information.

3. Lead the eight or three of hearts according to your agreements. I discussed what you should lead from three small cards in Chapter Eight. Leading from three small is not a good thing to do in general, but when you do decide on which card to lead, you and partner must be in agreement.

   Normally, you would consider leading a club. The QJ84 of an unbid suit is worth leading most of the time. Here, unfortunately, North bid clubs, making that lead dangerous. Actually, if you prefer leading the four of diamonds instead, that is a thoughtful lead. Be prepared for it to work poorly, but given the quality of choices on this hand, it is worth considering.

#1	W	N	E	S		**Problem Forty-Four**
				1H		North South Vulnerable
	3S	4H	DBL	P		
	P	P				

WEST
♠ 10986542
♡ 87
◇ K94
♣ A

#2	W	N	E	S
		1NT	3C	4H
	P	P	DBL	P
	P	P		

1. Lead the ace of clubs and decide how to continue from there. East has some entries so you should get a ruff or two with this lead. Leading a spade is fruitless unless partner has a void and there is no reason to believe that is happening.

2. Lead the two of spades. This is an amazing auction. East preempted to three clubs and then doubled four hearts. Definitely an odd sequence. What do you think this unexpected double means? East does not have high card points for this double and he does not have a lot of trump tricks either. Your doubleton heart tells you that East has at most three of them. Is it possible that East is making a takeout double? When something strange happens at the table, you must look at all the possibilities. If you refuse to think, you won't get many answers. It is unlikely that East is making a takeout double, but it was definitely worth the moment it took to consider it. There is a logical meaning for East's double which was discussed in Chapter Three, section eight. It feels, under the circumstances, that East is making a lead directing double. If so, you have to figure out what he wants you to lead. Surely it is a spade. East is ruffing spades. That is the easy part. The next question is how to take advantage of this. The answer is that you must lead a spade and not the emotionally automatic ace of clubs. The idea is this. Lead the two of spades. This is a suit preference lead. You are telling East that after ruffing the first trick, he can get you back in with a club. This defense works and you do end up setting four hearts one trick. Why not lead the ace of clubs first? The next page shows the entire hand.

NORTH
♠ AK3
♡ KQ
◇ QJ32
♣ J762

WEST
♠ 10986542
♡ 87
◇ K94
♣ A

EAST
♠ —
♡ 1052
◇ 1085
♣ KQ109853

SOUTH
♠ QJ7
♡ AJ9643
◇ A76
♣ 4

If you lead the ace of clubs, you don't beat four hearts at all. East will ruff a spade at trick two, but when he returns a club, declarer ruffs high and draws trump. Later you get a diamond trick, but that is only your third trick. Even if South has two clubs, the spade lead is best. You might get *three* spade ruffs, a club, and a club ruff. Maybe even a later diamond. By not cashing the ace of clubs, you keep the potential for an extra entry into your hand for more spade ruffs. Neat. Do not always make the automatic lead.

W	N	E	S
	1C	P	1H
1S	3C	P	3H
P	3S*	DBL	4C
P	4H	P	P
P			

*Asking for a spade stopper

Problem Forty-Six

No One Vulnerable

WEST
♠ AQ763
♡ 65
◇ K86
♣ J54

#2

W	N	E	S
			1H
1S	2S*	DBL	4H
P	P	P	

*Game forcing heart raise

#3

W	N	E	S
			1H
P	4D*	DBL	4H
P	P	P	

*A singleton with heart support

The answers to these three hands relies on what agreements you have with your partner. You ought to read the discussion on doubles in Chapter Four. I will use that discussion as my guideline here. If you do not play in tournaments, you are unlikely to see auctions like these.

1.   Lead the six of spades. This is a dramatic lead that goes against everything I have said earlier. The reason you make this lead is that your partner's double is a lead directing double promising one of the top three honors in the suit. The rule for this is simple. If you overcall and partner does not raise, a later double by him of a cue bid shows an honor. Given that you are playing him for the king of spades, you lead low in case he has a doubleton spade. You may have three tricks in the suit. Leading low ensures you get them.

2.   Lead a heart or a diamond. Definitely a tough nut. The important thing about this hand is the difference between East's double on this hand and his double on the previous hand. On this hand, the double is made at his first turn to bid. He is showing you spade support but not a good enough hand to do anything. Typically, your partner has a so-so hand worth a raise to two spades. You can use this information in the bidding if you wish. For instance, if you had another spade or much better shape, you might bid four spades over four hearts. The hand you have is balanced and minimum. Passing is wise. Your opening lead, unfortunately, is not helped by the double. East may or may not have the king of spades. I would not count on it and will guess to lead something else.

3.   On this auction, you will note that you passed over one heart. This is a possible action for someone who objects to going down a lot and often. Bidding is a wise idea, but passing hands like this can work. Anyway, given you chose to pass, North makes a singleton showing bid of four diamonds which East doubles. South bids four hearts making it your lead.

       Lead the four of clubs. This is in accordance with the suggestion I made earlier. If you double a splinter bid, a good theoretical usage is to play that you want partner to lead the lower unbid suit. In this case, spades and clubs are unbid. East is able to state with his double that he really wants a club lead. He might have as little as four clubs to the KQ97 and nothing else. This is definitely in the realm of an expert trick. Do not assume this agreement is in effect unless you have discussed it.

Problem Forty-Seven

No One Vulnerable

#1	W	N	E	S
			1S	P
	2S	2NT	P	3D
	P	P	DBL	P
	P	P		

WEST
♠ J102
♡ AJ76
◊ 42
♣ Q982

#2	W	N	E	S
			1S	P
	2S	P	P	3D
	P	P	DBL	P
	P	P		

1. Lead the two of diamonds. Poor South was asked to bid a minor suit and he did. It does not mean he was happy to do so. Declarer rates to have two or three diamonds and fewer clubs. One of the things he will try to do is ruff clubs in his hand. Lead a trump and stop that from happening. Given your high card strength and your good club holding, setting three diamonds three or four tricks is possible.

2. Lead the jack of spades. There is no reason to lead anything except the jack of spades. I stated earlier that you should think about your leads in this way. Mentally decide on the card you intend to lead and then consider if you can find a reason to do something else. If nothing else appeals, go ahead with your choice. There are many reasons in this book that you might think about when you are giving final consideration to your lead. If you thought North was going to have a ruffing value, you would lead a trump. On this hand, there is no clue or even a hint that a spade lead is not best so you should go with your normal choice.

#1	W	N	E	S
				1H
	P	1S	P	2H
	P	P	P	

Problem Forty-Eight
No One Vulnerable

WEST
♠ A65
♡ 98
♦ J764
♣ QJ76

#2	W	N	E	S
				1H
	P	1NT	P	2H
	P	P	P	

#3	W	N	E	S		#4	W	N	E	S
				1H						1H
	P	P	1S	2H			P	2H	P	P
	P	P	P				P			

1. Lead the queen of clubs. In the four auctions here, South got to two hearts on relatively uninformative auctions. On this auction, the queen of clubs is the best lead, not because it is a good lead, but because all other leads are poor. Spades are out of the question for two reasons. You have an ace-high suit and it has been bid on your left. Hearts are definitely out of the question too. Never lead a trump when declarer bids and rebids a suit without any indication of support from partner. Leading diamonds is legal but that is about the best that can be said for leading from a jack-high suit when you have a suit like clubs available. Clubs may not work, but they will if partner has as little as the ten.

2. Lead the queen of clubs for much the same reasons as before. Again, declarer is in a low level contract on an uninformative sequence. Basically, you are leading the queen of clubs because it is miles better than the alternatives. I admit to wishing I had the ten of clubs too. NOTE again that a trump lead is terrible.

3. Lead the queen of clubs. Don't lead trumps. Definitely, do not lead or think of leading spades. Leading an ace is terrible barring the few explicit occasions where you can do so. A very important aside here is that your partner will suspect you have the ace of spades. He will rationalize that you would normally lead his suit. If you don't lead his suit, he will reason that you may have the ace. This is a powerful inference for the defenders.

4. Lead the queen of clubs. But, if you chose to lead the nine of hearts, you get full credit. They have a fit and you don't have a strong alternative lead. I am not fond of trump leads, but they can be right.

All in all, this is not a dynamic set of questions. Still, it is a type of problem that you will run into. If you varied from the correct lead on any of these hands, you are likely guilty of over thinking or of indulging in one or more bad habits.

#1	W	N	E	S
				1NT
	P	3NT	DBL	P
	P	P		

Problem Forty-Nine
No One Vulnerable

#2	W	N	E	S
				1C
	P	1H	P	1NT
	P	2NT	P	3NT
	P	P	DBL	P
	P	P		

WEST
♠ KJ873
♡ 4
◊ J2
♣ 109853

#3	W	N	E	S
				1NT
	P	2C	P	2S
	P	2NT	P	3NT
	P	P	DBL	P
	P	P		

#4	W	N	E	S
				1D
	P	1H	P	2D
	P	2H	P	3C
	P	3H	P	3NT
	P	P	DBL	P
	P	P		

1. East's double is telling you that he wants a specific lead. Usually someone has bid a suit and you have a clue about what to lead. (See answers two and three below.) On the auction here, no suits were bid. East's double says he wants you to lead his suit, but you have to look at your hand and figure which suit he wants. From your hand, you can infer that East wants hearts. Lead the four of hearts. When the opponents bid as they did here, they imply that they do not have a good major suit fit. If they did, it would have been bid. When East doubles, he will have a major suit more often than not. This is why you lead a heart and not a diamond. NOTE that you did not lead a club or a spade. East's double is a demand that you look for his suit. Humor him. If you lead his suit and it doesn't work, he won't mind. If you lead another suit and it costs you the contract, he will not be in a good mood.

2. Lead the four of hearts. On this auction, dummy bid hearts. Lead one. East's double calls for dummy's first suit when your side has been quiet during the bidding. On this auction, the heart lead is automatic.

3. Once again, the four of hearts is right. If you look closely at the bidding, you will see that even though North did not say the word "hearts," he did bid the suit. North bid Stayman before going on in notrump. South showed spades and that did not interest North. The conclusion is that North has four hearts. East is asking you for a heart lead. Here is the complete hand.

NORTH
♠ Q2
♡ J852
◊ AK94
♣ 764

WEST
♠ KJ873
♡ 4
◊ J2
♣ 109853

EAST
♠ 96
♡ AKQ106
◊ 87653
♣ 2

A heart lead beats three notrump doubled one trick. A spade lead gives up an overtrick and any other lead holds declarer to just nine tricks. Look at East's hand. Knowing that North has four hearts, wouldn't it feel right to double for a heart lead? The result, down one hundred, doesn't feel like a big reward, but it is a huge improvement on letting the opponents make game, which is what would happen if West chose the opening lead without the double.

SOUTH
♠ A1054
♡ 973
◊ Q10
♣ AKQJ

4.   Once again, you should lead the four of hearts. North bid the suit three times, but his bids did not promise a good suit or a good hand. What has happened here is that North-South have bid very foolishly and are going down a ton. Here is the entire hand.

NORTH
♠ 102
♡ KJ87652
◊ 9
♣ J64

WEST
♠ KJ873
♡ 4
◊ J2
♣ 109853

EAST
♠ 9654
♡ AQ103
◊ AQ74
♣ 2

This contract is so bad that any lead will set it. But setting it as much as possible and doubling it in the process is nice. East will win the heart lead and return a spade. Declarer is in a mess and will do well to get more than five tricks. Horrible bidding is justly rewarded. North was right to bid hearts twice, but when South bid three clubs, North should have given it up.

SOUTH
♠ AQ
♡ 9
◊ K108653
♣ AKQ7

Mike's Bidding Newsletter

If you enjoyed this book and enjoy keeping up with bidding ideas and theories, you should subscribe to my bidding newsletter. It covers everything you need to know about bidding.

Conventions like DONT, Support Doubles, Bergen Raises, and the Law of Total Tricks get major coverage. Older treatments like Negative Doubles and Responsive Doubles also get reviewed and evaluated.

On occassion I present play and defensive problems that have caught my eye.

Recommended by Alan Truscott, the ACBL Bulletin, and Bridge World.

Sincerely,

Michael Lawrence

One Year Subscription
Six Issues of 26+ Pages $20.00

Contact me:

Michael Lawrence
131 Alvarado Road
Berkeley, CA 94705
(510) 841-8845